BAD
COMPANIONS

BAD COMPANIONS

SIX LONDON
MURDERESSES
WHO SHOCKED
THE WORLD

KATE CLARKE

The
History
Press

First published 2013

The History Press
The Mill, Brimscombe Port
Stroud, Gloucestershire, GL5 2QG
www.thehistorypress.co.uk

British Library Cataloguing in Publication Data.
A catalogue record for this book is available from the British Library.

ISBN 978 0 7524 9364 0

Typesetting and origination by The History Press
Printed in Great Britain

Contents

INTRODUCTION

M ost people find murder interesting; is it, perhaps, because the underlying passions that can result in murder are common to us all, though in the case of murderers they have become magnified, distorted and out of control? And is it our innate fear of violent death that enables us to so readily identify with the victim? Here lies the dual fascination with murder, expressed in the following words by the late lawyer and criminologist William Roughead:

> Murder has a magic of its own, its peculiar alchemy. Touched by that crimson wand, things base and sordid, things ugly and of ill report, are transformed into matters wondrous, weird and tragical. Dull streets become fraught with mystery, commonplace dwellings assume sinister aspects, everyone concerned, howsoever plain and ordinary, is invested with a new value and importance as the red light falls upon each.

London is the location for the six cases of murder highlighted in this book, and each of the women involved had one thing in common – they were all accused of murder or attempted murder and tried in the city's most famous courthouse, the Old Bailey. It would be impossible, in a book of this length, to highlight the many women in London who have committed equally vicious crimes, many of which may well have passed inadequately recorded, or not at all. It must be said, however, that despite the violence suffered by so many women, murders by men have always far outnumbered those committed by women.

In order to gain a little understanding of the women in this book, it is helpful to know something of the conditions in which they lived and the pressures, deprivations and limitations that dominated their lives in Georgian and Victorian London.

In 1891 it was estimated that, country-wide, more than a million – that is, one in three women between the ages of fifteen and twenty – were in domestic service; kitchen maids and maids-of-all work (sometimes referred to as 'slaveys') were paid between £6 and £12 a year. 'Tweenies', maids who helped other domestics, moving between floors as and when they were needed, were paid even less. There was a tax on indoor male servants – and their wages were considerably higher – so only the wealthy could afford to employ them. Women servants were cheap and generally more easily dominated and kept in their place. However, the close proximity of mistress and maids – interdependent yet still strangers under one roof – often led to squabbles and petulance – especially if the mistress's expectations were too high and the maid was overworked and probably feeling alienated and homesick. Despite the potential for violent outbursts only a comparatively small number of murders were committed by servants, pushed to the limit of their endurance by the drudgery of menial work, extremely long hours and meagre pay – that, and harsh treatment at the hands of their employers, sometimes led to retaliation and, in some cases, to murder.

The mistreatment of servants was commonplace, and young maids were especially vulnerable to being sexually exploited. Once hired, they found themselves in households in which a strict and unbreachable hierarchy below stairs ensured that they stayed on the lowest rung of that society. In 1740 Mary Branch and her mother were executed for beating a servant girl to death and, on the gallows, she admitted that she had considered all servants as 'slaves, vagabonds and thieves'.

In addition to severe chastisement in their place of work, tragically, many young women in domestic service were severely punished by the law, sometimes with their lives, for giving birth to illegitimate babies. Very often, in sheer desperation, they disposed of these new-borns in privies, ditches and on dung-heaps – and when found out, were tried by male judges and jurors. Although some were treated mercifully, others were hanged for their actions.

The briefest study of court records, the *Newgate Calendar*, contemporary newspaper reports or similar publications clearly illustrates the extent of the violence regularly meted out, not only to servants but also to women and children, by fathers, husbands and lovers. The ineffectual, amateur and largely unaccountable law enforcers, who were open to bribery and corruption; the ducking and diving to dodge the law in order to make some sort of living, one way or another; illiteracy, which made record-keeping random and incomplete; the frequency of premature death of women in childbirth, and the high mortality rate amongst infants – all these factors helped to mask and conceal criminal activity, even murder.

The alternative to a life of domestic drudgery for many women, ranging in age from those in early pubescence to those well past middle-age, was prostitution, especially for those females raised in institutions and without family support. Some were unable to find husbands to support them, whilst others may have been unwilling to become a chattel for life.

Domestic service was a precarious living, as girls could be sacked immediately for breaking house rules or committing some other misdemeanour. Once employed, young women would arrive with their boxes, containing their work clothes and undergarments, possibly a Bible and perhaps a few personal mementos of their lives before entering service. If a maid displeased her mistress, her box might well be retained after dismissal – possibly to make up a deficit from real or imagined thieving. However, without a box and a 'character', a written recommendation or reference, it was extremely difficult to find another position. Without the prospect of further employment some servants chose to become prostitutes; others, whilst still in domestic employment, would sometimes offer themselves in return for trinkets and small gifts – these were known as 'dolly mops'.

A few cases have been recorded of a client frequenting a brothel only to be confronted by either his cook, his children's nanny – she had ample opportunity to attract admirers whilst pushing infants in perambulators through London's parks and pleasure gardens – or a parlour maid, supplementing her meagre wages with a little 'dolly mopping' on the side. The mutual embarrassment can be imagined.

The number of prostitutes working in London in the nineteenth century was estimated at many thousands but, by its nature, the sex trade was clandestine, transitory and exploitative and it was therefore impossible to arrive at a true figure. With so many prostitutes at work in the city, perspective clients could purchase catalogues listing the women – and their specialities – available for hire, in *Harris's List of Covent Garden Ladies* and other similar publications. Those at the top of the pile, sometimes referred to as either 'gay' women or 'unfortunates', paraded in their brightly coloured clothing – but without hats – around the theatres along the Strand, Haymarket, and Covent Garden; the Vauxhall Pleasure Gardens were also extremely popular for business. But many more, women who were perhaps less appealing, were reduced to standing on murky street corners and wandering the dark alleys between the squalid tenements in the poorer districts of the city, plying their trade as best they could, and, as often as not, vulnerable to violent attack.

According to a report written in 1899 by The National Vigilance Association, entitled *Inquiries Concerning Female Labour in the Metropolis*, many young girls fell victim to agencies falsely luring them – including many from Germany – with the promise of domestic employment, only to find themselves forced to work in one of the city's many brothels – such as Mrs Harris's establishment in Great Tichfield Street, in Central London. Especially targeted were the droves of young, naïve girls coming into London from the countryside, or from abroad; they were frequently preyed upon by procurers employed by the brothel keepers. In 1731, Mother Needham, notorious for trafficking young country girls into prostitution, had been put in a pillory at the corner of St James Street and Park Place and pelted with rocks and other missiles for a period of two days, after which she died of her injuries.

The report also published lists of names and addresses of *bona-fide* householders throughout London who were offering work for domestic servants.

Christians of every persuasion attempted to address the problem. Midnight Mission Meetings were arranged in premises in the Strand to coincide with prostitutes leaving the theatres, music halls and taverns at midnight. In return for giving up their way of life, they were offered light refreshments, some intensive sermonising and a twelve-month rehabilitation in a Lock Asylum, learning to perfect their needlework and housewifery skills. It was noted by an observer at one of these meetings that this option was seldom met with any enthusiasm.

Many similar charitable schemes were launched in London to rescue these girls. The Female Servants' Home Society was one of many; also The Female Aid Society, established in 1836. It provided three 'safe' houses and, with a certain sanctimonious censure, graded the rescued women in the following manner: one in New Ormond Street, Bedford Row, catering for 'young, friendless servants of good character'; a second house in Southampton Row for 'respectable servants out of a place'; and thirdly, a house in White Lion Street for 'the fallen'. It was estimated that The Metropolitan Association for Befriending Young Servants also helped to protect some 8,000 'slaveys' by vetting households offering work.

And of course, from 1840 until shortly before his death in 1898, William Gladstone and others like him were making nightly forays through the city streets, gathering up 'fallen women' in an attempt to save them from degradation and disease.

The six women featured in this book had a chequered history in this respect. Two, Sarah Drake and Eliza Fenning, chose not to prostitute themselves, preferring to work in domestic service. Catherine Hayes and Elizabeth Brownrigg were supported by hard-working, successful husbands, so didn't need to – though in her youth, Hayes had been a prostitute (and even in later life was regarded as promiscuous). Catherine Wilson found a more congenial way of acquiring money – poison. As for Kate Webster, although she did occasionally seek domestic work, she had served time for prostitution and would have been quite willing to turn a trick or two whenever her coffers threatened to seriously restrict her alcohol consumption.

Murder is somehow more disturbing when committed by women. The women who feature in this book were very different in age, background and circumstances, but they all ended up charged with murder or attempted murder, and facing the grim prospect of the death penalty. Their stories clearly illustrate the part played by poverty and ignorance and – in at least two of the murders – extreme violence unleashed by drink.

Catherine Hayes was a vicious wife and adulterer who persuaded two of her lovers – one of which was her son – to murder her husband and cut off his head. She was sentenced to die at the stake for 'petty treason' and was the last woman to suffer that fate. She was burned to death in 1726, without, due to the executioner's fumbling with the burning rope, the benefit of being strangled first.

Elizabeth Brownrigg was a sadistic, vicious woman who beat three of her maids without mercy – all her venom was used on Mary Clifford, a fourteen-year-old maid from the parish poor house, with the result that she died of her injuries.

The year 1815 saw the tragic case of Eliza Fenning, a young cook, who was found guilty of the attempted poisoning of three members of the Turner family, for whom she worked, in Chancery Lane, London. The guilt of the other four women was proved beyond doubt, but in the case of Eliza Fenning – accused of mixing deadly poison into the dumplings she made for dinner, despite the fact that none of the recipients died – there was, at the time of her trial, deep public unease about her subsequent execution, and many notable social commentators, including Charles Dickens (who learned of her case some years later), were absolutely convinced of her innocence.

Sarah Drake was a young, unmarried mother, working as a cook and housekeeper for a family in Upper Harley Street, London, in 1849. Unable to keep up the payments for the care of her two-year-old son, Lewis, she killed him and sent his body in a box to her family in the country, hoping they would give him a decent burial. She had previously done the same with one – and possibly two – of her other babies.

A few years later, in 1862, Catherine Wilson, working as a nurse and housekeeper to a Mrs Soames, in Bedford Square, was charged with murdering at least five people; she was a calculating serial poisoner, classic in her methods, who killed for one reason – money.

Finally, the surly maid, Kate Webster, well-liked by her friends, but resentful of authority and, when cornered, extremely violent, murdered and dismembered the body of her elderly mistress, Julia Thomas, and threw the box containing parts of the torso into the River Thames.

Although a span of more than a century lay between the first case in this book – beginning with Catherine Hayes in 1726 and ending with Kate Webster, in 1879 – not a great deal had changed to improve the lot of women who were destined to spend their lives as chattels. But radical change was on its way; the suffragettes were already taking action on behalf of women denied a voice. Their case was further strengthened when, thirty-four years after Kate Webster was hanged, the country was embroiled in the First World War and, with much of the male population called to arms, women began to leave domestic service and find alternative employment. Some trained as nurses or worked on the land, whilst others manned the vital munitions factories. Many chose to work in the cotton mills and other manufacturing industries that had emerged during the Industrial Revolution, and where they felt less demeaned and were better paid. There were far fewer opportunities, moreover, for covert acts of cruelty away from the closed worlds of the households in which they had previously served, and frequently suffered.

CATHERINE HAYES

'A vile woman, scarcely to be paralleled'

On Saturday, 7 May 1726, two days before Mrs Catherine Hayes was due to be executed, a brief but damning summary of her life was published in the *Ipswich Journal*. It stated that, in 1690, Catherine Hayes (*née* Hall) 'was born of an Adulterous and Wicked Mother, who dropt her, (a Branch of her Lustful Embraces) near Birmingham, in Warwickshire'.

When she was fifteen Catherine left home, intending to make her way to London. She was a good-looking girl and, it would seem, sexually mature, for before she had travelled far she met a group of army officers who persuaded her – with the promise of some gold pieces – to go with them to their quarters at Great Ombersley, in Worcestershire. She remained in their company for some time, mainly supplying sexual services but occasionally working as a general housemaid. When the officers grew tired of her she went back to Warwickshire, where, it was said, she 'ran about the country like a distracted creature'.

At the age of twenty-three she met a gentleman farmer, Mr Hayes, who, ignoring the advice of his wife, took her into his house as a domestic servant. Mrs Hayes was right to be wary of Catherine, for she soon began an affair with one of the farmer's two sons, twenty-one-year-old John Hayes, and they were secretly married at Worcester in 1713.

The article in the *Ipswich Journal* continued its account of the events that followed:

> …but the Father endeavour'd all he could to prevent it, but to no effect, for she threaten'd to cut her Throat if he (John Hayes) did not marry her; on the Day they were marry'd she fell into the water and

had been drowned if her husband had not waded after her. That same night, as soon as they went to bed, some officers, by her appointment, had him impressed (press-ganged) but his father got him his liberty, but she prevailed upon him to enlist and go with those officers to Spain, where she attended him, whether more for the love of the Officers than for him.

Whilst in Spain, the article concluded, 'she acted all manner of Debauchery and Wickedness.'

Another account states that John Hayes enlisted and was sent to the Isle of Wight; it was then that his father paid £60 'to buy him out'. Although impressment – press-ganging – was a common form of enforced naval recruitment, the army also targeted the 'able-bodied, idle and disorderly Persons', usually men aged between eighteen and fifty-five 'without lawful trade'. 'Incorrigible rogues', who had left their wives and children to the care of the parish, were also considered fair game.

Army life, however, ended when Mr Hayes, senior, bought his son's freedom and provided the young couple with a cottage on his farm and a generous allowance.

However, by 1719, Catherine, after six years of marriage (during which, it was said, she took numerous lovers), grew restless and convinced her husband that they should move to London:

> They came to London, and his Father dying left them some money, which they lent out in interest, but he found her guilty of many slippery tricks, never trusted her with the keys of the drawers, but she by many cunning stratagems often got some of his gold to supply the wants of those she liked best and this way she continued till the committing of the horrid fact.

John Hayes worked hard and prospered in London. He bought a house – part of which he rented out to lodgers – and set himself up as a chandler and coal merchant. The business proved profitable and, furthermore, Hayes continued to supplement his income as a pawn-broker and money-lender. Catherine was given a generous allowance – and yet she still berated her husband for not providing her with enough money to keep a carriage and employ servants. She was never satisfied, and reportedly nagged him constantly. Yet her harassment resulted not in more money but in her husband resorting to violence: he began beating her, and thereafter reduced, not increased, her allowance. She later complained that he 'half-starved her'. Resentment continued to build in Catherine and she often cursed her husband, saying that 'it was no more a sin to kill him than to kill a mad dog. Some time or other I will give him a jolt!'

Whether or not her scorn was well-deserved – he may well have been a thoroughly unpleasant person – it soon became evident that Catherine Hayes was a foul-mouthed scold who often belittled her husband in public and, moreover, quarrelled constantly with her neighbours. Perhaps to escape the ill-feeling his wife generated, they moved to premises in Tottenham Court Road, and from there to Tyburn Road, now known as Oxford Street.

In 1725 an eighteen-year-old tailor, Thomas Billings (who, it was later discovered, was actually Catherine's illegitimate son), came to live with them – and he and Catherine soon embarked on a sexual relationship. Not only were the couple cuckolding John Hayes whenever he was away on business, but also the neighbours noticed that Catherine and Billings lived lavishly at his expense, indulging in riotous parties and prolonged drinking sprees. When he returned they wasted no time in telling Mr Hayes about his wife's behaviour, and a fierce fight ensued. John beat her so violently that she was confined to bed for several days. This, no doubt, brought to a head Catherine's hatred of her husband and engendered talk of 'getting rid of him' so that she and Billings could continue their incestuous relationship without restraint or censure.

It was at this point in the story that the third figure in the ensuing drama appeared. A butcher named Thomas Wood, a friend of John Hayes, arrived from Worcestershire (escaping, it seems, from the efforts of the army officers to get him to enlist). John Hayes gave him lodging, unaware that, within days, Catherine would not only be sleeping with him but also trying to persuade him to join in his murder. As a friend of John Hayes, Wood at first refused to become involved in their heinous plan – until, that is, Catherine told him that her husband was 'an atheist, and had already been guilty of murdering two of his own children, one of whom he had buried under an apple-tree, and the other under a pear-tree'. He had also, she said, murdered a business rival. As an added incentive, Catherine promised to give him and Billings the £1,500 which she claimed she would inherit once her husband was dead.

On 1 March 1725, when Wood returned to London after a few days away, he found John Hayes, Catherine and Thomas Billings drinking together, already having consumed a guinea's worth of liquor between them – though John Hayes boasted that he was not at all drunk. As part of the plan, Billings suggested that Hayes should prove to them that he could drink six bottles of mountain wine without getting drunk. If he did so, Billings promised, he would pay for the wine. The wager was agreed and the three went out to buy more drink, determined now to use this opportunity to carry out their murderous plan.

Catherine Hayes paid half a guinea for the wine for her husband while she and her two accomplices drank beer. Before long, John Hayes, well inebriated, began to dance around the room. Then he drank the remainder of the wine. Determined to render him completely helpless, Catherine sent out for another bottle of wine and watched him drink it before he fell senseless to the floor. He lay there for a while and then somehow managed to crawl into 'another room and [throw] himself on a bed'.[1]

It was at this point that Thomas Billings entered the bedroom and attacked John Hayes with a hatchet, striking him so violently that his skull was broken. Hayes's legs were hanging over the edge of the bed as the blow fell and, as the blows registered in his brain, his feet thumped repeatedly on the floor. This sound brought Wood into the room. Taking the hatchet from Billings, he delivered vicious blows (two); these blows finally killed the husband.

A fellow lodger, Mrs Springate, living in the room above, heard the thumping of Hayes's feet on the floor and came down to complain that the noise had woken her and her family. Catherine managed to placate her by saying that they were entertaining some rowdy visitors: as they were just about to leave, the noise would soon stop.

---

1   From *The Newgate Calendar*, an extensive record of those within the penal system, comprising not one account but many, and issued in various forms: prison Governors' monthly reports and prison Ordinaries' accounts; published as 'improving' tracts warning of the terrible consequences of a criminal and dissolute lifestyle. 'Penny Dreadfuls' and pamphlets, with a similar message, were often sold at public executions.

By the time Catherine returned to the bedroom her husband was dead, and the room was extensively splattered with blood. The killers were now faced with a dilemma: what to do with the body? If they deposited it somewhere – as it was – someone might inconveniently identify him. It was Catherine who suggested that, to avoid detection, they should cut off his head. Her two collaborators were sickened by the dreadful prospect of beheading their former friend. However, as there seemed to be no alternative, they finally agreed to carry out this plan.

Catherine remained remarkably calm throughout the events that followed: she fetched a bucket, lit a candle and then watched as Billings supported her dead husband's head while Wood began to saw through the neck with a kitchen knife. Catherine even positioned the bucket so that the severed head – and all the copious amount of blood issuing from it – would fall into it, thus reducing the staining to the floor. Once the head was in the bucket, they poured off all the blood into a sink. They then poured down several pails of water to sluice it out so that no trace of blood remained.

To further prevent identification of the remains, Catherine suggested that they boil the head to separate the flesh from the bone, but the three eventually decided that this process would take too long. Instead, it was agreed that their best option would be to throw the head into the River Thames and allow the tide to carry it away. With Billings carrying the severed head in the bucket, and accompanied by Wood, they made their way out of the house. While they were about their grisly business, Catherine made several trips down to street level and up again to the second floor, carrying buckets of water for scrubbing away all evidence of the murder.[2]

At this point Mrs Springate, still annoyed by the noise from below, called out to ask what was going on. Catherine replied that her husband was just leaving the house to embark on a journey; she then pretended to carry on a conversation with her husband, commiserating with him about having to set off at such a late hour. Mrs Springate heard her say, as though addressing her

---

2   Such rudimentary methods of removing incriminating evidence from a murder scene were, prior to the introduction of finger-printing and DNA analysis of blood and tissue, often adequate to avoid detection.

husband, 'Watch out for brigands and dress warmly against these bitter March winds.' While this deception was under way, Billings and Wood were clear of the house and making their way through the darkened streets to the banks of the River Thames, anxious to get rid of the head before daybreak.

It was their intention to dump the head in the river at Whitehall but, as the gates were shut, they hurried to the wharf at Horse Ferry, in Westminster. On seeing a watchman approaching, they panicked. While Billings held the bucket, Wood lifted out the head of John Hayes and threw it into the river, expecting it to be carried away by the tide – but it was not to be. They soon realised that in fact the tide was ebbing – and the head had landed in the mud. The two killers fled while the watchman, hearing the thud of something landing on the mud-bank, came to see what it was. He retrieved the head and took it to the authorities.

This account is from *The British Gazetteer*, dated 5 March 1726:

> Last Wednesday morning at day-light, there was found in the dock before Mr Paul's brewhouse, near the Horse-Ferry at Westminster, the head of a man, with brown curl'd hair, the Scull broke in two blaces [*sic*], and a large cut on each cheek; judg'd to be upwards of 30, and, by all circumstances, appearing to have been newly cut from off a living body; but by whom, or on what account, is yet a secret. There was found near it, a bloody pail; and some bargemen have since affirmed, that they saw two Ruffian-like fellows bring that pail to the water-side, and throw the head into the dock, and then run away. The head was the same day set up, and expos'd to publick view in St Margaret's Church-Yard; to the end, that any one knowing the features, might give some Account of the person. Several houses in Tuttle Fields, and about Westminster, have likewise been searched for the body...

Billings and Wood, no doubt believing they had effectively disposed of the head, returned to the house where Catherine was waiting to commence concealment of the headless body. She suggested burying it but a box brought for that purpose was found to be too small. Wood used his butchering skills to dismember the body and pack it into the box, which was then left under the bed during the remainder of that night. The next morning, fearing to arouse suspicion if they were seen carrying a heavy box, they decided to transport the chopped-up corpse in a blanket. It must have been with great relief that Catherine watched as her lovers left the house with the remains of John Hayes; she was no doubt anticipating a life of new-found wealth, unfettered by a brutal and parsimonious husband. Once clear of the house, Billings and Wood hurried to a field in Marylebone and threw the bundle of body parts into a pond.

Meanwhile, the severed head that had been discovered by the watchman stuck on a mud-bank at Horse Ferry wharf had been appropriated by the local magistrates. They ordered that 'the head should be washed clean, and the hair combed.' It was then placed on top of a wooden spike in the churchyard of St Margaret's, in Westminster, in the hope that someone would recognise the face and inform the constables. Many in the crowds that flocked to witness this grim sight thought they recognised the head of John Hayes. Some even mentioned their suspicions to Thomas Billings, but he assured them that Hayes was still alive and had gone away on business.

After four days, it was decided to halt the decomposition of the head by storing it in a large glass jar at the premises of a barber-surgeon, and a chemist, Mr Westbrook, was called upon to fill the jar with cheap gin as a preservative.

For some reason, Catherine Hayes then decided to move to new lodgings in the same street, accompanied by Mrs Springate (presumably with her husband and child), Thomas Billings and Thomas Wood. From there, she set about gathering all the monies owed to her husband and spent lavishly on both her lovers. This did not go down well with her neighbours, or with friends of John Hayes. Mr Ashby, a business colleague who had known Hayes well, called on Catherine and demanded to know where her husband was. Her husband, she told him, had got into a fight with another man and killed him; unable to bribe the man's widow with enough money to ensure her silence, he had fled London. Mr Ashby then asked if the head on the spike had been that of the man killed in the fight – but Catherine cleverly denied this, saying that the man her husband had killed had been buried whole. Where was John now? He had gone to work in Portugal.

Mr Ashby was not satisfied with this explanation, and voiced his doubts to a distant relative of Hayes, a Mr Longmore. They hatched a plan whereby Mr Longmore would call on Catherine and inquire about the whereabouts of John Hayes, to see if her explanation differed from the one given to Mr Ashby. As there were some discrepancies in her story, Messrs Ashby and Longmore (and another friend called Mr Eaton) decided to inspect the severed head more closely.

After carefully poring over the gruesome remains, they became convinced that the head had once belonged to their friend. They went straight to a magistrate, a Mr Lambert. On hearing their suspicions, he issued warrants for the arrest of Catherine Hayes, Thomas Billings, Thomas Wood – and Mrs Springate! The gentlemen went in person to the lodging house where the suspects lived and the landlord showed them to Catherine's room. Calling for her to come out, the magistrate threatened to break down the door if she didn't open it immediately. Catherine called back that she would open it as soon as she had put on her clothes. When she eventually opened the door, Thomas Billings was 'sitting on the side of the bed, bare-legged'.[3]

One of the officers asked him: 'Have you been sleeping with this woman?'

'No, I've been mending my stockings,' came the facetious reply.

The magistrate and Mr Longmore then went upstairs and arrested Mrs Springate; Catherine, Billings and Mrs Springate (there was no sign of Wood) were taken into custody and questioned separately, at length, at the magistrate's house. They all, however, maintained their innocence and it was decided that they should remain in custody until the following day, when they would be questioned further by Mr Lambert and other magistrates. Catherine Hayes was taken to Tothill Fields gaol, at Bridewell, Thomas Billings to Newgate Prison and Mrs Springate to the Gatehouse.[4]

---

3 Magistrates came from the powerful and wealthy property owners in the community and were often corrupt. Horace Walpole commented, 'the greatest criminals of this town [London] are the officers of justice'.

4 Bridewell Prison and Hospital (Tothill Fields, in Westminster) was established in 1553 (on the site of the former Royal Palace of Bridewell) to house the 'miscreant poor' and homeless children. As well as being a House of Correction, it also trained young apprentices referred by magistrates and parish officials, who were anxious to off-load responsibility for impoverished teenage boys in their care.

The next day, when fetched from prison to face further questioning, Catherine expressed a desire to see the head, which was in the possession of a barber-surgeon. On seeing the head in the glass jar, she exclaimed: 'Oh, it is my dear husband's head! It is my dear husband's head!' She then put on an exaggerated show of wifely grief by crying bitterly as she cradled the glass jar in her arms. This dramatic display was intensified when Mr Westbrook suggested that he should take the head out of the jar so she might inspect it more closely, just to make sure. As she held the head in her hands, she kissed it several times and then pleaded with Mr Westbrook to let her have a lock of his hair. On being told by Mr Westbrook that she 'had had too much of his blood already', she fell into a faint. Once recovered, she was led to Mr Lambert's house, where she was questioned again by the magistrates.[5]

On 26 March, whilst all these histrionics were being played out, the mangled remains of the body of John Hayes were discovered. A man and his servant, whilst crossing the fields at Marylebone, found the headless remains and Mr Lambert, still questioning the suspects, was informed.

Both the *Weekly Journal* and *Mist's Weekly Journal* informed their readers of the grisly find:

> The body of a man has been found without a head near Tottenham-Court-Road, much mangled and bruised; which, by the time of lying, is supposed to have belonged to the head lately found at Westminster. The wife and her gallant were taken, on violent suspicion of the said murder, together with another woman, and committed to several prisons. His name is John Hayes.

The *Weekly Journal* went into more detail:

> The arms, thighs and legs of a man cut asunder, as if done with a butcher's cleaver, were found last Wednesday in a pond at Marybone [*sic*] and on

---

5 There was a superstition at the time that held that if a person guilty of murder touched their victim, their guilt would be revealed. It was also common for people to clasp the hand of a corpse on the gallows as a cure for disease – the dead man's hand.

> Thursday they drag'd the pond and took out the trunk of the body wrapt in a blanket, but finding no head, 'tis suppos'd that which was exposed to publick view at Westminster in St Margaret's Church-yard, belong'd thereto.

Catherine Hayes was subsequently committed for trial and transported to Newgate Prison.[6]

The committal of Thomas Billings and Mrs Springate was deferred until Thomas Wood had been apprehended. On his return to London, Wood rode straight to Catherine Hayes's lodgings and was told to go to Mr Longmore's house. That gentleman's brother, however, was waiting for him and 'seized him, and caused him to be carried before Mr Lambert'. When questioned by the magistrate, Wood refused to confess to any involvement in the murder of John Hayes and was taken to Bridewell Prison. At the prison he was informed that the dismembered body of Hayes had been found; on hearing this, he begged to be returned to Mr Lambert's house and, once there, he admitted his part in the killing and signed a confession.

According to the *Newgate Calendar*, 'this wretched man owned that since the perpetration of the crime he had been terrified at the sight of everyone he met, that he had not experienced a moment's peace, and that his mind had been distracted with the most violent agitation.'

This done, he was escorted to Newgate Prison, protected from angry mobs in the street, by eight soldiers with fixed bayonets. A Mr Mercer visited Thomas Wood in prison and Wood pleaded with him to go to Thomas Billings and urge him to confess. Billings was subsequently brought before Mr Lambert and confessed to his part in the crime. He also implicated both Catherine Hayes and Thomas Wood, saying that she, Hayes, had paid for the drink to make her husband so drunk he was unable to defend himself and that, although he, Billings, had struck the murderous blows, it was Wood who

---

6 Conditions in Newgate Gaol were appalling – drunkenness, filth, disease and near-starvation awaited those prisoners without outside help from relatives or the resources to bribe the turnkeys. Many, like Thomas Wood, died of typhus (or 'gaol fever') and other diseases spread by such an insanitary environment.

had dismembered the body. It was now clear that Mrs Springate was completely innocent, and she was released.[7]

The *Weekly Journal*, on 2 April, published a lengthy article on the arrest of Catherine Hayes, Thomas Billings and Thomas Wood:

Margaret[8] Hayes, who stands committed to Newgate for petty-treason, for being concern'd in the most inhumane and un-heard of murder of her husband John Hayes, hath confess'd That she hath had fourteen children by her said husband; That having criminal conversation[9] with Thomas Wood, a butcher, and Thomas Billins, a taylor, both Worcestershire men, they put her upon complying with the execrable deed, that they might get into possession of her husband's substance, and keep her without molestation; That when her husband was murdered, they took out of his pocket 26 guineas, 9 King George's shillings, and 6 six-pence, 11 guineas whereof they return'd to her, and kept the rest themselves.

And on Monday the said Thomas Billins was removed from New-Prison to Newgate, by Justice Lambert's Warrant, and loaded with irons, and are since put into the condemn'd hold, but are not stapled down.

Also the same day in the evening, the abovesaid Thomas Wood was brought to Newgate in a coach, guarded by a Serjeant and two Files of Musqueteers and several constables; the mob all the way expressing their joy by loud huzzas. He confessed before Colonel Mohun and Mr Lambert, two Justices of the Peace, That himself and Billins first made the late Mr Hayes drunk with claret in his own gouse [*sic*]; (the wife having furnish'd money for that purpose) and that he falling asleep, Billins broke his scull as he lay on the bed with an ax, and knock'd out his brains, which causing a great effusion of blood, the good woman advis'd to cut the head off, which was done accordingly; she afterwards brought them a box to put the body in, but not being sufficient to receive it, they quarter'd the same, and carry'd it out as formerly mention'd.

---

7 Although conditions at Bridewell Prison were slightly better than many of the more notorious eighteenth-century gaols, it was customary for discharged prisoners to impale the free loaf of bread they were given on the railings outside the prison gates as a mark of relief or as an insult.

8 Early newspaper articles often misspelt or gave the wrong names; both Billings and Wood were sometimes referred to as 'John', not Thomas.

9 A euphemism for sexual intercourse outside marriage.

We hear the wife gave the murtherer her husband's hat, coat, and some silver, and assured him he should not want; and that last Sunday he came to town for more money, and calling at her lodging, the landlord said she was remov'd to the next street; and so carry'd him to a friend of the deceas'd, where he was secur'd.

Wood, upon his confession of having quarter'd the deceas'd, being ask'd if he was not a butcher by trade, said, he was not, but could kill and cut up a beast as well as any butcher at all.

The mangled corpse was carried out of town on Monday last in a hearse followed by several mourning coaches, to be interr'd at Ombersley in Worcestershire; his mother, who is come to town, having order'd the funeral, and a vigorous prosecution against the murderers.

The following week, on 9 April, the *Weekly Journal* added yet one more detail – only partially true – to the horrible case:

Last Saturday it was discover'd; That William [Thomas] Billins, by trade a taylor, the person that beat out Mr Hayes's brains with a hatchet, on the 1st of March last, at his house in Tyburn-Road; is the natural son of Margaret [Catherine] Hayes, begotten by a tanner in Worcestershire, before her marriage with the said Mr Hayes. [10]

There was a coroner's inquest, opened on 16 April, in a house near Soho. Having viewed the mangled remains of John Hayes, a verdict was reached, that of wilful murder against Catherine Hayes, Thomas Billings and Thomas Wood.

The Trial

Catherine Hayes and her cohorts stood trial at the April Sessions of the Old Bailey between Wednesday 20th and Saturday 23rd. They appeared before the Lord Mayor, the Recorder, several

---

10 The full facts of Thomas Billings's parentage were made known by Catherine Hayes while she was in Newgate, awaiting execution.

other judges and a jury of twelve men. Thomas Billings and Thomas Wood were both charged with murder, but the indictment against Catherine was more specific:

> Katherine Hays [Catherine Hayes] is indicted for Petty Treason, in being Traitorously present, comforting and maintaining the said Thomas Billings in the Murder of the said John Hayes, her Husband.[11]

Catherine attempted to dispute the charge against her by insisting that her part in the murder had merely been holding the candle while her two lovers dismembered the body. She was not guilty of the murder, she firmly believed, insisting that it was the work of the Devil.

Although both Billings and Woods had confessed their guilt, Catherine still maintained her innocence, on the grounds that she had not actually struck the mortal blows that killed her husband. Her protestations held no sway, however, with the jurors; they felt that her part in the murder made her equally culpable, and pronounced her guilty of 'petty treason'. They found all three prisoners guilty as charged.[12]

Wood and Billings were to be hanged at Tyburn and their bodies hung in chains from a gibbet. Catherine Hayes was sentenced to be burned at the stake. She begged the court not to inflict such a terrible retribution – one she had always dreaded – but to no avail.

Catherine and the other condemned prisoners were taken to the Condemned Hold at Newgate prison and, thereafter, only

---

11   The crime of petty treason, according to the Treason Act of 1351, applied to the killing of a master by a servant, a husband by his wife, or an ecclesiastic by an inferior Church member. Women convicted of petty treason were burned at the stake until the year 1793; after that date, until 1825, when the crime of petty treason was abolished and the offence was reclassified as ordinary murder, they were hanged in the usual way.

12   More than 200 crimes carried the death penalty, although the sentence was often commuted to transportation to Botany Bay, in Australia, via 'convict ships'. Many feared this more than the gallows, and only the fittest survived the horrendous journey. Also convicted during that April session were Thomas Wright, Gabriel Lawrence, George Reger and William Griffin, for sodomy; Mary Schuffman and Jane Vanvick, for felony; John Mapp, John Gillingham and Henry Vigas, for robberies on the highway; John Cotterell and another man, for burglary; and Joseph Treen, for horse-stealing. After he was hanged, the body of Gabriel Lawrence was dissected at Surgeon's Hall.

allowed bread and water. For a fee, paid to the turnkeys, members of the public were allowed admittance to the prison to gawp at the prisoners. Many were affronted by the way Catherine Hayes and Thomas Billings held hands and stood leaning closely together. Whilst awaiting the death sentence, Thomas Wood appeared full of remorse and, whilst suffering from a severe bout of 'gaol fever' or typhus, he was subjected to the fervent administrations of religious advisers[13], and dutifully declared that he felt that he deserved to die. Perhaps fortunately for him, he died of the fever before the sentence could be carried out.

Catherine Hayes, however, fought to escape the terrible fate awaiting her. She somehow managed to obtain a small phial of poison with which to kill herself, but her plan was thwarted when another female prisoner, thinking the phial contained liquor of some sort, grabbed it from her and tasted it.

She did eventually make a full confession to the Ordinary, the Revd J. Guthrie, though she still contested the severity of her sentence. The *London Journal* informed its readers that Catherine had also 'affirmed that Billings was her own son'. They then added the awful detail that he been 'got by Mr Hayes's father, when she lived with him as a servant [a common problem at the time, as servant girls and masters lived in such close proximity]. So that Billings murder'd his own brother, assisted in quartering him, and then lay with his own mother, while his brother's mangled limbs were under the bed.'

A different version appeared in the *Ipswich Journal*, dated 7 May 1726 (though in this one the identity of Thomas Billings's father is not given):

> She said she did not value Death, only the thought of burning was terrible to her. After the Deed Warrant came down, and she found she must die, she began to shew signs of repentance, and on Sunday before Execution she fainted at the sermon which was preached in the afternoon; and then she acknowledged that she was guilty of whatever had been sworn against her, and that she had had two Bastards; and that Billings was her son, who was about 22 years

---

13 A role generally taken by the prison Ordinary, usually an Anglican, though from 1735 ministers of other faiths were also admitted, aiming to squeeze a confession from the condemned. The Newgate Ordinary, Revd Guthrie, was Catherine's religious advisor; he managed to persuade her to confess.

old, and by her dropt in a basket at Holt-Heath, near Omersley, in Worcester and was put to nurse by the Parish to one Billings, from whence he was call'd Billings.

A third version of Thomas Billings's parentage was provided by the *Newcastle Courant*, on Saturday 14 May: after referring to Catherine Hayes as 'such a vile woman scarcely to be paralleled', it announced:

Upon taking the Sacrament at Newgate, she affirmed that Billings, who was hanged in chains near Tyburn Road, was her own son, got by Mr Hayes, this supposed before her marriage with him, so that the son killed his father, and assisted in quartering him, had Criminal Conversation with his mother, and lay with her when his Father's mangled limbs were under the bed.

They added that 'a special order from the Council' had been issued that she should be burned alive – as was customary in such cases – and not first strangled. It seems likely that the writer of the article misquoted the piece in the *London Journal* when it stated that it was the murder victim, John Hayes (and not his father) who had fathered Thomas Billings. However, in both accounts – one published two days prior to her execution and the other five days afterwards – Catherine had no opportunity to put the record straight by stating which Hayes was the father of Thomas Billings – her late husband or her father-in-law.

According to the *Newgate Calendar*, when asked the reason for murdering her husband she repeated her allegations, saying that, 'it was no more Sin to kill him than a Dog or Cat, because of the cruel Usuage he gave her, and his blasphemous Expressions which he too frequently used'.

The Execution

On the Sunday before her execution she attended a service which was held in the prison chapel. For a fee paid to the turnkeys – a practice that earned them a lot of money, until it was stopped in 1860 – members of the public were allowed admittance, ghoulishly anxious to hear the Ordinary's pulpit-thumping sermon and watch the look of terror on the faces of the condemned. Throughout the service the prisoners sat on either side of a table, draped in black cloth; on the table was a black coffin.

The following day, which would be her last on earth, 9 May 1726, Catherine Hayes received the sacrament in the prison chapel – available only to those condemned to die within one week – and was then taken to the Press Yard with the others who had been condemned to death. Their leg irons were removed and nooses put around their necks; they were then transported by three carts or wagons, sitting on their coffins, to Tyburn.[14]

Thomas Billings went in the cart carrying the two burglars but Catherine was strapped to a hurdle or sledge and dragged through the streets of London, stirring up all the dust and filth littering the streets – an easy target for both missiles and blows directed at her from the jeering crowds lining the route and baying for her blood.

The 2-mile journey to Tyburn could take as long as three hours – via Holborn, St Giles and the Tyburn Road (now Oxford Street) to Tyburn Lane (now Park Lane). The horse-drawn carts, sometimes draped in black cloth, were accompanied by a large posse of guards and officials – the Chief Marshal, on horseback in all his finery, the Under-Marshal, javelin men and constables, with the armed guards bringing up the rear. When the procession reached the church of St Sepulchre[15], its bell began to toll as family and friends gave the condemned nosegays. A church official then addressed them: 'You that are condemned to die, repent with lamentable tears; ask mercy of the Lord for the salvation of your souls.'

---

14 At the time, Tyburn was a village, west of London; the site of the gallows or 'the Triple Tree', was close to the present Marble Arch, now marked by a plaque on a traffic island. Public hangings at Tyburn began in 1196 and ended in 1783, with the execution of a highwayman, John Austin, after which public executions usually took place at Newgate Prison, Horsemonger Lane, Wandsworth (originally the House of Correction for Surrey) until 1868.

15 The hand-bell at St Sepulchre's was rung twice, once on the eve of an execution and again as the carts carrying the condemned passed the church on their way to the gallows. In 1555, John Rogers, a former vicar of St Sepulchre's, a married man with eleven children, was burned at the stake for heresy.

Then, turning to the huge crowds that had gathered, he urged them to, 'pray heartily unto God for these poor sinners who are now going to their death, for whom the bell tolls.'

As custom demanded, the procession stopped at various taverns on the way; it was here that the condemned were allowed off the wagon, though the hangman remained in the cart. Still tethered and guarded, they were given ale or gin to drink before resuming their dreaded journey. Mercifully, many were drunk by the time they reached the gallows. This may be the origin of the term 'off the wagon', meaning to take a last drink.

On reaching Tyburn, a huge crowd was waiting to witness the grisly spectacle; at street level, hordes surged forward as the carts approached and every window and rooftop was taken up with excited spectators. So great was the crowd that one of the spectators' grandstands, especially erected for executions two years before and holding about 150 people, collapsed, causing the deaths of at least two people – a gentleman and a snuff-box maker – and injuring many more.

The *British Gazetteer* informed its readers that some twelve men and women were 'maimed and wounded in a most cruel manner; some having their legs, others their arms, &c. broke. Some part of the scaffold [the spectators' stand] being left standing, the mob gathered upon it again in numbers; and in about half an hour more, that also fell down, and several were hurt.'

More drama ensued when the two highwaymen, John Mapp and Henry Vigus, attempted to escape from the carts, having freed themselves of their nooses and wrist ties. Sadly for the men, they were immediately seized. The prison chaplain would usually at this point exhort the condemned to repent their sins and, hopefully, provide the expectant crowd with some suitably anguished dying words – preferably with a last-minute warning about the dire consequences of sin. Especially dramatic or heart-rending dying speeches were often issued in pamphlets on sale on the streets very soon after the execution had taken place – and often before, the writers being rather unscrupulous. Some sought to delay the moment of death as long as possible by embarking on epic speeches, addressing the crowds at great length and with dramatic emphasis, either confessing to their crimes or vehemently denying any culpability; faced with such a large and attentive audience, others took the opportunity to rail against the injustice of their sentence.

Although the hangman was entitled to claim possession of the dead person's clothes, some of the condemned still chose to wear their finest apparel, anxious to cut a fine figure on the gallows. James Boswell described a young highwayman, Paul Lewis, in Newgate, awaiting execution in 1763: he was 'drest in a white coat & blue silk vest & silver, with his hair neatly queued & a silver-lac'd hat, smartly cock'd'. Others, however, wore little more than rags to ensure that the hated hangman didn't profit from their deaths.

On the same visit, Boswell recalled seeing Hannah Dagoe, convicted of robbery and under sentence of death, describing her as 'a big unconcerned being'. Hannah was a feisty, muscular Irish woman who, having managed to release the cords binding her arms, threw a hefty punch at the hangman, knocking him down. She then proceeded to strip off 'her hat, cloak and other parts of her dress' and to toss them into the baying crowd. The hangman managed to get the noose over her head but she suddenly threw herself out of the cart, breaking her neck in an instant. Highwayman Stephen Gardiner also cheated the hangman out of his dues by going to his death in 1724 wearing a shroud! As well as money for clothing, hangmen were permitted to sell off bits of the noose for sixpence an inch, probably the origin of the phrase 'money for old rope'.

Eventually – if the prisoner had not escaped, attacked the hangman or thrown themselves out of the vehicle – the carts would be positioned under the beams. The executioner – Richard Arnet, in this instance – would throw the loose end of the noose over the beam. Once it was secured the horses were whipped to make them surge forward, leaving the criminals hanging – and, more often than not, choking to death. Family members – and sometimes the hangman himself, if he had received a large enough bribe or was anxious to complete the assignment as quickly as possible and escape from a particularly hostile crowd – would often pull down hard on the legs in an attempt to quicken death and thus avoid the awful writhing on the end of the rope referred to as 'the Tyburn jig'.

On 9 May 1726 the corpse of Thomas Billings was left hanging in chains from a gibbet, close to the pond in Marylebone Fields, where he and Thomas Wood had dumped the butchered remains of John Hayes.

The fate awaiting Catherine, who, still strapped to the hurdle, had seen the hanging of her son, Thomas, was infinitely worse. She was taken from the hurdle and fixed to the stake by an iron collar around her neck and an iron chain around her body; the stake was close to the gallows on which the bodies of the nine men executed before her still hung. It was usual practice to strangle someone before the flames reached them, and for that purpose a cord was placed around her neck and through a hole on the stake. The order, however, had been given that, because her crime had been so heinous, she was not to be strangled first, but must burn to death.

Two cartloads of fire wood were piled around her and set alight. It was reported that 'she begg'd for the sake of Jesus, to be strangled first; whereupon the Executioner drew tight the halter, but the flame coming to his hand in the space of a second, he let it go, when she gave three dreadful shrieks'.[16]

As she became engulfed in the flames, she was seen to be desperately trying to kick away the burning logs; at this point Arnet, in an attempt to quicken her death, threw a large piece of wood at her head which 'broke her skull, when her brains came plentifully out. In little more than an hour her body was reduced to ashes.'[17]

There were a number of other women sentenced to burn at the stake for husband-killing in the eighteenth century, one being Elizabeth Broadingham, who, in 1776, was found guilty of petty treason for murdering her husband, John. She, too, was burned at the stake – but, unlike Catherine Hayes, she was strangled first. It was said that some of those spectators who watched her burn stooped to gather handfuls of her ashes as souvenirs. Her lover and accomplice, Thomas Aikney, was hanged and his body sent to the newly built Leeds Infirmary for dissection.

Another criminal offence that constituted treason and for which the sentence was death by burning was the common

---

16   *The Weekly Journal/The British Gazetteer.*

17   According to *The Newgate Calendar*, 'she survived the flames for a considerable time and her body was not perfectly reduced to ashes until four hours later.'

practice of 'coining' – filing off parts of gold coins. In 1788 Phoebe Harris, a life-long 'coiner', was burned at the stake at Newgate before a huge crowd of onlookers.

As for Catherine Hayes, there is little doubt that she had an extremely unfortunate start in life, and yet so many young women, before and since, have managed to overcome disastrous beginnings and lack of parental guidance yet still lived out their lives without resorting to murder. It may well be that John Hayes was a brutal, parsimonious man, successful in business but deplorably lacking in any endearing qualities. Clearly, after his marriage to Catherine, he realised she was a chronic malcontent, quarrelsome by nature, and morally and sexually incontinent.

Catherine Hayes has gained notoriety in the annals of crime, not only for the viciousness of her crime, but also her horrendous death at the stake. Yet she was a complex character – not merely a sexually voracious shrew – for she seems to have been able to seduce her illegitimate son, Thomas Billings, as well as young Thomas Wood – in addition to numerous other liaisons. Her husband also, it is worth noting, was not averse to sleeping with her either (if she was telling the truth when she said that he had fathered fourteen of their children during their fourteen-year marriage) – despite being under no illusion regarding her rampant promiscuity.

Two

ELIZABETH BROWNRIGG

'Wicked beyond belief'

Forty-one years later, in 1767, another notorious Londoner, Elizabeth Brownrigg, suffered a similar fate, though by a slightly less barbarous method – hanging. Many considered her even more evil than Catherine Hayes, for Brownrigg's particular brand of cruelty was sustained, an extreme form of sadism (and not, as in the Hayes case, the result of three people fuelled by alcohol and intent on drunken violence) – and moreover, her victim was a young, innocent, fourteen-year-old maid.

Even Londoners, hardened to the harsh reality of the city where many of its inhabitants were living in dire poverty and accustomed to the casual, often drunken cruelty meted out to women and domestic servants, were appalled when the crimes of Elizabeth Brownrigg came to light – so much so that on the day of her execution the streets leading to Tyburn were swarming with thousands of jeering spectators, noisily jubilant and eager to watch her die.

There were no obvious indications in Elizabeth Brownrigg's earlier life to suggest that she would, in middle age, commit such an appalling murder, meet such an ignoble and harrowing death or have her name become notorious, a byword for cruelty in the annals of crime.

Little is known of Elizabeth's early life except that she was born in 1720 to a working-class family named Hartley or Harkly, in Greenwich; many accounts of this case suggest that she married James Brownrigg whilst still in her teens. However, she later stated that they were married in 1745, which would have made her twenty-five at the time. To add credence to the date she gave, it was confirmed at her trial that, when the Brownriggs first took in apprentice girls in 1765, they had lived together as man and wife, on very good and affectionate terms, for twenty years.

James Brownrigg was described in some contemporary newspapers as a plumber, whilst others suggested he was a house painter. He probably took on either trade whenever the opportunity for employment arose. Elizabeth also worked as a midwife, and the couple lived in Greenwich for some years before moving to a house in Flower-de-Luce Court – sometimes called Fleur-de-lis Court, Fetter Lane – in the heart of London. At the time the Brownriggs took up residence the area had a reputation for bawdy houses and lewd behaviour. It was also the scene of several murders; in 1735, a fifteen-year-old girl, Sarah Thorn, was beaten and starved to death by her mother, who, though tried for the murder, was acquitted. In 1742, Thomas Homan was hanged in Fetter Lane, close to the scene of his crime (the murder of an elderly resident).[18]

At the time the population of London was rapidly expanding, reaching nearly one million by the end of the century. The numbers were greatly increased with the influx of Huguenot refugees throughout the seventeenth and eighteenth centuries. They were silk merchants and master weavers and soon established a flourishing textile industry, mainly in the Spitalfield area of the city. By the 1730s Irish weavers had arrived to work in the silk-weaving trade and, although there was conflict between the two factions, they were united in their protests against price-cutting and the import of French silks. The resulting skirmishes – the Spitalfield Riots – were in full force at the time of the Brownrigg case and continued well into 1769.

As London expanded there was an increased demand for builders, house-painters and men able to install and service the machinery vital to the many small workshops in the city. Plumbers also provided a much-needed service to the rapidly increasing population: there were constant and often abortive attempts to direct surface water, carrying with it vast amounts of disgusting detritus from the streets of London, towards the River Thames via covered culverts, ditches and drains. Maids could

---

18   Fetter Lane, close to Fleet Street, is where the Great Fire of 1666 ended.

be seen sweeping the cobbles in front of houses with their feet encased in wooden blocks to raise them above all the revolting mess of rotten vegetables, copious quantities of steaming horse dung – a magnet for swarms of feasting flies – and, if the communal cess-pits were full, human faeces, offal and the rotting carcasses of domestic animals and fowl.[19] It was not until the late eighteenth century that roads were improved and, in some cases, widened to accommodate carriages and the streets were, in theory at least, regularly swept.

The air was also thick with the soot and grime from the open coal and wood fires and the locally subsidised oil lamps lighting the busiest thoroughfares and market places. The streets were teeming with pedlars and street hawkers, shouting out their wares – coffee, milk, fruit and pies and, of course, copious supplies of gin – adding to the incessant bustle and cacophony of noise. The street traders and the increase in horse-drawn traffic caused chaos in the narrow lanes and alleys of the city. Accidents involving pedestrians being mown down by carriage wheels and under the clattering hooves of horses were commonplace.

Adding to the nauseating stench of the city of London at the time was the smell of putrefying corpses in the graveyards. An article in *The Morning Chronicle*, on 9 February 1778, highlighted the smells coming from 'some burial grounds, near the centre of the city, the graves, or pits, for the reception of the lower sort of people, are made sufficiently wide to contain four, five or six wooden coffins.' Many of these burial pits were vandalised – sometimes by 'grave-robbers' after easy pickings – and the exposed corpses added yet one more ingredient to the already heavily polluted air of London.

There would have been, therefore, plenty of work in the city for a practical and hard-working man like James Brownrigg, and he and his growing family prospered – so much so that they were able to afford country lodgings in Islington, a village north of London, somewhere for them to visit at weekends, a brief respite from the malodorous air and noisy, polluted streets of the city.

---

19   The cess-pits were emptied by the 'night-soil men' and, in more salubrious households, these primitive latrines were referred to as 'the necessary'.

During their marriage, Elizabeth Brownrigg gave birth to sixteen children. However, only three survived beyond infancy: two sons, John and Billy, and an unnamed daughter. The number of children she had, and the high mortality rate in her family, was not that unusual; at a time when disease was rife, in the pre-penicillin days – and rapidly spread by overcrowded living conditions, contaminated water and lack of hygiene – thousands of babies died, either at birth or in infancy.[20]

Well-versed, therefore, in pregnancy and childbirth, Elizabeth was in demand as a midwife and – such was her kindly reputation and efficiency – the overseers of the parish of St Dunstan's-in-the-West appointed her as their official midwife, responsible for the care of destitute women in labour. She also, no doubt, offered her services for laying out the dead, as did many midwifes at that time, finding that the management of both birth and death was a very lucrative business indeed.

By 1765 the Brownriggs were so successful that Elizabeth needed to employ some apprentices (or maids) who would also take on the domestic chores. She applied to the workhouse to find suitable young girls; every resident of the workhouse who was fit enough to work was compelled to undertake menial and arduous tasks to pay for his or her keep.

In this way, employers like Elizabeth Brownrigg were taking full advantage of the newly implemented scheme whereby young persons could be taken from workhouses and other charitable institutions as live-in apprentices, either to learn a trade or to work as domestic servants. In return for removing these youngsters from the dire conditions of the workhouse, they were given employment, food and lodging. The poor were not completely without help; they were given 'outside relief' from the parish, charities and individual philanthropists, but the workhouse was the last refuge of the destitute and desperate. The prospect of ending up in the workhouse loomed large in the psyche of the poor who were unable to scrape even the most basic level of

---

20 By 1770, there were about ninety workhouses in London, with some 15,000 inmates. The death rate for children in workhouses and other charitable institutions was over 90 per cent and, in the population as a whole, one in five children died in infancy.

sustenance. It was often viewed with scorn by more affluent city dwellers and, one suspects, by many of its inmates as well.

Traditionally there was a trial period of about a month – referred to as 'upon liking'- whereupon, if both maid and mistress were satisfied with the arrangement, an agreement was made and the term of employment or the apprenticeship began.

In February 1765, Mrs Brownrigg obtained a young girl called Mary Mitchell from the overseers of the Poor of White Friars' precinct and, at first, treated her well. After her probationary period, however, Mrs Brownrigg's reign of terror began; as well as administering regular beatings for the slightest infringement of her rules, she developed the nasty habit of grabbing the girl's cheeks and pulling them down so hard that her eyes bled. A full account of Mary Mitchell's ill-treatment at the hands of her mistress would be made known when she gave evidence against her mistress at the subsequent trial at the Old Bailey, two and a half years later.

Three months later, on 15 May, Mrs Brownrigg acquired another girl, fourteen-year-old Mary Jones, from the charitable institution the Foundling Hospital – established for the 'education and maintenance of exposed and deserted young children' – which, at that time, was situated in the countryside on the outskirts of the city. Mary had been in the hospital since 1751 – all her life, in fact – and this may have been her first employment. As with Mary Mitchell, Mary Jones was treated well during the month's trial period and both girls were employed to assist Mrs Brownrigg in her thriving midwifery business. As a side-line, Elizabeth Brownrigg would provide lodging for women with nowhere else to go during their lying-in period; they always left, she stated later, as soon as they had given birth.

However, once the girls were officially assigned to her, everything changed; their lives became blighted by constant harassment and meagre food rations; they were often given only bread and water and occasionally tossed scraps of food from the Brownriggs' plates as they dined. To add to their misery, their sleeping arrangements were both filthy and totally inadequate.

Mary Jones, in particular, was treated appallingly. She was ordered to wear dirty, lice-ridden rags instead of her own clothes and she became the butt of coarse ribaldry by James Brownrigg and his son, John. Mrs Brownrigg slapped and punched the girl, calling her 'nothing but a filthy slut'. She was kept working on domestic chores for eighteen hours each day and slept on a mat in the kitchen.

Whenever she incurred Mrs Brownrigg's displeasure – for instance, when she tried to escape – she was stripped naked and laid across two chairs and then repeatedly whipped until her mistress had to take a rest from her exertions. Her sadism knew no bounds; having established that Mary had a great fear of water, Mrs Brownrigg would often push the girl's head into a pail of water and keep it submerged to the point of drowning before reviving the girl to suffer yet more beatings. This form of torture (in essence still used today in the form of water-boarding) became a favourite pastime of, not only Mrs Brownrigg, but also her husband and her son. They also enjoyed abusing the girl in other ways. Whenever they found her on her knees, scrubbing the floor, they would creep up and grab her by the ankles and then force her head into the bucket of water. This vile practice was repeated several times each day.

Mary Jones, however, was less submissive than Mary Mitchell, and was determined to escape her tormentors, making several attempts before she finally succeeded. To keep her confined, the Brownriggs made her sleep under a dresser in their bedroom; the doors in the house were kept locked and the windows barred. Then, early one morning, when the Brownriggs were still asleep, she crept downstairs and saw that the key to the front door had been inadvertently left in the lock the night before. She saw her chance and ran from the house, never to return.

As she had probably never ventured far beyond the grounds of the Foundling Hospital she was unsure of her bearings, not knowing how to get back to the only place she regarded as home. Hurrying away from Fetter Lane, she roamed the unfamiliar and dangerous streets in the heart of the city, asking anyone she met where she might find the Foundling Hospital. Eventually a pedlar took her back to the hospital, where she was examined by doctors; they were appalled at the girl's condition. Not only was she starving, she was also covered in cuts and bruises and blind in one eye. The wound was caused when her head was repeatedly jammed into the water bucket, and had become infected. He informed the Governors of the hospital; they, in turn, ordered Mr Plumbtree, their solicitor, to write to James Brownrigg on 24 July 1765 [in which he was referred to as a 'house-painter'], threatening prosecution and demanding an explanation for the injuries inflicted on the girl.

This letter was ignored by Brownrigg – and yet the Governors failed to take any further action, merely notifying him that Mary Jones's apprenticeship had been formally terminated.

Meanwhile, poor Mary Mitchell remained in the Brownrigg household and became the butt of persistent cruelty, not only from her mistress but also, occasionally, from James Brownrigg and their son, John. The full extent of the cruelties she suffered, and the means the family took to keep her confined to the house, were revealed at the subsequent trial at the Old Bailey.

However, about a year later, when Mary Mitchell did manage to escape, her freedom was short-lived. She was met in the street by Billy, the younger of the two Brownrigg sons, who forcibly dragged her back to face her tormentors once more. Enraged by her attempt to escape, the poor girl was punished even more severely and, once more, confined to the house.

Unfortunately, another young girl, fourteen-year-old Mary Clifford, was allocated to Mrs Brownrigg by the overseers of the White Friars' precinct on 18 February 1766. She, too, was treated reasonably well during the 'upon liking' period but soon became the victim of jeers and insults; she was also stripped naked, made to work for hours on end and relentlessly beaten.

Little wonder that the wretched girl was a bed-wetter, thus enraging her mistress even more. She was not allowed to sleep on even the meanest, makeshift bed but instead she was forced to sleep on a filthy mat in the coal-hole with only, if she were lucky, bread and water to sustain her. After some time she was given some straw to lie on but her only covering was her few articles of clothing, and she suffered terribly from the cold.

Hunger drove this poor girl to break open a cupboard, hoping to find even a crust to eat – but it was empty. On another occasion, when she had been left without any water, she broke some boards (possibly covering a water butt or barrel) in an attempt to find something to drink but, of course, Mrs Brownrigg used these misdemeanours to punish the girl even more severely than ever.

Mrs Brownrigg's cruelty escalated; she even fixed an iron jack-chain around Mary Clifford's neck, tied the end to the yard-door and pulled it so tight it nearly strangled her. When the girl was eventually released from her labours she was locked away in the coal-hole at 'candle-light', with her hands tied behind her back and the jack-chain still around her neck.

James Brownrigg was responsible for providing clothes for the apprentices and maids under his roof, and he decided that he didn't want their garments damaged by bloodstains. For this reason, both Marys were stripped naked before having their hands tied above their heads, fixed to a water pipe that ran across the kitchen ceiling, before being beaten mercilessly until they bled. Fearing that such exertions might fracture the water pipe, Elizabeth Brownrigg persuaded her husband to insert a metal hook from one of the beams to provide a more robust mooring.

By doing this, James Brownrigg was clearly complicit in the cruel treatment of the two girls, and witnessed it without censure. Not only that – John, the elder of the two sons living at home, treated them heartlessly. He picked on Mary Clifford for special abuse and, on one occasion, he ordered her to put up a half-tester bedstead which was clearly too heavy for her to lift. Seeing that she hadn't the strength to do as she was bid, he taunted her and beat her viciously. He would even take over a sustained beating of Mary, tied to the hook in the kitchen ceiling, when his mother became fatigued by her exertions.

Mary Clifford's ill-treatment continued without mercy. One day, she mentioned her sufferings to a French woman who was lodging in the house at the time. Fearing further punishment, Mary begged her not to say anything. Later on, however – in the wake of a disagreement between the lodger and Mrs Brownrigg – the woman remonstrated with her. Furious at this interference, Mrs Brownrigg fetched a pair of scissors and yelled at Mary, 'I will cure you of your tattling!'

She then cut the girl's tongue in two places, adding a hideous warning: 'Next time I will cut that wagging tongue out completely!'

Nor did her cruelty stop there; it continued relentlessly. On the morning of 13 July, in the presence of Mary Mitchell, she made Mary Clifford strip before tying her to the hook in the ceiling. She then proceeded to beat her so severely that blood from her wounds pooled onto the kitchen floor. Her body was covered with sores and scabs from previous assaults, yet she was beaten severely at least five times that same day.

There was one person, however, who was concerned, if rather belatedly, about young Mary Clifford's well-being – her stepmother, Mrs Clifford, who had been living in the country for some time. On her return to London, she made enquires at White Friars and was told that the girl was apprenticed to the Brownriggs but when, on 12 July, she went to the house in Fetter Lane, James Brownrigg denied any knowledge of her daughter and became abusive when challenged.

By chance, as Mrs Clifford was leaving, Mrs Deacon, the wife of a baker who lived next door, drew her aside and told her of the awful sound of screaming and groaning that she had heard coming from the Brownriggs' house. She and her husband promised to watch their neighbour's house more carefully for signs of abuse and, having established Mrs Clifford's address, report their findings.

After sending Mrs Clifford on her way, James Brownrigg set out for Hampstead on business and decided to buy a pig, probably to fatten up in the back-yard ready for the Christmas festivities – a common practice in London at the time and even longer in rural areas. When the time came for it to be eaten, the poor creature would be straddled along a wooden bench and have its throat cut by a member of the family or a 'pig-sticker' doing his rounds of the city's fetid yards and alleyways.

The Brownriggs' pig was housed in a covered yard with the sky-light removed to help dispel the revolting smell. Seeing that the sky-light had been removed, Mr and Mrs Deacon next door ordered one of their servants, William Clipson, to look down into the pig-pen from one of their windows overlooking the yard.

He saw a crumpled heap lying in the pen and the alarm was raised. Mrs Deacon persuaded him to climb out on the roof leads for a better look. He tried to ascertain whether the inert girl was dead or alive by throwing down bits of dirt, but there was no response.

Mrs Deacon fetched Mary's stepmother, Mrs Clifford – not until that evening, though, as she was at work – and together they went to inform Mr Grundy, one of the overseers of St Dunstan's, of Mary's fate. All three proceeded to the Brownriggs' house and demanded to see Mary Clifford. As the family always referred to Mary Clifford as Nan or Nanny, the belligerent James Brownrigg tried to outsmart them by bringing out Mary Mitchell instead of Mary Clifford. But William Clipson declared that this Mary was not the one he had seen lying in the pig-pen; that girl, he said, had short red hair.

Mr Grundy then sent for a constable and a cursory search was made of the Brownriggs' house, but the girl was not found. Clearly, someone had moved her and somehow managed to conceal her successfully within the house.

Although James Brownrigg remained abusive, Mr Grundy took charge of Mary Mitchell and, in the safety of the workhouse, she was examined and the extent of her wounds was realised. When she tried to pull off her tattered leather bodice she screamed with pain – it had become stuck fast to her seeping lacerations. The horrified overseers promised her that she need never return to the Brownriggs and so, once she knew she was safely out of their clutches, she was able to give a true picture of the torturous treatment both she and Mary Clifford had received at the hands of the Brownriggs. She also confirmed that Mary had been brought in from the pig-pen earlier – she had seen the girl on the stairs shortly before the search was made of the house.

Determined to rescue Mary Clifford, Mr Grundy gathered reinforcements and returned to the house for a more thorough search. They were threatened with legal action by James Brownrigg but, unbowed, Mr Grundy sent for a coach to take Mr Brownrigg to the compter (a small lock-up) under arrest on suspicion of murder.

At this point, Brownrigg promised to produce the girl within half an hour if Grundy would dispatch the coach. This agreed, poor Mary was eventually brought from a cupboard under a cabinet in the dining room, wearing a pair of shoes quickly shoved on to her feet by the Brownriggs' son, John. She was in an appalling state, covered in old bruises and fresh bleeding lacerations; some of her old cuts had already begun to mortify. There was no longer any doubt whatsoever that she had been grossly mistreated – way beyond the usual and accepted levels of punishment administered by employers to their servants.

James Brownrigg was immediately arrested and taken to the Wood Street Compter, but – presumably while her husband had been stalling – Elizabeth Brownrigg and her son had managed to escape, taking with them a gold watch and other valuables. Brownrigg was later questioned by Alderman Crosby at Guildhall, remanded in custody and returned to the Wood Street Compter.

Meanwhile, both girls, having been examined by the doctor at the workhouse, were taken to Guildhall to be questioned by the city's Lord Mayor. Mary Clifford was in such a weak and pitiful state that she was carried there in a sedan chair.

Shortly after questioning, both Mary Mitchell and Mary Clifford were taken for treatment at St Bartholomew's Hospital, in the City of London, but, sadly, Mary Clifford died of her injuries a few days later, on 9 August.

A coroner's inquest was held and the verdict reached was one of 'wilful murder against James and Elizabeth Brownrigg and their son, John.'

Elizabeth Brownrigg and her son, however, were still at large, disguising themselves in clothing bought at the Rag Fair in Petticoat Lane, not far from Fetter Lane, where crowds of Londoners flocked at weekends to exchange old clothes or haggle for bargains from the numerous market stalls. The events that led to their subsequent arrest were described in an article written by John Wingrave, one of the constables who arrested Elizabeth Brownrigg.[21] It appeared in the *Derby Mercury*:

21   There were one or two constables to each parish, unpaid and chosen by the community; they were allowed to investigate crimes and assist in arrests. In 1750 Henry Fielding, writer and Westminster magistrate, established the Bow Street Runners, forerunners of the Metropolitan Police of 1829. Elderly night-watchmen or 'Charleys' patrolled the streets at night and could escort miscreants to a lock-up. For a small fee, they would rouse workers from their beds early in the morning by either banging on the door or tapping the bedroom window with his pole.

Elizabeth Brownrigg, who stands charged with the murder of Mary Clifford, her apprentice girl, and John Brownrigg her son, a youth of about nineteen years of age, were apprehended at a chandler's shop near the church in Wandsworth, Surry [*sic*] and brought to the Poultry Compter about four in the afternoon.

They took this lodging on Tuesday last, for a few days only, and passed for man and wife, cohabiting together and lying in the same bed;[22] that the first day they did not stir out of the room; but on the second the young man came down to light a candle when the landlord [Mr Dunbar] had a full view of him; though without any suspicion at that time, he being a labouring man who seldom sees a newspaper; but on Saturday evening by accident took one up and casting his eyes upon the advertisement relating to the apprehending of the above-mentioned persons, went home and told his wife what he had read and that he was sure the persons that lodged with them answered the description; the woman being greatly terrified thereat was for turning them out in the street immediately but her husband remonstrated against such a step as, in all probability, if the least scent should be got by the mob, they would be torn to pieces and themselves involved in the same calamity for harbouring them; whereupon it was agreed to keep the affair secret till he had made further enquiry.

Accordingly, on Sunday morning he set out for London and enquired at Peele's coffee-house in Fleet-street, where Mr Owen, the Churchwarden of St. Dunstan's lived; on the master's showing him the house, Mr Owen (who was then at church) was sent for; and finding the man's account very exact, Mr Deacon, baker in Flower-de-luce court, and Mr Wingrave, Constable, immediately went back with the person to Wandsworth, where they found the mother sitting by the bed-side and the son walking about the room; she was dressed in a brown and yellow stuff gown and a straw hat and had so well disguised herself that the parties who went to take her, and knew her personally, being her near neighbours, declared they should not have known her had they not received the previous suspicion from the person where she lodged; her son had on a livery thick-set frock.

---

22   There was no indication in contemporary accounts that there was any un-natural connection between mother and son – nor indeed was it ever insinuated that there was a sexual element in the family members' ill-treatment of the three servant girls.

On the Monday night preceding it is said they laid in Dean-street, Fetter-lane, which is not unlikely as they declared they went down Fetter-lane in a hackney-coach on Tuesday morning.

The taking of the above persons was conducted with such calmness and privacy that not the least bustle was made; and not even the coachman knew what they were about till when he had brought his fare to town he was ordered to drive to the Poultry Compter.

Yesterday morning a very great number of persons assembled before the Mansion-house and the Poultry Compter, expecting that the above Elizabeth Brownrigg and her son would be carried for examination before the Right Hon., the Lord Mayor; and they continued till near two o'clock when they dispersed on finding the prisoners were not likely to be brought out.

The mother was in convulsions all Sunday night and continued very ill yesterday; nor could the son with safety be conveyed to the Mansion-house; the Lord Mayor therefore sent for the Coroner who signed a warrant for her commitment to Newgate, in order to take her trial at the ensuing sessions at the Old Bailey. The son is to remain in the Poultry Compter till he can be examined.

The Trial

Elizabeth, James and John Brownrigg all stood trial in the Central Criminal Court at the Old Bailey on Friday, 11 September 1767, before the Lord Mayor of London, Sir Robert Kite, the Honourable James Hewitt, Esq. one of the judges of his Majesty's court of King's Bench, James Eyre, Esq. Recorder, a jury and various Justices of the Peace.[23]

23   Five years earlier, in 1762, Sarah Metyard and her daughter, Sarah Morgan Metyard, were tried at the Old Bailey for the murder – and dismemberment – of one of their apprentices, thirteen-year-old Anne (or Ann) Naylor, in Hanover Square. Parts of her body were found in a hole in Chick Lane. The case was re-markably similar to that of Elizabeth Brownrigg. Both women were found guilty and hanged at Tyburn; their bodies were sent to the Surgeons' Hall for dissection, where the public could pay to watch corpses being anatomised.

All three were indicted for:

> ...not having the fear of God before their eyes, but being moved by
> the instigation of the devil, did wickedly, maliciously, and feloniously,
> from the 1st of May, 1766, and divers other days and times, to the
> 4th of August 1767, make an assault on Mary Clifford... wilfully, and
> of malice aforethought, did make an assault, with divers large whips,
> canes, sticks, and staves, and did strike, beat, and whip, over the naked
> head, shoulders, back, and other parts of her naked body, in a cruel
> and inhuman manner, giving her divers large wounds, swellings, and
> bruises; and with divers large hempen cords, and iron chains, round
> the neck of the said Mary, did bind and fasten, giving her thereby a
> large and violent swelling on the neck of her the said Mary; and in a
> certain place, under the stairs, leading into a cellar, in the dwelling-
> house of the said James, did fasten and imprison; by means of which
> striking, whipping, binding, fastening, confining, and imprisoning her
> the said Mary, she did pine and languish till the 9th of August, when
> the said Mary did die.
>
> And the said James and John his son, of malice aforethought, were
> present, abetting, comforting, and maintaining her, the said Elizabeth,
> the said Mary to kill and murder.
>
> And the said Elizabeth and James her husband stood charged on the
> coroner's inquest for the said murder.

All these defendants pleaded not guilty to the charges.

The first witness called to give evidence was young Mary
Mitchell, a very brave young girl indeed to stand up in the
courtroom at the Old Bailey and confront her tormentors. She told
those present that she was nearly sixteen years of age. When asked if
she understood about taking the oath, and swearing to tell the truth,
she assured those assembled that she could say her catechism.

She confirmed that she had lived in the house of James
Brownrigg, in Flower-de-Luce Court, Fetter Lane, and that
in May she had served two years of her apprenticeship. Her
period of 'upon liking' lasted for two months, after which she
was bound over to James Brownrigg. As for Mary Clifford, she
confirmed that she had been with the Brownriggs for eighteen
months before she died and her 'upon liking' had been for one
month only, during which time she was treated very well. She
was even allowed to sleep on a bed – but about a week after

her probationary month was up, the ill-treatment began. When asked what form this ill-treatment took, Mary Mitchell said that Elizabeth Brownrigg had beaten Mary Clifford over her head and shoulders, using a walking-cane and an old hearth brush. She had also seen the Brownriggs' son, John, strike the girl.

Although there was a bed in every room of the house and only one lodger in residence at the time, soon after she became a bound apprentice Mary Clifford was made to sleep either on the floor in the parlour or in the passageway. More often she was forced to sleep in a coal-hole under the stairs or the cellar below, which was airless and pitch black. Mary Mitchell had been given the job of removing all the coals from the cellar to make room for Mary Clifford, and sometimes the witness herself was forced to sleep there as well, at which times they were locked in.

When asked the reason for this, Mary Mitchell said that the girl 'had the misfortune of wetting the bed' and at first was given a mat to lie on when she slept in the cellar. She was sometimes made to sleep naked and, despite the cold, she was only given 'a bit of a sack with some straw on it'. To cover herself she was given a 'bit of a blanket'; either that or she had to use the few clothes she possessed.

Mary Mitchell confirmed that, on one occasion, Mary Clifford had been so hungry she had broken open a cupboard in the hope of finding food. When Elizabeth Brownrigg saw the damaged lock she punished Mary by forcing her to strip naked while she spent the whole day scrubbing floors and doing the washing; at intervals she was subjected to severe beatings to her head and shoulders, using the stump of a riding whip.

Asked who locked the girls in the cellar at night, Mary replied that it was usually Mrs Brownrigg but occasionally one of the male apprentices was ordered to do it. At other times, Billy, the younger of the Brownriggs' sons, did it but it was more usually done by the other son, John, who used to stay in London at the weekends rather than go to the country with the family.

On several occasions, when the family went to stay the weekend at their country lodgings in Islington, both girls were locked in the cellar on the Saturday until they were released on the Sunday night. They were made to strip naked and sometimes only had a few rags and a boy's waistcoat to cover them. This was done to save the clothes provided by James Brownrigg from wear and tear. They were often left with only a piece of bread to eat but no water to drink. It was usually an apprentice who unlocked the door to the cellar on the Sunday night when the Brownriggs returned.

Questioned further, Mary said that although Mary Clifford had been, at fourteen, a little younger than her, she was much taller. Describing one particular beating inflicted on Mary Clifford by John Brownrigg, when his parents were away, Mary Mitchell told the court: 'Once he beat her with a leather strap for not turning up a parlour bed; she was trying to turn up a press bed, and could not, so he took a leather strap which my master used to put around his waist, for my mistress to hold by when she rode behind him.'

Asked how Mary was dressed at the time, the witness replied: 'She had on a boy's waistcoat, it was a very old rag, it did not cover her well; it came very high before, but was torn on each shoulder; it did not cover her behind.'

Mary told the court that John Brownrigg hit Mary Clifford:

…as hard as he could strike; she seemed as if she had not strength to turn up the bed; she had lifted it, but could not push it up; he said he would make her lift it up. He struck her eight or ten times, and then he would stop, to see if she would put up the bed; after that, he struck her again, and after he had beat her, he pushed the bed up himself.

The beating she received was made even more excruciating because the old wounds inflicted by Elizabeth Brownrigg's frequent beatings had not had time to heal, so when John Brownrigg beat her again her head and shoulders began to bleed so badly that it formed 'a little puddle' on the floor.

Mary Mitchell told the court that she had, on one occasion, seen her master, James Brownrigg, beat Mary Clifford with an old hearth brush. Asked in which part of the house Elizabeth Brownrigg used to beat Mary, the witness said it was usually in the kitchen, where the girl would be stripped and then tied by her hands to the water-pipe that ran under one of the beams, the length of the room. Her mistress often used a horse-whip and would keep beating the girl until she drew blood.

The witness then recalled an angry exchange between her master and mistress on the subject of the hook she had asked him to insert in the kitchen beam as an alternative to using the water pipe, which might get damaged. There was an added advantage – she could beat both girls at the same time. The hook was screwed into the beam and the rope used to tie up the girls was pulled through a ring.

Questioned about the use of the jack-chain on Mary Clifford, the witness said that a month or six weeks before the girls were rescued and taken from the house, the chain was fixed around her neck and the end fastened to the yard-door; it was as tight as could be, short of strangling her. This was a punishment for breaking some boards, when trying to find some water to drink. 'She was to scour the copper,' the witness said, 'and was chained to the yard-door all day, and loosed from the door on nights, just before dark, but sent down into the cellar with her hands tied behind her, with the chain on her neck.'

When asked who had put the chain around the girl's neck, Mary Mitchell replied;

> I saw it put about her neck, but cannot tell by whom; there was my mistress, and the youngest son, and my master by, when it was put about her neck; to the best of my knowledge, it was my master's youngest son Billy, that called her up by my mistress's order. I heard her beat her; there was a brass chain, a squirrel chain, added to the iron chain, to make it longer.

The court learned that shortly before the authorities arrived to take the girls away, Mrs Brownrigg had been in the country for the weekend, returning to London on the Sunday evening. On the Monday, after complaining that the girls had been slacking in their duties, she said she would deal with them 'as soon as she had time'.

She then left the house on business and did not return until Friday 31 July.

During the week their mistress was away, Mary Mitchell told the court, the wounds on Mary Clifford's head and shoulders had begun to heal.

> She was in a very pretty good state of health, only her head and shoulders were sore, they were scabbed over; there were very great scabs on each shoulder, and three or four on her head; them on the head were in a fair way to get well.

However, about ten o'clock that morning, after she had eaten her breakfast, Elizabeth Brownrigg went down to the kitchen and once again tied Mary by her hands to the hook above her head. The harrowing scene was described by Mary Mitchell:

> I was in the kitchen at the time, there was nobody there but us three; she horse-whipped her very much all over her, there were drops of blood under her as she stood, she struck her with the lash when she let her down as she was at her washing, and with the butt-end of the whip over her head, as she was stooping at the tub, and complained she did not work fast enough.
>
> I saw her tied up five times that day, and whipped by my mistress; I think my master and John were out that day, except their coming home to dinner; Mary Clifford had not her clothes on all that day, and my mistress gave her two or three strokes every time, but not so severe as before.

Mary saw her dressed in her own clothes, a gown and a petticoat, on the Friday night, but she didn't know where she slept that night. When she saw her on the Sunday she was wearing a boy's waistcoat and her head and shoulders looked badly wounded.

Asked to recall the day the authorities came to make enquiries, Mary Mitchell said that her master and mistress, and John, were all there. Elizabeth Brownrigg had already realised that Mary Clifford had been badly hurt by the iron chain and had boiled some bread and water to make a poultice to put around Mary's neck. Asked to describe the condition of Mary's throat, the witness replied: 'It was very much swelled, and her head also; her throat was so swelled that her chin and cheeks and all were quite even.'

When asked about the measures taken by the Brownriggs to prevent their escaping, she described the doors in the house: 'There is one that opens into Flower-de-luce court, and one in Fetter-lane, that was always double locked, and the key in the parlour; the street-door was never opened, unless somebody particular came, so that I and Mary Clifford could not go out.'

All the bedrooms were kept locked – except the two garrets – and only the best parlour was used by the family, not the parlour facing Fetter Lane. Asked why the girls could not have gone through the front parlour and into Flower-de-luce Court to ask for help, the witness explained that there was always somebody in the parlour or in the shop.

Though kept imprisoned in the house, Mary Mitchell admitted that she had accompanied the Brownrigg family on their weekend visits to their country cottage in Islington three or four times, the last time being eleven months previously. Before she had been bound as an apprentice Mary Clifford had also been to Islington, but she was never sent out of the house on errands.

Asked whether Mary Clifford cried when she was being beaten by Mrs Brownrigg, Mary Mitchell replied: 'Yes, but my mistress used to say, the more we cried the more she would beat us, and we endeavoured to stop it, but we could not help crying; but Mary Clifford cried out but very little.'

Under cross-examination, Mary Mitchell stood her ground surprisingly well when the reliability of some of her answers was questioned. It must have been extremely intimidating for someone as young and considered of lowly position to speak before the Lord Mayor and the other dignitaries in the auspicious atmosphere of the Old Bailey – and more so with Mrs Brownrigg's vile face glaring at her from the dock as questions were put to her. Asked why an additional hook was screwed into the beam in the kitchen when there were already two hooks in the room, she explained: 'We were tied up to the other because my mistress chose we should not have any thing to save ourselves by; the two hooks are just over the grate, the other was nearer towards the wall.' In other words, Mrs Brownrigg was determined that the girls' bodies should be hanging loose while she beat them without their being able to gain any leverage by pushing against either the grate or the wall with their feet.

Whilst trying to establish that James Brownrigg took little part in the ill-treatment of Mary Clifford, the witness admitted that most of the beatings administered by Mrs Brownrigg occurred when her husband was away from home.

Perhaps to suggest some of her injuries were not caused by any of the Brownriggs, the defence counsel asked her to recall the occasion when Mary Clifford fell down a flight of some eight or nine steps whilst scrubbing the stairs. She had caught her head on the pail of water, and as she fell the saucepan she was carrying banged the side of her face. Asked why the girls, so sorely misused, had not tried to escape by lifting the sash window in the kitchen – which was below ground level and with bars on the outside – Mary explained that there was always somebody around who might hear the window being lifted. It didn't need explaining that the punishment the girls would have received for any attempt to escape would have been severe beyond endurance.

Determined to probe further, the defence asked her whether she had ever complained about her treatment to one of the male apprentices. She replied that she did complain sometimes but nothing was done. She didn't think that James Brownrigg made any attempt to curb his wife's cruelty although he would sometimes remove his horse-whip and take it back to the stable; on the other hand, he may have done so as he needed it when he went out on horseback, which was very frequently. If, however, when he came back from riding and left it in the stable, Mrs Brownrigg would order one of the apprentices to fetch it and bring it back into the house.

At this point, Elizabeth Brownrigg addressed the girl from the dock, accusing her of hiding in the coal-hole to avoid work: 'Have I not sent down to you and the other girl, when you have been sitting with your clothes over your heads, to come up; and have I not beat you for lying there and neglecting your business?' she demanded.

'No,' replied Mary. 'We often chose to go up into the shop and grind the white lead [used in both plumbing and house-painting], rather than stay in the coal-hole; we never went there without we were sent there, and fastened in.'

Asked by the defence counsel whether Mary Clifford's head was shaved – presumably to prevent infestation by head lice – Mary Mitchell said the only time she'd seen Mary's head shaved was when she was admitted to the hospital after they were rescued. At this point, James Brownrigg interjected from the dock: 'I shaved both the girls' heads twice,' he protested.

It was then established that neither girls had any injuries or blemishes before they came to live with the Brownriggs. Though she admitted that she and Mary Clifford sometimes squabbled, they had never resorted to fighting each other or causing any physical harm.

Before leaving the witness box, the defence tried to establish that Mary Mitchell had been to the cottage in Islington on several occasions – once she rode there on a horse, sitting behind Billy Brownrigg, and another time she walked there – the implication being that she could have taken the opportunity to escape had she so wished.

One of the other apprentices, George Benham, was then called to give evidence. He told the court that he had been apprenticed to James Brownrigg since the previous December and had been given a two-month probationary period. Both Mary Mitchell and Mary Clifford, the only two servants employed by the Brownriggs at that time, were already there. Although he had not seen Mary Clifford tied up, he had witnessed his mistress beating her with 'the end of a horse-whip, or stick, or any thing that came in her hand as she ran by'. When he saw her being beaten, Mary was wearing a light camblet gown [probably a cheap version of an expensive, woven cloth made from camel or goat hair]. He declared that he had never seen her naked. Asked how he spent his Sundays, he said that he used to go to church in the morning, and sometimes in the afternoon he would visit his sister. He was then asked where his master and mistress went on Sundays, to which he replied: 'Sometimes they used to go out on the Sunday into the country, and sometimes they went on Saturday nights, and returned on the Sunday night.'

Mary Mitchell, he told the court, usually slept in the Brownriggs' bedroom, but Mary Clifford was made to sleep 'sometimes in the coal-hole and sometimes in the passage': 'Mrs Brownrigg used to say she be-fouled herself sadly, and rotted the bed to pieces, that was the reason she did not lie in a bed.'

The apprentice admitted that he had locked Mary Clifford in the coal-hole under the stairs under orders of Mrs Brownrigg. The girl was left there all night, and was naked except for shoes and stockings.

> She asked me to get her some clothes to cover her, and said she knew where the clothes were. I bid her go and take them in with her; she took in some old pieces of blanket, a piece of an old rug, and such things to lie on, and cover her. I was opening the door for her to go in when she asked me.

The lad was not given any reason for locking the girl in the coal-hole for the night but said that it 'made my heart ach [*sic*] to lock her up so naked'.

'Did you look at her back when she was naked, to see if she had any wounds upon her?'

'No, I turned my head away and would not look at her.'

'Why so?'

'I thought she might have some cuts from being beat, and my heart ached.'

Moving on to the subject of James Brownrigg's arrest and detention in the Compter, George Benham told the court that when he went to see his master the following day he was told to go and remove the hook from the beam in the kitchen. This he did: he put it in the top drawer in the shop. Brownrigg also ordered the boy to burn all the sticks he could find.

'There was a piece of rattan, a cane about a yard long, and a piece or two more of cane and the handle of a whip.' The horse-whip previously mentioned he had used two or three weeks before when he rode the horse to the country. He thought it was now in The Bell Inn, in Holborn.

Benham then confirmed that he had seen Mary Clifford wearing the iron chain around her neck when she was put in the coal-hole. He went on to recall Mrs Clifford, Mary's stepmother, coming to the house asking for her daughter. He had been ordered to lie to the woman and say that Mary was not there. Mrs Brownrigg told him that Mrs Clifford was 'a bad woman, and might teach bad things to her daughter'.

When Mrs Clifford returned to the house about a week later, James Brownrigg answered the door and denied that Mary was in the house. When Mrs Clifford returned with the overseers that afternoon James Brownrigg tried to trick them by presenting Mary Mitchell instead but eventually the right Mary was brought out. She was wearing a light camblet gown, said the apprentice, and 'her face was swelled. She had a cap on, and a handkerchief put all round her neck; I fancy she had on a poultice.' He had often seen blood on the girl's cap as 'the sores used to run'.

At this point, the defence counsel rose to question the boy. Asked if James Brownrigg had ever struck Mary Clifford, he replied:

I have heard him say to the girl, go along about your business, and push her along the parlour, when my mistress was going to beat her. My master met me once going home with the whip in my hand; my mistress had sent me for it; he asked me what I was going to do with it; I said, to take it home; he said, take it back with you, and go and dress the horse.

The apprentice then repeated that he had only locked Mary Clifford in the coal-hole once and that sometimes she wore the camblet gown and at other times a 'bit of a waistcoat'.

There followed questions that inferred that the girls were allowed out and the key to the front door was kept in a place that was easily accessible; in other words, the girls could have escaped whenever they chose. It was also suggested that the blood on Mary Clifford's cap came from old stains, not fresh ones, as her cap had not been washed.

From the dock, Elizabeth Brownrigg reminded the court that at one time Mary Clifford had been left at the cottage in Islington – implying that she could have escaped but did not. She also referred to one of her lodgers, possibly a lying-in client, who had a fear of sleeping alone: she had shared a bed with Mary throughout the winter, yet the girl didn't complain to her or try to escape. She also said that Mary Clifford was often so exhausted she would be found curled up asleep in the coal-hole, implying that she went in there at night of her own accord.

Mary Clifford's stepmother, also called Mary Clifford, was then called to give evidence against the Brownriggs, describing how she had been repeatedly turned away from the door, how they had denied that Mary was there, how Mr Brownrigg had 'threatened, if I came to breed any disturbance there, he would have me before my Lord-mayor'. Then a neighbour 'came and told me the girl was there, and sadly used; I went up to the parish-officers, and told them of it.' Eventually, after several visits – and after Mr Brownrigg had first claimed Mary 'wanted for nothing, and did not want to see [her mother]', forcing the officers to order him to produce her or 'they [the officers] would make him suffer' – Mrs Clifford saw her daughter:

She was in a sad condition indeed; her face was swelled as big as two, her mouth was so swelled she could not shut it, and she was cut all under her throat, as if it had been with a cane, she could not speak; all her shoulders had sores all in one, she had two bits of rag upon them.

Her shoulders were all cut to pieces… I suppose they were cut by whips and sticks, they had that appearance; her head was cut, she had a great many wounds upon it, and cuts all about her back and her legs; when I pulled her shoes and stockings off at the workhouse, I found her legs cut cross and cross, as if done with a thin end of a whip, and her back worse than her legs, and a very bad wound upon one of her hips.

Next to be called to give evidence for the prosecution was William Clipson, who told the court:

I am apprentice to Mr Deacon, a baker in Flower-de-luce court, the next door to Mr Brownrigg; my master and mistress both told me Mr Brownrigg had apprentices there … on Monday the 3rd of August I was up … on the staircase that commands Mr Brownrigg's skylight; the sky-light window being taken off, I saw through that down into the yard; there I saw Mary Clifford, her back and shoulders were cut in a very shocking manner, and likewise her head; I observed her hair was red, she had no cap on. I saw blood and wounds on her head.

…I had never seen her before as I know of; then I went down to the one pair of stairs, and crawled out at a window upon the leads; I crept on my belly to the sky-light, and laid myself cross it; I looked down, there I had full view of her; I spoke to her two or three times, but could get no answer; I tossed down two or three pieces of mortar, and the third piece fell upon her head; then she looked up in my face, I saw her eyes black, and her face very much swelled; she made a noise something like a long *Oh*; and then drew herself backwards; I heard Mrs Brownrigg speak to her in a very sharp manner, and ask what was the matter with her.

William Clipson said that he recognised her voice, as he had heard Mrs Brownrigg scolding the girls before:

Then I went down and told my mistress what I had seen, and what a shocking condition the girl was in; then a watchmaker's wife, that lives opposite to us, went and found the girl's mother-in-law [stepmother], and she came to our house; we told her what we had seen, and what a condition the girl was in; she cried and went the next day to the overseers of the parish; they came on Tuesday the 4th with her; they went into the house; James, the father, said the girl was at Stanstead in Hertfordshire, and had been there a fortnight; I went in and said that I would take my oath I saw her the day before, which was the third; he said, she was looking after his daughter that had the hoping [*sic*] cough; I said, according to the description Mrs Clifford gave of her, I believed it was she, and that she was in a very deplorable, bloody and shocking condition, with several wounds upon her; he swore by G–d she was not in the house; when Mr Grundy insisted upon seeing the girl, I just saw Mrs Brownrigg; she turned about, and shut the door, and went off; we were in the house about half an hour, arguing with Mr Brownrigg; he produced Mary Mitchell, and said, by G–d, that was all the girls he had in his house; our maid was standing at the door; she went in and said to Mary Mitchell, what is the matter with your cap; she pulled off her cap and handkerchief; then I said I would take my oath that was not the girl that I saw, for the other girl was worse than [this], a great deal, both on her head and back, as far as I could see; (I could see her shoulders, and near half way down her back when she stooped) besides, the other girl had red hair cut short.

When Mr Grundy saw Mary Mitchell, he said, is this usage! And took the girl out into the court; Mr Brownrigg then desired he would not expose him; then Mr Grundy sent for Mr Hughes, the constable, from Brown's coffee-house; when he came, we searched the house from top to bottom; and could not find the girl in the house; we searched everywhere where we thought any body possibly could be; the key of the garret could not be found, and Mr Brownrigg broke that door open for us to search there; then they took Mary Mitchell away to the workhouse; in about half an hour after they came back again and searched the house again, and could not find her; then they called a coach to take Mr Brownrigg to the Compter; he then, when he found he must go, gave the coachman a shilling, and said that he would produce the girl; I was then standing at the door, presently the girl was brought.

William didn't know from where in the house Mary Clifford was eventually brought, but he took hold of one of her arms and the porter took the other and they 'led her away to the workhouse'.

William Clipson's place in the witness box was then taken by Mr Grundy. He described how the father had pretended Mary

Clifford was 'in Hertfordshire', insisting on this story for several hours.

> ...upon that a neighbour knocked at the window and said the children were in the house, and desired me to insist upon seeing them; then I insisted on seeing the other girl; in about half an hour I got sight of Mitchel, she was brought down stairs; I seeing what a bad condition she was in, asked her after Mary Clifford; she said Mary Clifford was at Stanstead in Hertfordshire, as her master had said; I said to her, my dear, you shall never come here any more, if you tell the truth where Mary Clifford is; it was some time before I could get it out of her, at last she said she left her upon the garrett-stairs...

Next called to give evidence was White Friars' Overseer John Elsdale, who addressed the court. 'When Mr Brownrigg was informed he should go to prison,' went on Mr Elsdale, 'and the coach was waiting at the door, he desired to leave to go into his house to speak to two or three friends.'

> [Then] he said he would agree to produce the girl, provided that would satisfy us; I told him we should be satisfied, provided he could produce the girl, and asked him how long he would be before he would produce her ... he brought out a bottle of red wine, and handed round a glass a piece for us to drink, and, I think, in about half an hour he said he would produce her; she was led in by a tallish young man, about such another as the son at the bar [John Brownrigg] ... I went up to the girl, and asked her how she did; she could not speak, her mouth was extended; she could not shut her lips, her face was very much swelled; I thought the best method I could do was to take her away to the workhouse; there was a surgeon came; he said she was in very great danger.

It was clear that James Brownrigg had procrastinated to avoid showing the overseers the state Mary Clifford was in. During this time the girl was probably warned to keep quiet about her terrible treatment and, no doubt, some attempt was made by Elizabeth Brownrigg or her son, John, to clothe her and clean her up as much as possible before they allowed her to be seen by the authorities.

Brought into the witness box, Thomas Coulson corroborated the evidence given by the previous witness. He added that when Mary Clifford was eventually brought into the room she was told to sit on a chair next to Mr Coulson who asked her to name the person who had beaten her. At first she shook her head and refused to answer but when Coulson asked her directly if James Brownrigg had beaten her, she said 'by pronouncing it very incorrect and long, n − o; I asked her if it was her mistress; she, in that same way, answered y − e − s ; she could only say yes or no.'

When cross-examined, Mr Coulson was asked to give his opinion as to the character of James Brownrigg: 'I have known him between three and four years. I know him to be a sober industrious man from three years observation, and I believe him to be a humane good-natured man.' Asked if he could think of any reason why James Brownrigg had done nothing to prevent the ill-treatment of the girls, Coulson replied:

> No, I cannot, I did not know there was a maid-servant in the house; I have never been with his wife, I have been with him often; I have invited him to my house to spend an hour or two with me, but I never was at his house; I know nothing of his family business.

William Denbeigh was next to give evidence: 'I am an apothecary; I take care of the people in that workhouse; the deceased was brought in on 4th of August; the girls were both in bed together.'

When curtly told to confine his evidence to Mary Clifford, he went on to describe her injuries;

> The top of her head and shoulders and back, appeared very bloody; I turned down the sheet and found from the bottom of her feet to the top of her head almost one continued sore, scars that seemed as if cut with an instrument upon the body, legs, and thighs; upon one hip was a very large wound; it spread about half the palm of my hand.

When he attempted to take off the girl's shift he found that it was stuck to the wounds, and they started to bleed. He told the court that the girl's hair was 'almost an inch or two long' and her head 'was almost one continued sore, there were five or six wounds on her head'. He could not suggest the type of instrument used to inflict such injuries, but agreed that a horse-whip might cause such wounds:

> I put four or five pledgets [small dressings made of cotton or lint] upon her, and took some blood from her; she had a fever upon her; her neck was swelled a great deal, to such a degree that she could not speak or swallow; she was in a most shocking condition, I never saw such an object in my life; I dressed them both (that is the two girls) that night; when I came home, I told the gentleman I live with the case; it was requested they should be removed to the hospital, because we did not practise surgery. I got up the next morning and told the officers of the parish, the sooner they were removed to the hospital the better; they were removed.

Mr Young, the doctor who examined Mary Clifford when she was brought to St Bartholomew's Hospital from the workhouse, was sworn next and gave this account of her injuries:

> I found upon her head six wounds, three of them very large, and three small; they appeared to be bruised wounds, such as might be given by the butt-end of a whip; her head and throat extremely swelled, she could not speak or swallow; from her head to her toes was wounded, in such a manner as was impossible to number them, but particularly upon her hip; the other wounds appeared to have been done by the lash of a whip, that is, from the head to the toes; and they appeared to be in a state of mortification from neglect.

The court was told that Mary Clifford had died on Sunday 9 August, and, in the doctor's opinion, her extensive injuries had been the cause of her death. When asked to explain the cause of the swelling of the neck, the doctor said that there was evidence of something having been tied tightly, leaving a clear mark of restriction: 'When I saw her on the Friday, the swelling on her head and neck did a good deal subside and she was able to swallow; after that, she was in a high fever and delirium, and died.' The doctor added that the girl had been in so much pain that, even when the swelling had subsided, they thought it unwise to make her speak. She said nothing, therefore, to implicate anyone in her predicament.

At this point, James Brownrigg's defence representative[24] told the court that he proposed to bring forward several witnesses but first Brownrigg himself rose to make a statement in his own defence:

> Here are several witnesses I can call, that have brought me word of the deceased girl's saying that I never beat her, nor suffered her to be beat. With regard to denying this girl, my dear partner for life, whom I have had sixteen children by, and the girl alive, they have always deceived me; I have been most bitterly deceived; they told me the deceased was out of the house; my wife told me herself the girl was gone to Stanstead … the woman that keeps the house where my lodgings were in Islington, can prove the girls used to go there by turns.

Elizabeth Brownrigg also rose to speak in her own defence. She said: 'I did give her several lashes, but with no design of killing her; the fall of the saucepan with the handle against her neck occasioned her face and neck to swell; I poulticed her neck three times and bathed the place and put three plaisters to her shoulders.'

That is all she had to say. Her son John was also given the opportunity to make a plea but merely said, 'I am not capable of recollecting any thing, so I leave it to our counsel.'

At this point, several witnesses were called to vouch for both James and John Brownrigg. John Manton told the court: 'I asked the girl that is now living, where her master and the rest of the family were when she was beat; she said they were out; I asked her whether her master beat her or the other girl; she said he never did hurt them but he would give them a stroke or two.' Eleanor Peirce, who lived close by in Fetter Lane, was present when Mary Clifford, barely able to speak, was questioned by the Alderman at the Guildhall and indicated that it was only Elizabeth Brownrigg who beat her – although she may have indicated that the son also ill-treated her. However, she admitted that Mary Mitchell had

---

24 There was no mandatory defence counsel; a defendant's statement could be read to the court at the end of a trial, though this advantage excluded those who couldn't read or write. Defendants could pay someone to speak for them, the precursor to hiring a lawyer – once again excluding the poor from any form of justice.

said that 'the sons used now and then to correct her, but not as severe as the mistress did.'

John Williams told the court that, whilst visiting another patient at the hospital, he had spoken to Mary Mitchell. She had told him that James Brownrigg never beat her but would sometimes 'hit her a tap on the head'.

Others came forward with character statements of varying quality. A friend from Islington had seen Mary Mitchell in that town, and said that he 'never saw any ill of Mr and Mrs Brownrigg'; another witness from Islington, Dinah Harrison, told the court that the Brownriggs had taken lodgings in her house for a period of twelve months and 'they behaved well in my house, but what was private at home I know not.' John Lucas and Jarvis Reeves both testified on oath that they had known the defendants for ten or fifteen years and could vouch for their good character. The latter said that he had 'been several times at his house; I never heard but he was an honest industrious man.' The final character witness for James Brownrigg was Alexander Willes, of St Dunstan's Court, Fleet Street, who had known James Brownrigg for two years but did not know his wife. 'He was a man of an agreeable chearful [*sic*] disposition,' he told the court.

Having heard these testimonies, the counsel for the Crown had to admit that 'the neighbours in general give the man and woman the best of characters, he as a sober, industrious, good-natured man, and she deserving the same character.'

Notwithstanding, the jury (after eleven hours of evidence, and fifteen minutes of deliberation) found Elizabeth guilty of wilful murder, but acquitted the two male Brownriggs, 'it not appearing that were present at the several beatings and ill-treatment of the girl nor specially at the last beating which was thought to be the occasion of her death.' The *Derby Mercury* dated Friday, 18 September 1767 described the trial for its readers:

> At the time of her receiving the sentence she was asked what she had to say she said that as she did not beat the girl intending to kill her, she therefore did not consider herself guilty …
>
> [The verdict received] the entire satisfaction of the whole court and a very numerous audience.

The judge addressed Mrs Brownrigg as she stood in the dock:

> It is my duty to pronounce sentence in accordance with the law, that you are to be taken from hence to the prison from whence you came; that you be removed on Monday next, the 14th instant September, to the usual place of execution, and there to be hanged by the neck until you are dead; your body afterwards to be dissected and anatomised, according to the statute – may God have mercy on your soul.

After the sentence of death was passed, Elizabeth Brownrigg was returned to Newgate Gaol to await her execution on the following Monday. She was confined to the condemned cell, fettered and given only bread and water. This, of course, gave the Newgate Ordinary, Revd Joseph Moore, and other ministering clergy the opportunity to spend the Sunday offering comfort to the condemned and also bombarding them with tales of hell-fire in an attempt to elicit a confession.

Revd Moore, in his lengthy Ordinary's account published in the *Newgate Calendar*, rather pompously announced that:

> it was a most pleasing sight to the great assemblage of persons who attended their trials, to behold, not only the judge who tried them, but even the counsel for the prosecutors, in the midst of their zeal for justice, using with humanity every means in their power to guard the minds of the jury from the pernicious consequences of prejudice, and to direct their attention to the evidence produced, as the only legal foundation for their verdict.

He went on to say that 'happily for the two persons acquitted the jury composed of men of sense and virtue, capable and inclined to resist the torrent of public prejudice; their verdict is a lasting proof of their integrity and justice, and gave entire satisfaction to the court and all who were present.'

Once Elizabeth Brownrigg had been incarcerated in the condemned cell at Newgate Prison awaiting trial, Revd Moore had wasted no time in descending upon her, determined to extract a full confession of her heinous crimes, recalling his efforts in the following account:

As soon as I was informed of Mrs Brownrigg's commitment to Newgate I attended her, and endeavoured by the most mild and pathetic means to convince her of her deplorable situation, but all my endeavours for some time were ineffectual, but on my repeated attendance on her, for which I took every opportunity, and using my utmost endeavours to impress in her mind the awfulness of death, and the certainty of eternal punishment for the impenitent, she appeared to be much affected, and began to acknowledge her guilt, and with agony and distress cried out, 'O Lord God, cleanse me of this horrid fact and let the blood of Christ speak better things for me that the blood of that innocent child I have so cruelly and barbarously murdered!'

And, turning to me she said, 'Do you think that God can forgive such a wicked creature as I am?'

Suffice it to say that Revd Moore's reply was both long and sanctimonious. He went on to outline all Mrs Brownrigg had told him of her affection for her husband and children and how she had been a practising Christian for many years and:

…when she had a large family of small children she was constantly, for several years, at the early sacrament of Bow Church and constantly read prayers to her family; but she had lately neglected the same, by which means, and frequently breaking the Sabbath, she believed to be the first inlet to the wickedness she had unhappily fallen into; and that having left her God, he had hardened her heart, and permitted her to commit those acts of cruelty for which she was justly prosecuted.

After her trial was over and she had received that sentence which her crime merited I attended her in her cells, when she appeared quite resigned and perfectly at ease. She said, although Mary Mitchell, the surviving child who was evidence against her, had sworn many things that were not true, yet the material part of her evidence was not to be contradicted, and acknowledged that her sentence was just and that she deserved to suffer long ago for her cruelty to the poor girls…

Responding to rumours abroad that she was responsible for the deaths of other apprentice girls besides Mary Clifford, Mrs Brownrigg assured the Revd Moore that she had only ever had three young girls working for her. After relating all the details of the events in her household leading up to the death of Mary

Clifford, 'she seemed to be considerably eased, and applied herself with great chearfulness [*sic*] and earnestness to prayer.'

According to the Ordinary's account, she also addressed some spurious rumours in the press that she was involved in the vile occupation of 'baby-farming'.[25]

'But she assured me,' continued Revd Moore:

> …in a manner that forced belief, that all such stories were groundless, and mere inventions to blacken her character, already sufficiently darkened by the load of iniquity she was really guilty of, and for which she acknowledged she was most deservedly to suffer. She admitted that she often had unfortunate women to lie-in at her house, but that she never undertook to provide for their children, they being always taken away and provided for by friends, and she heard no more of them; and that she never had a child dead in her house, which was still born; and that, during her whole practice, only two women had died under her care, and that not through neglect, or want in judgement or tenderness in her; but this she assured me would be confirmed not only by the officers of the parish of St Dunstan but also by her neighbours, and many others now living.

The Ordinary was prepared to believe Mrs Brownrigg's protestations of innocence in this respect and went on to lament 'the depravity of the age in inventing and propagating such horrid untruths, which have with too much success been impressed into the minds of the people, in prejudice of this unhappy family'.

When Revd Moore visited her again in Newgate on Sunday 13 September, on the eve of her execution, he found her 'in great distress of mind, crying out, "What must I do to be saved?" After praying with her for a considerable time, she seemed much comforted.'

Meanwhile, James Brownrigg and his son, John, having been acquitted on the charge of the murder of Mary Clifford, were held in custody on a charge of assaulting and abusing Mary Mitchell, for which they were subsequently given six months' imprisonment and 1*s* fine apiece.

---

25 It seems that many of these pamphlets and newssheets have not survived, so we only have Elizabeth Brownrigg's repudiation of the damning rumours they contained. The deplorable practice of 'baby-farming' is referred to at the end of this chapter and also, more fully, in the chapter on Sarah Drake.

The Execution

On the morning of her death, Mrs Brownrigg was taken to the prison chapel and was there joined by her husband, James, and their son John.

The *Ipswich Journal* of 19 September 1767 stated that at first Elizabeth Brownrigg was:

> … in a very violent agitation of spirits that morning about what was to become of her in the next world but after she had received the Sacrament, accompanied by her husband and son, she was more composed and took leave of them very affectionately; after she came into the Press Yard, lamenting her wickedness and hoped that her fate might be a warning to mankind, to behave with more compassion to their fellow creatures. She was then led trembling by two men [the Newgate Ordinary, Revd Mr Joseph Moore and a prison missionary, Silas Told] out of the Press Yard to the cart; but her face could not be distinguished, having a hat on which was put very forward.

The *Derby Mercury* of Friday, 25 September 1767 gave its readers a more detailed account of the scene. All three Brownriggs, it revealed:

> …received the Holy Sacrament in the chapel, after which she prayed with great fervency, crying; 'Lord deliver me from my blood-guiltiness. I have nothing to plead or recommend me to thee but my misery; but thy beloved son died for sinners; therefore on his merits I rely and depend for pardon.'
>
> She was quite resigned and prayed with her husband and son upwards of two hours, when she took leave of them, which exhibited a scene too affecting to be described and which drew tears from all present.
>
> On her husband's assuring her that he would take care to maintain their two younger children, when he should be released from confinement, she begged him to seek a release from the prison of sin; and for her children, God was all-sufficient and hoped he would not suffer them to be used as she had treated the unhappy girls put under her care.

Her son fell on his knees and begged his mother's blessing; on which she fell on his face and kissed him while her husband fell on his knees on the other side, praying to God to have mercy on her soul. Which occasioned her to say; 'Dear James, I beg that God, for Christ's sake, will be reconciled and that he will not leave nor forsake me in the hour of death and in the Day of Judgement.'

As with Catherine Hayes, some forty-one years before, the procedure was carried out meticulously. Elizabeth Brownrigg was brought into the Press Yard and released from her manacles and leg irons; the noose was then put around her neck and the loose end wrapped around her body. Her arms were then pinioned with a cord in such a way that left her with insufficient movement to reach up and remove the noose yet still allowed her to raise her forearms and hands in prayer.

Accompanied by the Newgate Ordinary, Revd Joseph Moore and a prison missionary, Silas Told, she was tied to the horse-drawn cart and transported – with her back to the horse – through the streets to Tyburn. Catherine Hayes, of course, found guilty of petty treason (for husband killing) had been dragged through the streets strapped to a sledge, but other than the mode of travel, the whole ritualistic drama was played out in the manner of all executions – the prayers, the tolling of the bell at the church of St Sepulchre, the stop for a last tipple at the inns on the way and then, finally, the waiting gallows at Tyburn with the hangman – in this case, Thomas Turlis[26] – ready to launch her into eternity.

Once there, in full view of the huge crowd of spectators, she remained standing in the cart, the noose about her neck and the loose end of the rope first flung over the beam of the gallows and then tied securely. Before the horse was whipped into motion:

...she composedly assisted in prayer and desired the Ordinary to acquaint the spectators that she acknowledged her guilt and the justice of her sentence. And her last words were, 'Lord Jesus, receive my spirit.'

---

26 Thomas Turlis was hangman for twenty years, from 1752 until his death in 1771. He was the first executioner to introduce a slightly raised platform which, when removed, allowed a little longer length of rope, which was more likely to dislocate the neck – a device that preceded the trap-door 'new drop' at Newgate after 1783. Earl Ferrers was the first person to be hanged by this method in 1760, but Elizabeth Brownrigg was not afforded this concession.

She repeatedly before her death declared her husband innocent of ill-treating the girls, and that the son never did so but by her order.

The exclamations of the people on her way thither were very shocking and unchristian; one said he hoped the Ordinary would pray for her damnation, not her salvation. Others, that they hoped she would go to hell and were sure the devil would fetch her soul.

The reporter for *The Ipswich Journal*, published five days later, observed that 'she stood under the gallows almost insensible as a statue, seemingly unconcerned, and never shed a tear.'

The following account was later published by the prison missionary, Silas Told, who had, along with the prison Ordinary, Revd Joseph Moore, accompanied the condemned woman in the cart that day.[27]

'When we had fixed ourselves,' he recalled:

I perceived that the whole powers of darkness were ready to give us a reception. Beckoning to the multitude, I desired them to pray for her, at which they were rather silent, until the cart began to move. Then they triumphed over her with three huzzars; this was followed by a combination of hellish curses. When we passed through the gates [of Newgate Prison] carts had been placed each side of the street, filled principally with women. Here I may say, with the greatest truth, nothing could have equalled them but the damned spirits let loose from the infernal pit. Some of the common cries from the thoughtless concourse were, 'Pull her hat off, that we may see the bitch's face!' accompanied by the most dreadful imprecations.

So it was that Elizabeth Brownrigg made her way to Tyburn through streets teeming with jeering onlookers, raucously shouting obscenities, no doubt enjoying a day off from their labours and, moreover, looking forward to watching another, and a particularly wicked woman, swing: 'all the way, from Newgate

---

27   From his book, *The Life of Mr Silas Told*, published in 1786. He was a Methodist preacher and visitor to Newgate for twenty-one years (between 1754 and 1775).

to Tyburn, is one continued fair, for Whores and Rogues of the
meaner sort,' Silas Told recalled.

Such were the numbers that it was said that the crowds
exceeded those of any other execution. And such was the fury
of the mob that it was feared, by the authorities trying to control
such large numbers, that her fellow citizens might fight their
way to the scaffold in an attempt to get to her first and tear her
limb from limb. In the eyes of many Londoners that day, it would
have been no more than she deserved and a most fitting end to a
despicable monster.

Many had booked costly seats in 'Mother Proctor's Pews'.
She was a cow-keeper's widow who took advantage of the new
spectator stands constructed on her land in 1758, and she made
a fortune selling seats close to the gallows; not only did they
provide an excellent view of the whole ghastly spectacle, but also
they enabled her customers to see the anguished faces of those
about to die and, moreover, to hear their last speeches.

The *Leeds Intelligencer*, on Tuesday, 22 September 1767,
described the scene in this way:

> A few minutes before she was turned off, being very weak, the
> clergyman at her desire informed the spectators that she owneth the
> justice of her sentence and desired all persons to take warning by her
> fate and not give way to cruelty. She moreover urged that all overseers,
> etc. would look now-and-then after the poor young persons of both
> sexes, to see that their masters and mistresses used them well.

A similar scene had been enacted at an execution in Somerset
in 1740. Elizabeth Branch and her daughter, Mary, had savagely
beaten their servants, the abuse culminating in the death of young
Jane Butterworth. Both women were hanged; Mary Branch made
a long speech at the foot of the gallows: whilst admitting the
crime she said she had considered servants as 'slaves, vagabonds
and thieves.'

At the scene, clergymen preached sermons on the treatment
of servants to a vast and jubilant crowd surrounding the gallows.

The *Derby Mercury* published the following report:

> This morning Elizabeth Brownrigg was carried from Newgate to
> Tyburn, where she was executed, pursuant to her sentence of Saturday

[*sic*, Friday] last for the murder of her apprentice Mary Clifford. She
behaved with great composure of mind, joining with the ministers in
prayer and singing a hymn.

She was a thin woman, of a brown complexion, sharp visage and
seemed to be above 50 years of age.

As the volatile and rampaging crowd surged through the narrow
streets there must have been a great deal of pushing and shoving
in the ensuing melee – giving the city's pickpockets a field day. It
was reported that 'a woman with a child in her arms, was thrown
down in the crowd, near St Giles's Church; the woman was
greatly bruised and the child taken up for dead.'

After hanging on the scaffold for the usual time – about half
an hour – the body of Elizabeth Brownrigg was taken down and
conveyed to the Surgeons' Hall in a hackney-coach where it was
dissected and anatomised.[28]

The *Derby Mercury* announced on Friday, 25 September 1767,
that: 'It is said that the skeleton of Mrs Brownrigg will be fixed
in the niche opposite the front door in the Surgeons' Theatre,
and her name will be wrote under it, in order to perpetuate the
heinousness of her cruelty in the minds of the spectators.'

In fact, it was not until Thursday 11 August of the following
year that the *Bath Chronicle & Weekly Gazette* informed its readers
that the skeleton of Elizabeth Brownrigg had been placed in a
niche at the Surgeons' Hall.

There was no doubt about Elizabeth Brownrigg's guilt and
therefore, unlike the case of Eliza Fenning, forty-eight years later
(featured in the following chapter), no press reports were printed
supporting her or pleading for a reprieve.

In the case of Elizabeth Brownrigg, once she was dead there
appeared to be little interest in her case; no letters in the press
disagreeing with the verdict at her trial or disputing the sentence
of death. This may have been because her guilt was so certain,

---

28   Hangmen were not always popular and sometimes wore masks to disguise
themselves. They were often attacked by the criminal's family and friends. To
comply with the law that the bodies of murderers should be sent for dissection –
doctors were allowed ten bodies a year – there was often a frantic and unseemly
tussle to claim the body once it had been cut down from the gallows.

and may also have been because Elizabeth was 'ill-favoured' in her looks, described as almost witch-like in appearance.

Secondly, incidents of the harsh treatment of domestic servants by their masters and mistresses were common, though maybe not as extreme as in the Brownrigg case, and did not therefore merit much press coverage.

One can only speculate why Elizabeth Brownrigg, herself a mother of sixteen children and, apparently, a practising midwife with a reputation for kindness and care – so much so that the Trustees of the White Friars St Dunstan's-in-the-West precinct put her in charge of the welfare of destitute women and their children in the parish workhouse – should have resorted to such uncontrolled violence. It must be remembered, however, that there were no stringent controls over the youngsters bound over as apprentices and domestic servants. This, undoubtedly, led to undetected abuse. With so many impoverished citizens of London at the time, the workhouses and charitable institutions were full to capacity. The trustees and overseers were therefore only too glad to find positions for some of their inmates and thereby delegate the burden of their care to others.

Although Elizabeth Brownrigg had given birth to sixteen children, only three had survived infancy. The birth rate and the rate of child mortality were, of course, extremely high throughout the Georgian period, the latter due in part to disease, rapidly spread by crowded living conditions, polluted water, filthy streets and putrid cess-pits; in addition, many new-born, unwanted babies were victims of infanticide. Given Elizabeth's propensity for violence, there is a possibility that the death of those thirteen children may have resulted from maternal neglect, malnourishment or even injuries inflicted by Elizabeth Brownrigg herself. It was remarkable that, on the eve of her execution, whilst she was trying to convince the Newgate Ordinary that the rumours about her were incorrect, she boasted of her exemplary record as a midwife, completely overlooking the thirteen children she herself had lost. If she did indeed dispatch some of those thirteen babies, was she, as the rumours about her suggested, also in the murky business of 'baby-farming'?[29] It is perfectly possible that she was: women approaching confinement, and with nowhere else to go, were often accommodated at the Brownriggs' house in Fetter Lane. Women in such a situation often left their babies with the midwife, if she was willing to act the role of baby-farmer. The promise was that the child should be found a good home with a nice family; in practice, however, some of these women simply starved or strangled the infant to death and disposed of the body, under cover of night, on a stinking dung heap or in the foul, rat-infested waters of a ditch. If Elizabeth Brownrigg was a baby-farmer, then the women must surely have imagined that a well-known and respected midwife could be trusted to 'do the right thing'. Some, of course, if they did indeed leave their babies with Elizabeth, may not have cared what became of their babies. After all, yearly pregnancies were commonplace, and life was cheap.

Today, we attempt to understand the cruelty in human nature, rather than simply to condemn it. There appeared to be a dichotomy in Elizabeth's Brownrigg's character. Her husband declared that they had lived together on very good terms throughout the twenty years they had been married, and that she had been an 'affectionate' mother. Despite this claim, however, the records show that Elizabeth's youngest son, Billy, and her unnamed daughter did not visit their mother in Newgate on the morning of her execution. Also, at the trial, though James managed to find several witnesses prepared to speak favourably on his behalf – people who described him as 'industrious', 'honest' and 'cheerful' – not one person came forward to speak well of Elizabeth, save James himself. Clearly there is more to this story than meets the eye. If this woman was indeed a loving wife and mother, then why did she suddenly become a monster?

From all accounts, James Brownrigg seems to have been rather ineffective at preventing the daily cruelty going on his house. As he was often away working, he left the management of the household to his wife. (It was generally considered the wife's

---

29 Amelia Dyer, fifty-seven, was hanged in 1896 by James Billington, at Newgate, for the murder of a four-month-old baby, Doris Marmion, who she had been paid £10 to look after. (The subject of 'baby-farming' is further addressed in the chapter on Sarah Drake.)

responsibility to oversee the management of the household and the welfare of servants.) He was obviously aware of the abuse going on – as his apprentice mentioned in court, he attempted to remove the horse-whip from the house and he was also known to push the maids out of harm's way when his wife was on the rampage, in an attempt to spare them further punishment. However, he did of course insert the metal hook into the kitchen beam to facilitate more merciless beatings of both girls at the same time (though Elizabeth managed to convince Revd Moore that her husband didn't know what she intended to use it for). Was James Brownrigg in fact in thrall to an ill-tempered and violent wife, and reluctant to infuriate her by voicing any criticism about her treatment of the maids? Her sadism seems to have been stirred up and stimulated by power over the well-being of another human being. Was that why she vented all her anger and resentment on her maids – simply because she could?

Or did the thirteen children she lost, mentioned above, play a part? Was she perhaps inwardly grieving for her lost infants? Did she somehow, submerged in grief, resent the young girls that had, unlike her own children, survived into adolescence? The fact that, in her professional capacity, she brought new life into the world on a daily basis – apparently in a kindly and professional manner – makes this seem rather unlikely.

One must consider also the possibility that, at forty-seven, some measure of hormonal imbalance associated with the menopause might have occasioned a sudden change in her personality, expressed in an uncharacteristic behaviour towards the young.

Or was she perhaps party to the prejudice against the Irish that was so prevalent at the time? This attitude was still rife in 1780, as manifest by the Gordon Riots; it was also evident in the attitude of many when Eliza Fenning stood trial in 1815. There had been a proclamation, issued on 25 February 1744, ordering 'all papists to depart Westminster and the city, and 10 miles hence. Suspected papists who remained are to be put under house arrest.' Furthermore, the Spitalfield Riots occurring at the time of the crime, which in part had an anti-Irish agenda, might have had some influence on Mrs Brownrigg's attitude towards her maids. Added to which Mary Clifford was particularly Celtic in her looks, with bright red hair; could that have been the reason that Elizabeth singled out Mary Clifford for especially cruel treatment?

Such a radical change in behaviour may also, of course, have had a quite different and physical cause – a brain tumour, perhaps? (Although it must be said that when her body was dissected and anatomised at the Surgeons' Hall there was no report of finding a tumour or any other obvious physical malfunction.)

As nothing is known of the early life of Elizabeth Brownrigg, we cannot know if she was ill-treated as a child, or whether she came from a large family, raised in poverty, with all its harsh deprivations. Nor can we know whether James was a tolerant spouse or a bully, or if Elizabeth Brownrigg was a heavy and habitual gin drinker, all of which might have had a part to play in her crime. (Not only was gin very cheap and easily available, but also drinking gin was actually safer than drinking the lethally polluted water supplies – though of course it had its own dire consequences, including drunkenness, ill-health and criminality.)

We can only know for certain that Elizabeth Brownrigg grossly mistreated all three of her young charges, and moreover that she went on to cause the death of Mary Clifford. Whether she killed before this case came to light remains unknown.[30]

Some readers might wonder why neighbours living in such close proximity to each other, with any sort of privacy at a premium, didn't investigate the cries which they must have heard emanating from the Brownrigg household, or, at the very least, report the suspected maltreatment to the authorities. Months of torture had passed before Mary's body was seen lying in the pig-pen, only days before her death. But it must be remembered that the violent and regular beatings, in the most part meted out by husbands to their wives, were commonplace. The most cursory study of the Old Bailey trials, the *Newgate Calendar*, the *Terrific Register* or the contemporary press reports contained in pamphlets, almanacs and Penny Dreadfuls will testify to the appalling treatment and cruel punishments inflicted on women and domestic servants. The young apprentice in this case, George

---

30 The following announcement appeared in *Freeman's Journal*, on Monday, 18 January 1830: 'Mrs Mary Curry [

⅞ITCHELL) APPRENTICE TO LIZABETH ROWNRIGG AND WITNESS AT HER TRIAL, DIED AT T NDREW S fiORKHOUSE, ⅝ITTLE ¼RAY S ¾NN ⅝ANE; SHE WAS ASSISTED BY CHARITABLE FUNDS. OR A WOMAN WHO HAD BEEN BEATEN SO BADLY AT FOURTEEN AND PROBABLY WORKED IN SERVICE ALL HER LIFE, SHE LIVED TO THE REMARKABLY ADVANCED AGE OF SEVENTY-NINE.

Denham, clearly felt great sympathy for Mary Clifford – his heart ached to see her – but didn't dare risk the consequences of telling anyone what was happening. It was therefore probably unusual for Mrs Deacon and young Mary's stepmother to take the trouble – and risk suffering a violent reaction – to investigate the girl's predicament. Had they turned a deaf ear to the pitiful cries from the pig-pen, young Mary Mitchell might well have been next to suffer the brunt of Elizabeth Brownrigg's pathological compulsion to inflict pain and degradation on those in her power.

Fittingly, the thousands who swarmed to see her hang at Tyburn, even in an era of hardship, cruelty and disregard for human life, were appalled by her extreme cruelty – and even reading about it now can still shock, horrify and sicken.

An equally vicious crime occurred in 1733, not far from Fetter Lane. Twenty-two year old Sarah Malcolm, an Irish laundress, was hanged on the portable gallows erected between Fetter Lane and Mitre Square, close to the scene of her crimes – robbery of a dwelling and the murder of her mistress, Mrs Dunscomb, and two servants, Elizabeth Harrison and Ann Price, in Tanfield Court, Inner Temple. Whilst admitting the robbery she denied the murders; during her trial at the Old Bailey she conducted a spirited defence, declaring that the stains on her clothing came not from the throat of the maid she was accused of killing but from her own menstruation. This rather earthy defence so shocked the gentlemen judging her that within fifteen minutes they found her guilty on all counts and sentenced her to hang. Such was her notoriety that the painter William Hogarth visited her at Newgate. He produced a painting of her sitting in the Condemned Hold. Afterwards, he commented that he thought her 'capable of any wickedness'. At the gallows her cheeks were heavily rouged and she scornfully ignored the insults of the huge crowd that had gathered to watch her die.

Three

Eliza Fenning

'Spiteful minx or tragic martyr?'

Regency London was the setting for the dramatic but disturbing case of Eliza Fenning and the poisoned dumplings. Whereas Elizabeth Brownrigg had been a middle-aged, gaunt and ill-favoured woman, Eliza Fenning was described as being both young and pretty. It was 1815, the year that saw the end of the Napoleonic Wars, and many Londoners took to the streets to celebrate. Though it was an era of great creative energy in architecture, art and literature, it was also a time when society was starkly divided between the idle rich – as epitomised by the decadent lifestyle of the Prince Regent and his circle – and the working classes, the servants, artisans and labourers who often toiled long and hard in unhealthy conditions to ensure the comfort and well-being of their masters.

In January of 1815, young Elizabeth Fenning, usually known as Eliza, was employed as a cook in the home of Robert Gregson Turner, a prosperous law-stationer, and his wife, Charlotte, at 68 Chancery Lane, London. The Turners employed three other live-in servants: a housemaid called Sarah Peer (sometimes called Pearse or Pear), and two male apprentices, one of whom was called Roger Gadsden and the other Thomas King.

At the time Eliza went to work for the Turner family she was twenty-one years old, and engaged to be married. She had been in service since the age of fourteen. Her father, William Fenning, had been a soldier in the 15th Regiment of infantry and, whilst stationed in Ireland in 1787, he married an Irish woman (whose name was never mentioned in the numerous newspaper reports). Together they had ten children, of which Eliza was the only one that survived into adulthood. Three years after the marriage, the regiment was sent to Dominica, in the West Indies, where Eliza was born on 10 June 1793. Contrary to some subsequent (and, at the time, offensively prejudicial) reporting, the Fennings were Baptists, not Roman Catholics, and Eliza was raised in that faith.

William Fenning's regiment returned to Dublin in 1796 or 1797, having incurred many casualties during battles at Martinique and St Lucia; he was by this time a non-commissioned officer and obtained his discharge with a certificate of good character. He moved to London and worked for three years as a potato dealer with his brother, in Red Lion Street, Holborn. His wife, despite bearing so many children, worked as an upholsterer for a number of years and was of good character.

Eliza's life began to spiral into a nightmare when, on Tuesday 21 March, seven weeks after joining the Turner household, she prepared lunch for the family, a meal that consisted of rump steak, potatoes and dumplings. Those present at the dinner table that day were Robert and Charlotte Turner – who was heavily pregnant at the time – and Robert's father, Orlibar Turner (some press reports refer to him as Haldebart), who, though he lived in Lambeth, was in partnership with his son in the Chancery Lane office. His wife, Margaret, was not present. It was the routine of the house that the servants would eat their meal downstairs in the kitchen at two o'clock, whilst the family upstairs were served theirs at three o'clock. Within minutes of eating the dumplings all three members of the Turner family were taken violently ill with stomach pains and vomiting. Eliza and one of the apprentices, Roger Gadsden, were also seized with the same symptoms and a local doctor, Mr Ogilvy, was called to the house (although he was not called to give evidence at the subsequent trial).

At 8.45 p.m. that evening another doctor, John Marshall, who lived at Half Moon Street, Piccadilly, was sent for and, after further treatment, all those affected soon recovered. The other apprentice, Thomas King, may have been away from the house at this time for he was not mentioned in any of the press reports and was not called to give evidence in court.

For some reason Mr Orlibar Turner immediately suspected Eliza of attempting to poison the family. His suspicions were, from the start, focused on the dumplings. It was well known by everyone in the house that two packets of arsenic were kept in a drawer in the office to be used to kill mice that might damage the 'parchments and papers of consequence'. These were wrapped separately and clearly marked: 'Arsenic, poison'. They were kept in the same drawer as scraps of spare paper; one of Eliza's jobs was to light the fire in the office each morning, and it was said that she often went to the drawer to find paper to start the fire.

The next day, for some reason intent on searching for evidence that might incriminate Eliza, Orlibar Turner inspected the residue in the pan that Eliza had used to make the dumplings. When the doctor, John Marshall, called at the house, he showed it to him. After examining it, Marshall professed that the residue contained arsenic and, after he and Orlibar had informed the authorities, a warrant was issued.

The following day, 23 March, Eliza was found in her attic bedroom, still suffering from sickness. She was arrested and charged with attempted murder. A sedan chair was requested to convey her to prison but, as none was available, she was transported in a coach and put into the infirmary at New Clerkenwell Prison. During a final hearing at the Public Offices, Hatton Garden, on 30 March, Orlibar Turner, Robert and Charlotte Turner, John Marshall and Sarah Peer all gave the briefest of testimonies, after which Eliza Fenning was committed for trial at the Old Bailey and sent straight to the notorious Newgate Prison.[31]

On 3 April, Eliza wrote to Edward, her fiancé: 'Thank God I shall stand trial at the Old Bailey, where I shall have a Counsellor to plead for me, so I have nothing to fear as my conscience tells me I am not guilty.'

The Trial

The trial at the Old Bailey was opened on 11 April 1815, before the Recorder of the City of London, Sir John Silvester, and a jury of twelve men. Eliza's parents had managed to raise £5 for her

---

31 Two years earlier the Quaker prison reformer Elizabeth Fry (1780-1845) had visited the female section of Newgate Gaol and found the conditions appalling – women and children kept in squalid, overcrowded cells, rife with conflict and drunkenness; some prisoners were manacled or wearing leg-irons. In 1817, the *Association for the Reformation of the Female Prisoners* at Newgate was formed.

defence and a Mr Alley was paid £2 2s to watch proceedings on her behalf.

The charge against Eliza Fenning was that she 'feloniously and unlawfully did administer to and caused to be administered to, Orlibar Turner, Robert Gregson Turner and Charlotte Turner, his wife, certain death (to wit, arsenic) with intent the said persons to kill and murder'.

Through the testimony of the witnesses the events of that fateful day became clear.

Called to give evidence, Mrs Charlotte Turner told the court that she had recently caught Eliza in the apprentices' room 'in a partly dressed state', and, since she had reprimanded her, the girl had been sullen and resentful, and treated her disrespectfully. She also emphasised the fact that on several occasions Eliza had specifically asked to be allowed to make dumplings, saying, 'You cannot believe how well I can make them'.

Mrs Turner usually made dumplings with ready-mixed dough supplied by a local baker, but Eliza took it upon herself to order some yeast from a brewer in Gray's Inn so that she could make her own. On the Monday 20 March, the maid, Sarah, took delivery of the yeast from the brewer and gave it to Eliza in a white basin. Charlotte Turner then agreed to let Eliza use it to make dumplings from scratch the following day:

> I told her she might make some, but, before she made the dumplings, to make the beef-steak pie for the dinner of the young men.... [She had already bought the beef-steak from Brooks Market that morning.] This was about half past eleven; she carried the pie to the baker's before the kneading of the dough commenced. I gave her directions about making the dough.

When Eliza made it clear that she didn't need to be supervised whilst making the dumplings, her mistress left her alone in the kitchen and went upstairs. She went back into the kitchen two or three times during the morning, but had nothing to do with the making of the dumplings. At this time, the maid, Sarah, was also upstairs, in the bedroom, repairing a counterpane.

When questioned further about the dough Eliza had made, Mrs Turner said that when she came back to the kitchen the mixture was in a covered pan, left by the fire to rise. When she inspected the mixture, she told the court, it looked 'odd' and hadn't risen at all. When she mentioned this to Eliza the girl had seemed unconcerned and declared that it would rise, given time.

The court then heard that the family sat down to eat their lunch at three o'clock. Charlotte Turner had remarked to the housemaid, Sarah Peer, that the dumplings 'were black and heavy, instead of white and light'. After eating a small amount of dumpling Charlotte felt faint and was so stricken with severe stomach pains that she had to leave the room. She was upstairs for about half an hour, vomiting profusely, and when she came back downstairs she found the rest of the family, her husband, Robert, and her father-in-law, Orlibar, also stricken with similar symptoms.

Mr Orlibar Turner was called next to the witness box and told the court that he was taken ill within three minutes of eating some dumpling. 'The effect was so violent,' he said, 'that I hardly had time to get into the yard before my dinner came up. I felt considerable heat across my stomach and chest, and pain.'

When asked if Eliza had offered any assistance, he replied: 'None in the least.'

Nor, he insisted, did he see her eat any of the dumplings.

'I suspected it was poison,' he said:

I observed, the next morning, in the pan in which the dumplings had been mixed, the leavings of the dumplings; they stuck around the pan. I put some water in the pan and stirred it up with a spoon with a view to form a liquid of the whole. Upon the pan being set down for a moment or two, or half a minute, and taking it up slowly, and in a slanting direction, I discovered a white powder at the bottom of it. I showed it to several persons in the house; I kept it in my custody until Mr Marshall came; no person had access to it.

The witness then confirmed that two packets of arsenic were usually kept in the office drawer – at which point his wife, Charlotte, was asked to testify that Eliza could 'read and write very well'. This supply of arsenic, Orlibar Turner announced, had been missing since 7 March. He then drew from his pocket two blackened knives, which he said had been used to cut the dumplings.

Next to give evidence was the apprentice, Roger Gadsden, who confirmed that the packets of arsenic had been missing from the drawer since 7 March. He also told the court that Eliza had made dumplings for supper the night before and that he, Eliza and Sarah had all eaten them. 'They were quite different from these dumplings in point of colour and weight and very good,' he said:

> On Tuesday, the 21st of March, I went into the kitchen between three and four o'clock in the afternoon; I had dined at two: I observed there a plate on the table with a dumpling and a half; I took a knife and fork up and was going to cut it and eat it; the prisoner exclaimed, 'Gadsden, do not eat that – it is cold and heavy, it will do you no good.'

Ignoring her advice, the lad ate a piece of dumpling the size of a walnut and then consumed the remains of the sauce, soaking it up with a piece of bread. Within minutes he felt ill but did not vomit until later; it was then that he was told to go to Lambeth and fetch Mr Orlibar Turner's wife, Margaret.

Margaret Turner confirmed this, saying that when she reached the house about eight o'clock that evening: 'I found my husband, son and daughter extremely ill and soon after I came the prisoner was sick and vomiting. I exclaimed, "Oh, these devilish dumplings," supposing they had done the mischief; she said, "Not the dumplings, but the milk, ma'am".' She then said she blamed the half-penny worth of milk that Sarah had fetched for Charlotte Turner to make the sauce.

Robert Gregson Turner was called next and gave the briefest of testimony. He was not questioned in any depth and he merely said that he had eaten some of the dumplings but had not touched the sauce. He said he had suffered more than the others as he'd eaten more of the dumplings.

The maid, Sarah Peer, testified that on 21 March she went for the milk after she and Eliza had eaten their meal of beef-steak pie at two o'clock, and then she had served the Turners with the dumplings, potatoes and rump-steak at three o'clock. Immediately after that she left the house, having been given permission to visit her sister in Hackney.

'I came home at nine o'clock exactly,' she told the court. 'I ate none of the dumplings myself. In eating the beef-steak pie I ate some of the crust. I was not at all ill. I had eaten some dumplings she [Eliza] made the night before; I never tasted better. They were all made out of the same flour.'

Sarah admitted that she and Eliza sometimes quarrelled about petty things. At one time, for instance, they fell out when Eliza had taken something from Sarah's box to use as a duster. According to Sarah, when Mrs Turner had reprimanded Eliza about the incident in the apprentices' room, Eliza had said that she didn't like Mr and Mrs Turner. Finally, the maid said that she hadn't known about the poison kept in the office drawer, nor had she ever had any reason to go there.

William Thiselton, the police officer from the Hatton Garden office who had arrested Eliza, told the court that he had asked her whether she thought the flour was to blame for the sickness. She thought not, as she had used the same flour to make a beef-steak pie with no ill effects and, in her opinion, it was more likely to be the yeast, as she had seen a 'red sediment' when she used it to make the dumplings. If not the yeast, she had suggested, Sarah might have put something in the milk she had fetched that morning, as she was 'sly and artful'. Thiselton then informed the court that when he searched Eliza's box he found 'nothing of a suspicious nature'.

Mr John Marshall, the doctor who attended the family, told the court that he had arrived at about a quarter to nine on the evening of the outbreak. He found Eliza lying on the stairs, vomiting and 'apparently in great agony'. Robert and Charlotte were in the bedroom and both were in 'excruciating pain in the stomach and retching violently'. 'All the symptoms attending the family,' the doctor asserted:

> ...were produced by arsenic; I have no doubt of it by the symptoms. The prisoner was also ill, by the same, I have no doubt. Mr Orlibar Turner showed me a dish the next morning; I examined it; I washed it with a tea-kettle of warm water; I first stirred it and then let it subside; I decanted it off; I found half a tea-spoonful of white powder; I washed it the second time; I decidedly found it to be arsenic. Arsenic cut with a knife will produce the appearance of blackness on the knife; I have no doubt of it. There was not a grain of arsenic in the yeast; I examined the flour-tub; there was no arsenic there.

That was the case for the prosecution. When Eliza was asked if she had anything to say in her own defence, she said this:

> My lord, I am truly innocent of all the charge, as God is my witness: I am innocent, indeed I am: I liked my place, I was very comfortable; as to my master saying I did not assist him, I was too ill. I had no concern with the drawer at all; when I wanted a piece of paper, I always asked for it.

Some accounts added the following words: 'Gadsden behaved improperly to me; my mistress came and saw me undressed; she said she did not like it; I said, "Ma'am, it is Gadsden that has taken liberty with me".'

Five witnesses were then called and they all vouched for her sobriety, cheerfulness, integrity and humanity. However, when one of these witnesses testified that Eliza had told him, a few days before the Turner household became ill, that she was extremely happy in her work and liked her master and mistress the Recorder stopped him – his testimony, the Recorder said, could not be accepted as evidence.

Nor did he accept the evidence of Eliza's father, William Fenning, who handed over a piece of paper to Mr Alley on which was written a statement to the effect that, on 21 March, he had gone to the Turners' house to see his daughter and was told by Sarah Peer that Eliza had been sent on an errand by Charlotte Turner – when in fact she was being violently sick at the time. He had gone away none the wiser. The Recorder looked briefly at the piece of paper when it was handed to him by Mr Alley, but then totally disregarded it.

At this point, Eliza requested one of the apprentices to be called to the witness box. When Roger Gadsden was brought into the court, however, Eliza vehemently protested that it was the older of the two apprentices, Thomas King, whom she wanted to question, not Gadsden. Only Thomas King, she insisted, could testify that she never went to the office drawer where the arsenic was kept. In fact, whenever she needed spare paper for the fire he always gave it to her. Her request was dismissed by the Recorder. When asked, Roger Gadsden said that both he and Thomas King had seen Eliza go to the drawer for spare paper to light the fire many times.

At this point, Mr Alley, counsel for the prisoner, left the court, not even bothering to listen to the Recorder's address to the jury. Clearly, he felt that he had done all that he could in the circumstances. It was not until 1836 that defence lawyers were permitted to address the jury with a summary of the case. According to the *Newgate Calendar*, the judge's summing up ran as follows:

Gentlemen, you have now heard the evidence given on this trial, and the case lies in a very narrow compass. There are but two questions for your consideration, and these are, whether poison was administered, in all, to four persons, and by what hand such poison was given. That these persons were poisoned appears certain from the evidence of Mrs Charlotte Turner, Haldebart (Orlibar) Turner, Roger Gadsden, the apprentice, and Robert Turner; for all these persons ate of the dumplings, and were all more or less affected – that is, they were every one poisoned.

That the poison was in the dough of which these dumplings were composed has been fully proved, I think, by the testimony of the surgeon who examined the remains of the dough left in the dish in which the dumplings had been mixed and divided; and he deposes that the powder which had subsided at the bottom of the dish was arsenic.

That the arsenic was not in the flour I think appears plain, from the circumstance that the crust of a pie had been made that very morning with some of the same flour of which the dumplings were made and the persons who dined of the pie felt no inconvenience whatever: that it was not in the yeast nor in the milk has been also proved; neither could it be in the sauce, and yet they were violently affected with retching and sickness.

From all these circumstances it must follow that the poisonous ingredient was in the dough alone; for, besides that the persons who partook of the dumplings at dinner were all more or less affected by what they had eaten, it was observed by one of the witnesses that the dough retained the same shape it had when first put into the dish to rise and that it appeared dark, and was heavy, and in fact never did rise.

The other question for your consideration is, by what hand the poison was administered; and although we have nothing before us but circumstantial evidence, yet it often happens that circumstances are more conclusive than the most positive testimony. The prisoner, when taxed with poisoning the dumplings, threw the blame first on the milk, next on the yeast, and then on the sauce; but it has been proved, most satisfactorily, that none of these contained it, and that it was in the dumplings alone, which no person but the prisoner made.

Gentlemen, if poison had been given even to a dog, one would suppose that common humanity would have prompted us to assist it in its agonies; here is the case of a master and mistress being both poisoned, and no assistance was offered.

Gentlemen, I have now stated all the facts as they have arisen, and I leave the case in your hands, being fully persuaded that, whatever your verdict may be, you will conscientiously discharge your duty both to your God and to your country.

Following only a few minutes' deliberation, the jury returned a verdict of guilty.

After her conviction Eliza was taken back to her cell in Newgate Prison to await her fate. From there she wrote to Edward, her fiancé: 'They have, which is the most cruellest thing in this world, brought me in guilty. I may be confined most likely six months at least.'

Her hope for release was ill-founded. The following day she was once more in the dock at the Old Bailey, where she was sentenced to death by hanging. Reporters at the scene told their readers that 'she was carried from the dock convulsed with agony and uttering frightful screams.'[32]

To many who read about the trial in the newspapers, the verdict and sentence seemed particularly harsh – and, moreover, the case for the prosecution left many questions unanswered. The disquiet and scepticism was felt by many in the general public but also by men of influence. The day before the date set for Eliza's execution, two urgent meetings were convened by Mr Basil Montagu, of Lincoln's Inn – supported by several other persons who felt uneasy about the verdict – during which their concerns were expressed before the Lord Chancellor and the Recorder, Sir John Silvester.

---

32 Though the penalty for the crime of attempted murder was sometimes commuted to transportation, it remained a capital offence until 1861.

However, after much deliberation, it was decided that there were no grounds for any change in either the verdict or the sentence issued by the judge.

The full extent of the efforts of a number of professional people on Eliza's behalf became common knowledge from press reports after her execution. On 5 November 1815, for example, *The Examiner* published a letter of protest that had been written by a chemist, Corbyn Lloyd, after various press comments had suggested that he and others campaigning for a reprieve were swayed by the fact that Eliza was a pretty young woman – an assumption dismissed by the columnist:

Without having personally witnessed the unfortunate Elizabeth Fenning's prettiness as Mr Recorder unquestionably did when she was personally on her trial before him, it cannot be expected that those who are sincerely earnest in the exercise of their judgement upon her case should think, with the Recorder, that nothing but a woman's prettiness could be a motive for humanity towards her; and it is not any thing favourable in Elizabeth Fenning's person that these gentlemen, who, like Mr Corbyn Lloyd, never saw her, have interested themselves in her case.

On Monday evening, before the execution, a conversation took place at Mr J.M. Richardson's, in Cornhill, between a Mr Braithwaite and another gentleman, wherein the circumstances hereafter mentioned were stated by Mr B, with his persuasion of the innocence of the girl. Mr Richardson, finding that no steps were taken to make these circumstances properly known, and though, until then, wholly ignorant of the case, thought it his duty to write immediately to the Secretary of State, the Sheriffs and the Recorder, briefly stating the facts; and the next morning, Tuesday, Mr Richardson addressed a letter to Mr Basil Montagu, entreating that gentleman instantly to interfere with the Recorder on behalf of the unhappy girl whose execution was fixed for the next morning.

The strong ground of that interference and the Recorder's answer to Mr Montagu, will appear from that gentleman's letter to Mr Richardson:

This letter was sent on 10th August, 1815, less than two weeks after Eliza's execution:

'Sir, – I am to apologise for my apparent inattention to your letter respecting Elizabeth Fenning by stating that the instant I received it I waited upon the Recorder and informed him of the communication you had kindly made to me; and, as I was wholly ignorant of the merits of the case, I requested the Recorder to inform me, "whether any alteration could be formed in the opinion respecting the propriety of her execution, if satisfactory evidence were adduced that there was an insane person in the Turners' house, who had declared that he would poison the family", as it appeared by your Letter that such evidence could be produced. The Recorder assured me that the production of such evidence would be wholly useless. I therefore retired. I, at the time, had not read the trial of this unfortunate young woman; and she was executed early the next morning.

I am very sensible of your kind exertions, and I trust you will forgive my apparent neglect – I am, Sir, your faithful servant,
B. Montagu.
Lincoln's-Inn, Aug. 10, 1815.

Mr Richardson's letter to Mr Montagu, and that gentleman's application to the Recorder on Tuesday, were in consequence of information received only the night before, that circumstances of a nature tending to throw great doubts on the guilt of Elizabeth Fenning had been publicly stated, and that these circumstances could be clearly proved by most respectable persons. Upon this information, the following proceedings were likewise adopted:

Application being made to appoint a meeting of the parties at Newgate, at a meeting which was held at Mr Newman's house (chief gaoler), Mr Gibson, of the house of Corbyn and Co., Chemists and Druggists, No. 300, Holborn, stated the circumstances alluded to in the presence of Rev. Mr Cotton, the Ordinary, the Rev. Dr Perkins, Chaplain to H.R.H. the Prince Regent, Mr Under-Sheriff Leigh, and several other gentlemen.

It was then agreed that the proper course to be taken was to lay the circumstances before the Under-Secretary of State for the Home Department, Lord Sidmouth, the Secretary of State, being out of town.

Accordingly, between three and four o'clock in the afternoon, Mr J.B. Sharpe, Mr Ogle, Mr Braithwaite, Mr Aberdour and Mr Gibson, waited upon Mr Becket at the Secretary of State's office and Mr Gibson stated to that gentleman the circumstances as hereafter particularized. After listening to them, Mr Becket recommended Mr Gibson to attend at the Recorder's house, in Bloomsbury-square,

the same evening at eight o'clock; and before they separated it was
agreed that one other person should attend also.

At eight o'clock, Mr Gibson and Mr J.B. Sharpe attended at the
Recorder's house and there met the Recorder and Mr Becket, to
whom Mr Gibson made a statement of facts in the following words,
or words to the following effect:-

'About the month of September or October last, to the best of
my recollection, Mr Turner, junior [Robert] called at our house,
appearing in a wild and deranged state. I invited him into a back
room, or counting-house, where I detained him, whilst Mr Crockford,
another gentleman at Messrs. Corbyn's house, went to his father's. In
this interval, Mr Turner, junior, used the most violent and incoherent
expressions – such as, "My dear Gibson, do, for God's sake, get me
secured and confined, for, if I am at liberty, I shall do some mischief;
I shall destroy myself and my wife; I must and shall do it, unless all
means of destruction are removed out of my way; therefore do, my
good friend, have me put under some restraint; something from above
tells me I must do it, and unless I am prevented, I certainly shall do it."

Mr Gibson, to whom Mr Robert G. Turner thus addressed himself,
also stated to the Recorder and Mr Becket other circumstances
exhibiting the general symptoms of a deranged mind. He further stated
that Mr Crockford, a gentleman associated with him, could confirm
the fact of his – Mr Robert G. Turner's – mental derangement at more
periods that the instance then alluded to: but that Mr Crockford was
unfortunately at that time out of town.

Mr Gibson concluded by saying that, in the interval between
Elizabeth Fenning's apprehension and her trial, he waited on Mr
Turner, Sen, [Orlibar Turner] and strongly urged the impropriety
of proceeding with the trial, entreating him to consider the state of
his son's mind, and the language he had used, and trusting that the
consideration of these circumstances would induce them not to press
the trial. He acquainted Mr Turner, sen, that they were not alone his
sentiments; but that some mutual friends of the Turners' family and
himself had mentioned the impropriety of Mr Robert G. Turner's
being at large under the circumstances with which he was afflicted.

In the course of the conversation with the Recorder and Mr
Becket, it was mentioned by Mr Gibson that the arsenic had been
purchased some time previous to the conversation with Mr Robert
G. Turner above mentioned: and on leaving the Recorder's house,

Mr Gibson, with some laudable and honourable anxiety that he had shown during the whole of that day, expressed his sincere hopes that the knowledge of these circumstances would lead to an extension of mercy to the poor girl – at least a respite until some further enquiry should be instituted.

In twelve hours afterwards Elizabeth Fenning was executed.[33]

The debate over Eliza Fenning's fate continued in the press, an example being a report in *The Examiner*, dated 12 November 1815, in which the validity of some of the Recorder's comments at her trial was contested. In particular, they decried his comments to the jury ('Gentlemen, if poison had been given, even to a dog, one would suppose that common humanity would have prompted us to assist it in its agonies; here is the case of a master and a mistress being both poisoned and no assistance was offered.').

What were the conclusions which the Recorder evidently meant that the Jury should draw from these statements? Why, in the first place, that as the dough made by Fenning was heavy and would not rise, there must have been arsenic in it – (though it is clearly proved that arsenic will not prevent the dough rising but that the want of skill in the making it will) – and, in the second, that as the family above stairs were poisoned and very ill, and Fenning did not offer her aid, it was a mark that she either wanted common humanity; or she had her reasons for not assisting the sufferers… He, of course, did not know that arsenic would not prevent the dough from rising and he did not know that the girl had partaken of the poisoned food, was herself extremely ill and could not afford that aid the not rendering of which, even to a dog in agony, was a clear proof of the absence of common humanity…

That the Recorder might reasonably know nothing of the effects of arsenic upon dough, may be readily supposed; but why in his ignorance did he venture on conveying such a notion to the Jury when the life of a fellow creature was at stake!

That he could not have known of the illness of Fenning when he spoke of no assistance being offered and must have imagined she was

---

33 The article finished by stating that, 'It is highly essential that the statements asserting that the Lord Chancellor was present at the meeting on Tuesday should be contradicted – The Lord Chancellor was not present at either of the meetings above mentioned.'

able though unwilling to give it, must be concluded; but his strong allusion to the girl's apparent misconduct must have had a decided influence on the minds of the Jury and the Recorder's misconception of the fact must be allowed to be deplorable in the extreme. Had he altogether omitted these two points in his charge it appears more than probable that the Jury would not have returned a verdict of guilty; and he ought to have suppressed them both is now quite clear, we dare say, even to himself.

The piece ended with some strong words for the Recorder: 'How dare any man, official or unofficial, presume to tell a gentleman, that his interference could only have arisen because the object of it was a pretty woman!'

A detailed list of the dumplings originally made and the portions that remained uneaten was published in a letter from 'A Friend of the Poor and a Lover of Justice' on 3 October 1815. The writer stated that: 'I can no more shut out from a firm conviction of her innocence than I can shut out the day-light from my open eyes at noon day.'

The debate over Eliza Fenning's guilt or innocence continued in the press both before and after her execution. The doctor, John Marshall, issued a pamphlet – extracts of which were quoted in *The Times* – that was adamant in its conviction that Eliza was guilty as charged. She didn't assist other members of the household when they were taken ill, he said; she refused his suggestion to take milk and water for her pain and vomiting. This, of course, is quite understandable when it is remembered that she felt sure it was the milk in the sauce that had made everyone so ill! He even suggested that she had eaten some of the dumplings in order to 'destroy herself to evade justice'. He also referred to a book found in her box which contained advice on procuring abortion – yet the policeman, Thiselton, searched her box after her arrest and found 'nothing incriminating'. He declared that Eliza had made 'spiteful and revengeful' remarks about her mistress. *The Times* pronounced that 'these facts serve to illustrate how greatly Mr Turner and his family have been exposed to unmerited rancour by the artful and revengeful conduct of the wretch who has inflicted on them so much suffering and anxiety.'

A ground-breaking and incisive pamphlet offering the opposite view was written by John Watkins and published by the radical campaigner William Hone, entitled *The Important Results of an Elaborate Investigation into the Mysterious Case of Elizabeth Fenning*.[34] Watkins pointed out the many inconsistencies in the testimony given at the trial – one being that Orlibar Turner had said that he had not seen Eliza eat any of the dumplings – but then he wouldn't, as she and the other servants ate in the kitchen. Why, he asked, had the first doctor, Mr Ogilvy, who was called to attend the family as soon as they had fallen ill, not been questioned and allowed to testify in court? The only medical evidence heard had been from John Marshall, who had arrived nearly six hours after the dumplings had been eaten and he had been quite clearly convinced from the start that Eliza was guilty.

It seems that Watkins was present at the Old Bailey trial, for he also referred to evidence given that was not recorded by the court's shorthand writer. The presence of Eliza's father, William, and his offer to give evidence as to the Turners' hostility towards his daughter, was not included. As noted, Sir John Silvester's summing up of the case was highly prejudicial. John Watkins also pointed out that both John Marshall and Orlibar Turner were acquainted with the clerk of the court and the solicitor to the prosecuting barrister; some reports suggested that Orlibar Turner and Sir John Silvester were on friendly terms.

He then turned his attention to the toxicology evidence in the case. He estimated that the half-teaspoonful of arsenic that John Marshall said he had extracted from the pieces of dough stuck to the pan would have amounted to 1,800 grains of arsenic in the six dumplings made. If a total intake of five grains – or even less in some cases – was considered to constitute a fatal dose, how was it that nobody died? He also stipulated that arsenic would not blacken a knife and, secondly, contested Mrs Turner's assertion that the reason the dough had not risen was because it contained arsenic – the presence of arsenic does not prohibit the action of yeast.

Having dealt with the anomalies and false assumptions in the medical evidence, Watkins turned his attention to the shockingly speculative defamation of the character of Eliza Fenning. Vicious rumours about her were widespread after

---

34 William Hone (1780-1842) was a writer and bookseller. He campaigned vigorously on Eliza's behalf in his newspaper, *Traveller*. A fearless political agitator, he was tried three times for satirical works in December 1817.

Orlibar Turner made public a letter from a former employer, a solicitor, who maintained that she had once tried to poison him – and moreover, that she had tried to cut the throat of another employer. When questioned by Watkins, the solicitor admitted that Eliza had not tried to poison him at all, but that 'he thought Mr Turner had done what was proper in hanging the girl – as nobody would be safe if these Irish wretches were suffered to get into respectable families.' Furthermore, the woman whose throat Eliza was supposed to have cut admitted to Watkins that she had never even met the girl.[35]

Of course, John Watkins's pamphlet was received with outrage by those who were determined to see Eliza Fenning hang. The *British Critic* was unequivocal in its condemnation: 'Of all the wretched attempts which have ever been made to shake the confidence of the people in the administration of public justice, this is the most audacious.' Sadly, the efforts of the reporters, pamphleteers and petitioners who had tirelessly campaigned for a reprieve for Eliza Fenning came to nothing. The date for her execution was set for Wednesday, 26 July 1815, and it was to be held in public outside Newgate Prison. Two other convicts were to be hanged at the same time.

In the meantime, the press continued to publish articles and letters from the public commenting on the case; they also posthumously printed some of the letters that Eliza Fenning had written during her time in Newgate Gaol awaiting execution. The following were printed in a booklet entitled, *Affecting Case of Eliza Fenning, who suffered the Sentence of the Law, July 26 1815*:[36]

The *Examiner*, 14 May 1815:

It has been observed by many gentlemen that if they had been on the jury of Eliza Fenning they would not have found her guilty because

---

35 Prejudicial and virulent remarks against Roman Catholics were freely expressed without censure at this time. The *Newgate Calendar* accounts written by the Ordinary were often detrimental in tone to criminals of that faith. At the time of the Eliza Fenning case, the Monument to the Great Fire of London still had an inscription on it which attributed the outbreak of the fire to 'Popish frenzy'.

36 Published by John Fairburn, 2 Broadway, Ludgate Hill, London. Price, 2*s*.

there was no proof that she was the actual person that put the poison into the pan, knowing it to be poison.

I visited the unfortunate young woman a few days ago, she still declares her innocence, she still says she did not know there was arsenic in the house, nor never saw any there, she burst into a flood of tears, and said she wished she might drop down dead if she knew what arsenic was. Here her father became deeply affected on hearing his daughter declare her innocence in so solemn a manner. He said he had fought for his king and his country and now he was deprived of his only child for a crime of which he believed her to be totally innocent.

The mother of this unfortunate young woman was so affected that it was thought that she could not live.

[The observations of our Correspondent prove nothing: but still many persons are of the opinion that the guilt of this young woman has not been sufficiently shewn. The arsenic, it appeared, was kept in an open drawer with waste paper to which every one might resort – this was a very negligent practice, to say the least of it – *Examiner.*]

The following letter appeared in the *Morning Chronicle* on 18 May 1815:

Mr Editor.

I trust you will give the following lines a corner in your valuable paper. Having been present at the trial of Eliza Fenning at the Old Bailey Sessions, where she stood indicted for attempting to poison the family of Mr Turner, Chancery-lane, I witnessed a very extraordinary circumstance, which I think ought to be made public, previous to the Recorder's making his report of those under sentence of death at Newgate.

When the Recorder (in his usual clear and comprehensive manner) had summed up the evidence, the Jury consulted five or six minutes, when they returned a verdict of Guilty with the observation from the Foreman (addressing himself to the Recorder)-

'My Lord, we should have returned the verdict sooner had it not been that one of our brother Jurymen is deaf and we have been obliged to explain to him.'

Now, Mr Editor, an English Jury ought to consist of twelve persons in the full possession of all their faculties; and had this person been so, he perhaps might have dissented from the rest and the girl been acquitted.

Two days earlier, the *Morning Chronicle* had quoted a letter printed in 'the British Press' but declined to name the newspaper:

Sir – permit me through the medium of your esteemed paper to lay before the public the information which I have acquired in the extraordinary case of Eliza Fenning – I say extraordinary for I have never read or heard of a case equally wicked in one light and foolish in the other – wicked in the extreme for contriving to take away the lives of those who had never offended her – insane, by taking such a quantity of the bane, as subjected herself to as great a degree of affliction as any one of the family.

Far from being wickedly cunning does she appear to me, as it is evident she left the pan in which the dumplings were made unwashed till the next day, nor did she attempt to put the remainder of the dumplings out of the way, the doing of which the perpetrator of such a crime would not have omitted.

The unfortunate young woman in question is in the 21st year of her age, is a diminutive person, not such a one as my Lord or Lady would have either for the housemaid or cook, a place of all work was, therefore, the situation of this little female previous to going into Mr Turner's family, which made her feel perfectly contented with her late situation.

Mr Smyth, of the Colonade, No 8, Brunswick-square, gave the prisoner an excellent character, he swore that he had met the prisoner two evenings previous to the melancholy catastrophe; she declared that she was very comfortable in her situation and that she was never happier in her life.

There are two other persons who can prove similar expressions made use of by the prisoner, two days before the accident, when she happened to be out on business for her employers.

Now, sir, after such proof of her being satisfied is it likely that she could have conceived such a diabolical plan of murder and then suicide? I have been informed that a professional man has had some arsenic mixed in dumplings for experiment and that they rose as is customary, were neither black nor heavy, nor did they particularly colour the knives.

Now Sir, it was a pity, as two surgeons attended the family that they did not both attend the trial. For Surgeon Marshall says he had no doubt of the arsenic having a particular effect on the knives. Now, as Surgeon Ogilvy attended the family at five o'clock and Mr Marshall did not arrive till nine, I repeat it is a pity Mr Ogilvy had not been called as a witness.

I am informed that a professional gentlemen in the law, from the unsatisfactory statement of this case in the papers, waited on Mr Ogilvy who informed him that on his arrival at Mr Turner's he found the prisoner in as distressed a state as any of the family.

She has been informed by the officers one evening that she was to die next morning which deeply affected her. I must express my opinion that alarming prisoners, and repeatedly, as she has been, shews but very little feeling in the doers, to say the least of it.

However, she asked for paper to write to her inconsolate parents, in doing so she professes her innocence in the most solemn and affecting way. She requests to be buried by her little brother who met his death by an accident. She expresses a confident hope of meeting her father and mother hereafter in heaven and in this world she bids them an everlasting adieu.

The Paymaster-General of his Majesty's land forces, under whom the prisoner's father had served as serjeant of the band, in the 15th regiment of foot, at the taking of Martinique, Guadeloupe and St Lucia, on seeing the letter above alluded to, declared he would not believe that it had been written by a guilty hand.

A number of respectable people have signed a petition praying for the royal clemency, among whom I believe there are at least two Noble Lords – Mr Turner, however, contrary to the expectation of the prisoner and many of her friends, refused to set his name thereto.

The petition, her letter from prison, together with her father's discharge, I flatter myself is, by this time, before his Royal Highness the Prince Regent and the prayers of everyone who believes her innocent, as I do, I trust will accompany them. I visited her deeply afflicted parents yesterday, the bleeding tear rolled quick over their aged cheeks, their souls seemed heavily oppressed with poignant grief, my heart was rent for misfortunes which it was not in my power to alleviate.

F.M. BARREN.   Pleasant-retreat, Blackfriars-road, May 15, 1815

This letter, sent by Eliza to the editor of the *Examiner*, was published on Sunday, 23 July 1815:

July 18, Felons' side, Newgate,

Sir, – With the greatest submission, I most humbly beg leave to return my grateful thanks and acknowledgements for your humane charitableness that has been extended towards me, an unfortunate victim, in endeavouring to restore a lost and only child to her distressed and afflicted parents; and I trust and hope all those who help the afflicted in mind, body, or estate, will bear reward in heaven. Believe me, cruel and pitiable is my distressing case; to be even confined in this abode of wretchedness, much more to be continually warned of my approaching destiny.

Dear Sir, I do solemnly declare with firmness and perseverance my innocence to God and man, I am innocent of the crime that is laid to my charge; but how can I convince the world when brought guilty at the bar of man? Yet there will be a grand and great day when all must stand before the tribunal bar of God, then where will the guilty criminals stand or fly to secure themselves from the vengeance of the Almighty just God, who knows the secrets of all hearts, and will reward all according to the work done in the body. What a pleasing consolation within my distressed mind to think I am clear of such a heinous and dreadful crime, and never hurted man or mortal, in thought, word or deed – My dear parents and myself will feel in duty bound to pray for your kind interference in my behalf in your paper, as you have done – I remain your much injured and humble servant,

ELIZA FENNING

On 25 July, the day before her execution, this letter was printed in the *Day* newspaper:

…there is in the nature of the crime of which she has convicted a degree of improbability arising from its very enormity which is only surmounted by the most ample and unanswerable evidence of guilt and I have looked in vain for such evidence in the proof which has been adduced.

It is a maxim consecrated by the tenets of our religion and adopted in the practice of our laws that the guilty should escape rather than that the innocent should suffer and, in this case, where the scales of justice hang in equal poise, may we not yet hope that his Royal Highness the Prince Regent may extend over this young and wretched female the protecting sceptre of his mercy, without sacrificing the cause of justice or compromising the interests and safety of his people…

But what is the proof that is to justify the public immolation of this victim? The most desperate malignity of the practiced offender would not incite him to commit these many murders without a motive. Yet no evidence has been adduced of any motive that should excite this young woman to rush at once into such complicated guilt.

Without a motive, then, we are to believe that she has formed and attempted to execute the desperate offence of poisoning a whole family, and herself with them, for she had administered the poison, not only to an individual against whom she nourished an unmitigable spirit of revenge but to an entire family, not only to the family but to other individuals and to herself.

It has, indeed, been said she participated in the poison that, by an artifice, she might escape suspicion... It seems to me incredible that this person should have taken a mortal poison to escape the suspicion of administering it to others. She knew that arsenic would produce death but she could scarcely believe herself competent to balance nicely the quantity, greater or smaller, which was requisite to produce a mortal effect.

The writer suggests that all members of the household could have had access to the arsenic in the office drawer and, as it was stored so negligently, it might also have been mixed in food accidentally. He continues:

There seems to me no positive proof that the crime imputed to her was ever committed. There is certainly no positive proof that she committed that offence. It is not improbable that it should have been committed by others. Every circumstance from which her guilt is inferred is susceptible of an easy and rational explanation and, on the other hand, the very nature of the offence renders its commission by such a person, and under such circumstances, highly improbable.

I trust the high importance of this subject may excuse my laying these crude and hasty suggestions before the public.

I am, Sir, Your respectful and obedient servant, C.A.

The pamphlet also printed the following letters written by Eliza Fenning herself:

To Lord Sidmouth
Newgate, 27 June 1815

My Lord – With deference I most humbly beg leave to address your lordship; at the same time, am entirely at a loss how I dare venture such a presumption; but your lordship's well-known goodness and mercy, which has repeatedly been extended to many miserable creatures under calamities like myself, encourages me, with all submission, to state my real situation to your lordship.

I most humbly beg leave to inform your lordship, that I am under the awful sentence of death, on suspicion of poisoning Mr Turner's family, which heinous crime I never was guilty of, I most solemnly declare to a just God, whom I must meet, and my blessed Redeemer, at the great and grand tribunal, when the secrets of all hearts will be known.

Innocence induces me to solicit a fuller examination. I am the only child of ten, and to be taken off for such an ignominious crime strikes me and my dear parents with horror.

I, therefore, most humbly beg leave to solicit your Lordship's merciful interference in my behalf to spare my life, and my parents, with me, will be ever bound to pray for you.

I remain,
With due submission,
Your poor, but innocent servant,
ELIZA FENNING.

Eliza also wrote to Mr Robert Turner:

Honoured Sir, – With due submission I most earnestly entreat you to sign my petition, to save my life, which is forfeited for what I am not guilty of.

Honoured sir, I do here most solemnly declare I never meant to injure you or any of your family; picture to yourself the distressed mind of my dear parents, to see their only child suffer such an ignominious death; but innocent I am.

May the blessed God give my ever dear parents strength to bear the dreadful affliction to see their only child suffer; but may you never feel the pangs of a broken heart, which your unfortunate servant endures.-

Prayers for you and your family.

ELIZA FENNING

PS. If your goodness will comply with my request, I shall be bound to pray for you.

It appears, states the pamphlet, that Mr Turner did not sign the petition. The following letter, which Eliza wrote to her parents, was also published:

Felons' Side, Newgate,
21 July 1815

Dear and affectionate Parents,

With heart-rending sighs and tears, I, for the last and ever last time, write these solemn lines to you, hoping and trusting the Almighty will give you strength and fortitude to bear the distressing, awful, and dreadful scene that is about to take place. Believe me, cruel and pitiable is my unfortunate and affecting situation but God's will be done, and with humble resignation I must bear my untimely fate. But what a pleasing consolation within this tortured breast to suffer innocently.

Dear parents, I do solemnly declare, was I never to enter the heavenly mansion of heavenly rest, – I am murdered – dear father and mother, believe I am your only child that speak the sentiments of a broken heart; do not let me distress your breaking hearts. I wish to comfort you, dearest of parents; be happy, pray take comfort, let me entreat of you to be reconciled, and I will be happy in heaven with my dear sisters and brothers, and meet you bye and bye [*sic*].

Pray read the blessed Bible and turn your hearts, and live religious and holy lives, and there we shall be where sorrow and trouble will be no more. I grieve more to think I had an opportunity once and did not make use of it, yet there is time to pray to my Heavenly Father to forgive me all my sins and offences in my life past.

It is only the passage of death that I have to go through, and I hope and trust in God that will soon be over. Oh, my blessed and beloved parents, think what are my present distressing feelings, to part from you who gave me my being, and nourished me at that breast, and was my sole comfort, and nursed me in helpless and infant years, and was always a direction to me in the sacred path of virtue, which I have strictly kept; it will be one sin less to answer for, as a spotless frame will be acceptable in the eyes of God; I mention this as I let you know I have not done amiss. – Oh, dear parents, what an affecting scene to part from you, which must be endured by the laws of justice, but justice has not been shown at the bar. Man judges man, but God will judge us at the last, who knows the secrets of all hearts, and they who swore my life away will never enter with me into rest.

God bless you both, and may you live happy. Adieu, from your injured and unhappy child. Keep these few lines in remembrance of me, as this is all the comfort I can afford with my imperfect prayers. Adieu, dear parents, – God bless you both.
ELIZA FENNING.
Aged 21 Years.

Eliza received a number of compassionate letters from supporters as the day of her execution drew near, mostly couched in religious and repetitive terminology.

London,
21 June 1815

Dear Eliza,

I have done all I can to save your life and now we must leave it to the will of Kind Providence to turn the scale for the time draws near when you will know your fate, but be of good comfort for if you are innocent God can deliver you out of prison as easy as he did Peter. Pray to God to give you grace to save your soul, and that will enable you to forgive your prosecutors, for when Stephen was being murdered he prayed to God not to let the sin be laid to their charge. If it should be the will of Providence that you should suffer, it is better to die innocent than to die guilty.

Dear Eliza, be of good comfort; if the summons should come from a better world, I hope you will experience what Stephen did when he was going to die, for we read in the New Testament that he saw the heavens open and Jesus ready to receive his soul in glory.

Dear Eliza, it was this glory that the Apostle felt in his heart which made him say, I have a desire to depart and be with Jesus, which is far better.

Dear Eliza, my heart feels for you, but I hope we shall at last meet in heaven where trouble and sorrow will be no more. A friend has been to the Rev. Mr C[37] and I believe he will come and see you. May God bless you in this world and the next, if there is anything more I can do for you, I will do it with all my heart, I am anxious to do all I can.

Dear Eliza, read the 7th chapter of Acts, the 56th verse. Send me any particular you can.

I remain your dear Friend until death.

It is not clear, but it seems likely, that the following letter written by Eliza was to the writer of the letter above:

Felons' Side, Newgate,
30 June 1815
Dear Friend,

I feel extremely sorry at your being disappointed at not receiving my letter which must be the neglect of the person who I entrusted to put it in the post; believe me, I feel at a loss for words to express my gratitude for all the kind services you have so generously bestowed on an unfortunate victim but I hope and trust the Lord will bless those who help the afflicted in mind, body or estate and they may bear record in heaven, for the Lord has been good to me and has not let me want in my distressing and wretched case – believe me, cruel and pitiable is my forlorn situation but yet this trouble may be for some divine purpose which the Lord thought proper to bring me to himself, and next Sunday I think I feel prepared, respecting of taking the Holy Sacrament, as I firmly know I never injured any person, and trust, with safety, I have not violated the sacred laws of God or my country; believe me, I do, with a solemn vow, declare myself innocent of the crime laid to my charge for we must give an account before an Almighty just God who knows the secrets of all hearts, at whose tribunal bar we must all appear and give an account for every action done in the body. Once more, God bless you for all your kindness to me, an innocent victim.

---

37 Revd Horace Cotton, Newgate Ordinary, an Anglican chaplain active in extracting confessions from convicted prisoners and providing evidence of contrition. With this agenda he supplied Eliza with books entitled *Thoughts on Death* and *The Punishment of the Wicked in the Next World*. The Ordinary wrote accounts of those executed – later to be reused in the various versions of the *Newgate Calendar* – in part to illustrate the wickedness and weak character of offenders but also as cautionary tales to deter others from taking a similar path. He was eventually censured for over-doing the hell-fire rhetoric in his pre-execution sermons.

I remain yours, with gratitude,
ELIZA FENNING

The reply to this letter was written the following day:

Dear Eliza,

I received your letter this morning which I very gladly received.
I hope you will not be offended at me, the reason of my writing
to you is that I understand you have a desire to receive the Holy
Sacrament but, I will ask you one question, Eliza, from what quarter
does that desire spring. Is it only to convince Mr C (chaplain/
ordinary) that you are innocent and the people that may see you?

Dear Eliza, if this desire springs from this quarter, I would say, in
the language of a father and a friend and as a Christian, for God's
sake and your soul's sake do not take the Sacrament on such a
motive if Mr C will not believe you are innocent he cannot take
your life. Consider, my dear girl, God does not let men always have
their way, therefore be of good comfort, God can deliver you out of
prison without your taking the Sacrament to convince them you
have a clear conscience of this crime. I wish I had wrote to you
before on this subject. I hope it is not too late; consider, my dear girl,
the Sacrament is a very solemn subject …

Here the writer lapses into religious dogma and returns to
preach some more in a letter of 3 July 1815. They informed her
that, 'God forbid any Christian should try to screen a guilty
offender from the laws of justice for such a crime as you are
supposed to be guilty of', and that, though they felt inclined to
believe her:

God knows the secrets of all hearts, man judges man, but God will
judge all men. I hope your life may be spared if you are innocent,
to see the guilty offender brought to justice; but, if you should not
live to see it, the time will come when the guilty offender must
appear before an Almighty Judge which cannot be deceived by false
witnesses.

Dear Eliza, I hope you do not think that dying for a crime for
which you are innocent will atone for your past sins; there is nothing that will save your soul but the pardoning love of Jesus…

These thoughts may have brought some solace to Eliza as she languished in the condemned cell at Newgate. The latter part of his letter, however, can hardly have given any comfort to a young woman about to hang:

> Cheer up, don't be down-hearted, I hope you will be enabled to say, in truth, I am only going to die to live again with Christ in glory and there to sing the praise of God and the Lamb that bore the curse for guilty man, so you may perceive that death is only a kind friend to take you to eternal glory.
>
> Dear Eliza, as long as there is life there is hope but if it should be the will of Providence that my expectation should be cut off, send me a lock of your hair, that I may say this is the lock of a female whose life I tried to save and may the hand of kind Providence bless all those gentlemen who have exerted their abilities in the cause of an injured female.
>
> I remain your faithful friend till death.

Eliza replied on 6 July: 'I will grant you the request respecting a lock of hair if it is the will of God for me to suffer, believe me, the word suffer strikes me with awful horror: to think I am innocent of the crime and to indure [*sic*] the sufferings; suffer me to remain yours until death doth me call.'

Letters in this vein continued throughout Eliza's imprisonment. It is not entirely clear whether the following letter from Eliza was written to the 'Dear Friend', or someone quite different, called Charles:

> Felons' Side, Newgate, 21 July 1815
> Dear Charles,
>
> I am so deprest [*sic*] with woe and affliction that I scarce know how to direct my trembling and faultering [*sic*] pen I did not expect I should have fortitude to direct my words to you, oh, the blow is dreadful and distressing to me! It is impossible to describe to you my feelings in my awful situation, but time draws on a conclusion to my unfortunate case I must bear the smart with patience and humble resignation to the closing scene of mournful and eternal parting, farewell to my dear, unhappy, affectionate parents whose breaking hearts cut my tortured breast but God bless them and

give them consolation amidst the awful scene of their oppressing woe. You have been a sincere and dear friend towards me and I trust the Almighty will reward you for all is vanity and vexation of spirit. Oh, I trust the God of all mercies will receive me in the heavenly mansions above where sorrow and trouble will be no more.

Oh, believe me, I die innocent of the crime. I am sensible what I am going now to reveal to you, which is this, was I never to enter the kingdom of God, whose presence I must face, that I die a shameful and ignominious death for the guilty person, how cruel that they should be screened from the laws of justice; but God will reward according to their wicked deeds.

Pray God forgive them that they may never be destroyed in that world where everlasting burning must be endured, which is the portion of all wicked persecutors, who take the life of the innocent.

Pray comfort my dear parents and God bless you. Adieu, dear Charles. Pray call once and bid me farewell for ever. Adieu.

Your unhappy

ELIZA FENNING

PS Pray keep these few lines and this lock of hair in remembrance of me. God bless you. Adieu for ever.

Two days later, Eliza wrote again to her friend: 'it is hard and pitiable,' she said, 'and, indeed, distressing beyond description, to suffer such an ignominious death, innocent as I am.'

Believe me, my words are the real sentiments of a dying heart, I may justly say I have but a few hours before I shall leave the world of sorrow and woe, to enter the heavenly mansions of eternal rest, where troubles will be no more.

...the end strikes me and my dear parents with silent horror:– what a pity the guilty and dreadful character should be screened, by the sufferings of the innocent, which remains in the house of Mr Turner.

If they knew within their breast they were innocent, why not call and beg of me to forgive them, which, injured as I am, I freely forgive them and hope the Almighty will forgive them and trust this dreadful sin will never rise up against them in the grand and awful day of judgement when the secrets of all hearts will be judged before the tribunal bar of an Almighty just God.

According to the pamphlet, 'to a gentleman who had been kind to her in prison', she wrote: 'it's for some divine purpose the Almighty has ordained this trouble to bring me to himself. If it should be so, I must pray the Lord to give me strength to bear it. I dread the awful moment of bidding an eternal farewel [*sic*] to my dear parents and friends. Think what a scene may probably arise to my parents if I suffer.'

During the evening of Tuesday 25 July, on the eve of her execution, Eliza sent some earrings to her mother with the following note: 'Wear my ear-rings, dear mother, for my sake. Don't part with them, dearest mother. I die innocent of the crime, indeed ——.'

The Execution

At least Eliza Fenning was spared the terrible journey through the streets of London to Tyburn. There are a number of accounts of Eliza's execution, perhaps the most comprehensive being recorded in the *Newgate Calendar*. However, some interesting details omitted from that account can be found in the pamphlet published soon after the event by John Fairburn:

> On the Sunday before her execution she received the sacrament and heard the condemned sermon during which she was overcome by the intensity of her feelings which brought on violent hysterics that continued the greater part of the day.
>
> On Monday she wrote a letter to her late master and mistress, Mr and Mrs Turner, requesting they would favour her with an interview in the prison. This they complied with and visited her in her cell. She then protested to them, in the most solemn manner, that she had not administered the arsenic and expressed a hope ere long Providence would point its finger at the real criminal and relieve her character from the foul aspersion with which it had been undeservedly blackened.
>
> Of her approaching fate she spoke with firmness and took leave of her visitors in the most affecting manner. She was afterwards visited by her father and some of her friends to whom she expressed her perfect resignation.

On Tuesday evening, about four o'clock, she was visited for the last time by her mother, to whom, in taking a last leave, she said, 'now, my dear mother, I embrace you for the last time and with this embrace receive the only consolation I can give you and that is a solemn and sincere declaration of my innocence of the horrid crime for which I am to suffer.'

When her mother hinted at some hopes of mercy yet reaching her, she rejected the plea and requested her to spare herself the unavailing task, nor attempt to unhinge her mind by any sublunary objects.

She was then locked up for the night and at an early hour in the morning was visited by Revd Mr Cotton who continued with her and her wretched companions to the last moment of their existence. The unfortunate woman, although short in stature, was a very pretty figure. Her face was expressive and she had none of the characteristics of a woman capable of committing the foul deed of which she had been, after a patient and impartial trial, pronounced guilty. She was betrothed to a young man of industrious habits, to whom she wrote several affecting letters and who has exhibited the strongest feelings of misery in the contemplation of her fate.

On Wednesday, July 26th, Eliza Fenning was executed, pursuant to her sentence, before the Debtors' door, at Newgate. The morning was wet, gloomy and disagreeable; but the unfavourable state of the weather did not prevent the accumulation of an immense crowd at an early hour. Public curiosity was strongly excited and perhaps to a greater degree than on any similar event... For, in the case of Eliza Fenning, many had taken up an opinion that guilt was not clearly established.

A great portion of the public have taken an uncommon interest in the fate of this young female ever since her conviction and the feeling which generally prevailed was that she would on the scaffold make an open and decided disavowal of any participation in the crime imputed to her.

The following account is from the *Newgate Calendar*:

During the early hours of the Wednesday morning the large portable gallows was brought out of Newgate and made ready outside the Debtor's Door. It was normal for prisoners to be hanged in groups for unconnected crimes although this was to be the only triple hanging of 1815, a year in which 12 people were executed at Newgate. Long before eight o'clock, hoards of people were thronging the streets and jostling for the best positions from which to witness the executions.

Eliza was led from the condemned cell into the Press Yard around eight o'clock in the morning, where her hands were pinioned. She was dressed in a white muslin gown with a high waist, tied with a fashionable ribbon, a white muslin cap and wearing a pair of light laced lilac boots. This was her wedding outfit and she was to have been married on this day, instead she was to be hanged.[38]

From the Press Yard it was a short walk to the steps of the scaffold. The Reverend Horace Cotton, the Ordinary of Newgate, accompanied her[39] and asked her if she had anything to communicate to him in her final moments. She told him:

'Before the just and Almighty God, and by the faith of the Holy Sacrament I have taken, I am innocent of the offence with which I am charged.'

She proceeded up the steps of the gallows and the large crowd that had come to see her die fell silent. She stood calmly while the Reverend Cotton intoned prayers for her. John Langley, the hangman, drew the traditional white cotton nightcap over her head. Owing to the size of her muslin cap, he was unable to get it on. He then tried to bind a muslin handkerchief over her face but it proved too small. Then he pulled out his own dirty pocket handkerchief to tie over her face. This disgusted her.

'Pray do not let him put it on, Mr Cotton!' she implored. 'Pray make him take it off. Pray do, Mr Cotton!'

'My dear, it must be on. He must put it on.' Cotton told her.

So she now stood silently, with her arms bound, while the dirty handkerchief was tied over her face. Then Langley placed the rope around her neck. She continued to wait stoically, pinioned and noosed, praying with the Ordinary while the other two criminals who were to hang with her, fifty-one-year-old Abraham Adams, convicted of

---

38 According to John Fairburn's account the execution was delayed for an hour as the hangman, John Langley, was running late, having just hanged a woman in Ipswich.

39 Another report stated that 'a gentleman of the Methodist connection' was also in attendance. In his journal, the Methodist preacher Charles Wesley (brother of John) records that, in July of 1738, he visited Newgate Prison to preach to criminals destined to die on the gallows the following day. Whilst commenting that the Ordinary preached 'most miserably', he proceeds to congratulate himself on his own ability to so inspire the wretched condemned that they were filled with 'inexpressible joy' and euphorically longed for death.

sodomy, and twenty-four-year-old William Oldfield, who was 'guilty of an odious crime' – the rape of a nine-year-old girl – were prepared. Oldfield had apparently asked permission to hang beside her. As the noose was placed around his neck, Oldfield continued to rave and chant prayers.

Just before the drop fell she told Dr Cotton, once again, that she was innocent.[40]

At around half past eight, when the preparations were complete, Langley withdrew the pin releasing the trap and giving the prisoners a drop of about 12-18 inches.[41] It was reported that Eliza died easily 'almost without writhing'. Mercifully, she did not suffer long. Hangings were often grotesquely bungled, resulting in death by slow strangulation rather than a quick dislocation of the neck.

Another account, also taken from the *Newgate Calendar*, described the scene differently:

On the 26th of July, the day appointed for the execution of Elizabeth Fenning, William Oldfield and Abraham Adams, the public curiosity was strongly excited…. In the case of Fenning many had taken up an opinion that her guilt was not clearly established for she had uniformly protested her innocence. The last interview between her and her parents took place about half-past one o'clock on Tuesday. To them, and to the last moment, she persisted in her innocence. About eight o'clock the sheriffs proceded [*sic*] from Justice Hall along the subterraneous passage to the press-yard.

Fenning was dressed in white, with laced boots and a cap. Oldfield went up to her in the press-yard and enjoined her to prayer and assured her that they should all be happy.

The sheriffs preceded the cavalcade to the steps of the scaffold, to which the unfortunate girl was first introduced. Just as the door was opened the Reverend Mr Cotton stopped her for a moment to ask

40 According to the Fairburn account the last words spoken by Eliza were: 'I know my situation and may I never enter the kingdom of heaven to which I feel confident I am going, if I am not innocent.'

41 James Berry, executioner 1884 to 1892, devised a 'table of drops' based on the weight and stature of the prisoner and the length of the rope to ensure a quick and more merciful death, a practice perfected by Albert Pierrepoint, executioner from 1932 to 1956.

her if in her last moments she had anything to communicate. She paused for a moment and said: 'Before the just and Almighty God, and by the faith of the Holy Sacrament I have taken, I am innocent of the offence with which I am charged.'

This she spoke with much firmness of emphasis and followed it by saying what all around her understood to be:

'My innocence will be manifested in the course of the day.'

The last part of this sentence was spoken, however, so inaudibly that it was not rightly understood and the Reverend Cotton, being anxious to hear it again, put a question to get from her positive words; to which she answered:

'I hope God will forgive me, and make manifest the transaction in the course of the day.'

She then mounted the platform with the same uniform firmness she had maintained throughout.

A handkerchief was tied over her face and she prayed fervently, but, to the last moment, declared her innocence. Oldfield came up next, with a firm step, and addressed a few words in prayer to the unhappy girl.

About half-past eight o'clock the fatal sign was given. One movement only was perceptible in Fenning. After hanging the usual hour the bodies were cut down and given over to their friends for internment.

During the remainder of the day numerous groupes [*sic*] of people assembled at the Old Bailey and also, in the evening, opposite the house of Mr Turner (the prosecutor) in Chancery-lane, conversing on the subject, with whom, pity for her sufferings and a firm belief of her innocence, seemed to be the prevailing sentiment. At the last-mentioned place, the tumult became so great it was found necessary to send for the assistance of the police to disperse the multitude and preserve the peace.

It is remarkable that no part of the body of this unfortunate female, from the crown of her head to the sole of her foot, changed colour in the least after her execution until the evening of the following Friday, with the exception of a small mark under her chin, made by the rope. She lay in her coffin seemingly as in a sweet sleep, with a smile on her countenance.

Eliza's father had to pay 14*s* 6*d* for the 'executioner's fees' before he could redeem his daughter's dead body for burial. This, in addition to the cost of the funeral and wake, had clearly caused considerable financial hardship for the Fennings; in the Fairburn pamphlet readers were informed that:

Early in the day the friends and relatives of Eliza Fenning assembled at the house of Mr Millar, Picture-Cleaner and Repairer, No 14, Eagle-Street, Red-Lion-Square, (where the body lay) who had been maligned in some of the public prints as having made a shew of the body of the girl for interested purposes. We have, however, the solemn assurance of this man and his wife that they with reluctance admitted many of the numerous applicants to see the corpse, and such of them as chose to leave a donation for the relief of the distressed and unhappy parents, were permitted, the donations were faithfully paid into the hands of the father. Those persons, in the trying hour of affliction, had opened their doors for the reception of the father and mother of this unfortunate female, after they had disposed of every article of their furniture and were compelled, in consequence, to quit their usual lodging.

Their daughter was buried five days later, in the churchyard of St George the Martyr, behind the London Foundling Hospital, in Bloomsbury[42] and her funeral was attended by several thousand people.

Her funeral took place on 31 July 1815. It began to move from the house of her father, in Eagle Street, Red Lion Square, about half-past three o'clock; preceded by about a dozen peace officers and these were followed by nearly thirty more; next came the undertaker, immediately followed by the body of the deceased. The pall was supported by six young females, attired in white: then followed eight persons, male and female, as chief mourners, led by the parents.[43]

---

42 In 1777, at St George the Martyr, a grave digger, John Holmes, and his assistant, Robert Williams, were found guilty of digging up the corpse of Mrs Jane Salisbury to sell to anatomists at the city's teaching hospitals. Both men served six months' imprisonment but escaped the sentence of being whipped along the half-mile journey from Kingsgate Street to Dyott Street, in the St Giles area of the city.

43 In the John Fairburn account 'the coffin was neatly covered with a sky blue cloth, and with white nails. On the coffin plate was inscribed, 'Eliza Fenning, died July 26, 1815, aged 22 years.'

These were succeeded by several hundreds of persons, two and two, and the whole was closed by a posse of peace officers. Many thousands accompanied the procession and the windows, and even the tops of the houses, as it passed were thronged with spectators. The whole proceeded in a regular manner until it reached the burying-ground of St George the Martyr. The number of persons assembled in and about the churchyard was estimated at ten thousand.

The press was divided in its opinions on the case – some were staunchly pro-Eliza Fenning and others were extremely hostile. A lengthy article in the *Caledonian Mercury* on Saturday 5 August was revealing – and intensely hostile to Eliza:

The body of this young woman, whose fate has excited such interest, was, on Monday evening at four o'clock, consigned to its 'last home', in the burial ground of St George the Martyr, Bloomsbury. An intention had existed that the melancholy ceremony should not take place till five o'clock; the clergyman who was to perform the service, however, having given notice that he should be at the ground at four o'clock to receive the corpse and would not wait beyond that period, it became necessary that the procession should commence its movement from Eagle Street, Red Lion Square, where the body had lain, at half past three. Notwithstanding this alteration of the time, however, the multitude which assembled, from a feeling of curiosity to witness the scene, was immense.

As early as two o'clock the crowd began to assemble in Eagle Street and in all the avenues leading to the burial ground. Every window was thronged and in many places the tops of houses were covered with spectators. Every precaution had prudently been taken by the Police Magistrates to preserve the peace and nearly a hundred constables were in attendance to prevent confusion.

At half past three the coffin was brought forth, carried by six men in black. It was covered with a rich pall which was borne by six young girls in white dresses and was followed by eight mourners in mourning scarves and cloaks: the father and mother being, of course, the chief mourners. Several constables went before to clear the way and a posse also followed to prevent the encroachments of the mob which pressed in thousands behind.

The whole proceeded in a steady and solemn pace and the most perfect order prevailed, till the arrival of the procession at the gate of the burial ground, when, although the constables endeavoured to keep back the crowd, a vast number forced their entrance and thus a temporary confusion was excited. This soon subsided, however, and the body having been lowered into the grave, the Rev. Mr Force, curate of St George's, Bloomsbury, read the service of the dead with becoming solemnity. We lament to state, however, that towards the conclusion, a man, dressed in livery, made use of an expression relative to the deceased, which excited the indignation of the crowd.

According to the account in the Fairburn pamphlet, the outraged spectators were angered not only by the use of the offensive word, but also because the man was without a hat, which was considered 'a violation of all decency'. They waited until the distraught parents had left the graveside before following the man, shouting, 'Shame! Shame!' and spitting in his face; he was 'shuffled and hissed off the ground over the wall' and 'the men shook him and pulled him by the ears': He was knocked down and the church-yard became a scene of great disorder. Some gentlemen at length interfered, quelled the riot, and having obtained the name of the offender's master, declared their intention to complain of his misconduct.'

Meanwhile, 'the unhappy mother of the young woman was dreadfully affected throughout the whole of the ceremony, and was in fits three times, and indeed the whole of the persons connected with the procession exhibited the strongest marks of sympathy.'[44]

Fairburn described the group which gathered at Mr Turner's house in Chancery Lane, where they 'conducted themselves in the most unbecoming manner … Straw was brought for the purpose of setting fire to the house and we fear, but the interference of the civil power, much real mischief would have been done … the most dreadful threats were uttered by the crowd.'

Rumours and lies began to spread, including the tale that 'Mr Turner himself had been the mixer of the poison, a circumstance which is utterly disproved by the facts that transpired on the trial. It was then said that he had shot himself in despair; and if not him, that his apprentice, who had given evidence against the

---

44 The John Fairburn account states that towards the end of the ceremony Eliza's mother 'fell on the ground in strong hysterics'.

culprit, had committed suicide but that his death was concealed. To these are added other reports, all equally incorrect.'

In Red Lion Square, meanwhile, crowds came to see the body:

> There an immense crowd was attracted by curiosity to see the body which, to use an Irish expression, was waking in all due form, being placed in the kitchen of the house and dressed out in ribbons, flowers, etc. All persons who presented themselves obtained admission to the house. As fast as one set came out another went in, and although no money was actually demanded for this exhibition, we learn that the pecuniary contributions towards defraying the expenses of the wake and funeral, exceeded forty pounds...

In order to quell the growing unrest, the authorities were forced to issue the following statement:

> London(to wit) Samuel Davis, one of the principal turnkeys of his Majesty's gaol of Newgate, maketh oath and saith that in an interview which lately took place between the late convict Elizabeth Fenning, who was executed on Wednesday last, and her father (at which interview this deponent and the Revd Mr Cotton, Chaplain of the said prison, were both present) and on several other interviews between them prior to her execution, her said father urgently entreated her in the following words or words to the like effect (that is to say):
>
> 'Oh, my dear child, when you come out on the gallows, tell everybody that you are innocent and then I can walk the street upright as a man; but if you say you are guilty I shall never be able to hold up my head among the public any more.'
>
> Sworn at the Mansion-house, in the city of London, the 28th of July 1815. Samuel Davis.
>
> Before Samuel Birch, Mayor.

It did little good, and eventually the police were called to surround Mr Fenning's house and disperse the crowds there; '[on] Saturday, however, the multitude again assembled, although we have the pleasure to state, they were not so violent in their conduct as on the preceding days.' Another menace to the authorities then emerged: 'To the circumstances already detailed we have to add that a vast number of anonymous letters have been sent to the Reverend Mr Cotton, the Ordinary of Newgate, and to Mr Newman, the head gaoler, in which threats are held out in a variety of forms'.

Fairburn's pamphlet also contains a brief and rather unflattering biography of Eliza:

> It appears that her father and mother are both from Ireland and that they are both Roman Catholics: the former is a servant to Mr Hutchins, a potatoe [*sic*] seller, in Red Lion Passage; the other is, as far as we have been able to learn, an industrious woman and the mother of eleven children, of whom Eliza was the last living.
>
> Eliza, at a proper age, was sent to the Gate Street (Lincoln's Inn Fields) Charity School for education which is made the protection of dissenters. Here it was endeavoured to instruct her in the Christian religion and whatever instructions she received in that way, was derived from this source. Notwithstanding every effort to correct a wayward and vicious disposition which at this early period manifested itself, however, it became necessary, at twelve years of age, for the preservation of the morals of the other children, who were her school-fellows, to expel her; and in the books of charity is this memorandum, written on that occasion:
>
> 'Eliza Fenning, aged twelve years, turned out of the school for lying and lewd talk.'
>
> From this period she did but little to redeem her lost character. Truth was a practice with which she seemed to be at war and there was not a place in which she was employed [for she went out to service almost immediately afterwards] that she did not leave behind the character of a confirmed liar.
>
> In the service of Mr Hardy, a grocer in Portugal Street, Lincoln's-inn Fields, she gave particular manifestations of her vicious disposition. She there denied her mother and applied to her language which none but the most abandoned could use when speaking of a parent. She was also in the constant practice of inventing falsehoods; and by her general demeanour, impressed her master with an opinion, to use his own words, 'that she was capable of any act, however malevolent,' and so strongly did this impression weight on his mind that he was not happy till she was out of the house.
>
> Mr Hardy had also a suspicion that there was something deleterious mixed in a pot of porter which she brought from the public-house for the use of the family but which was not, from the idea that was

entertained of it at the moment, used. Of any attempt to poison here, however, though strongly reported, there is no positive proof.

In every place in which she lived afterwards she unhappily obtained for herself the character of being most spiteful and malicious: She did not live long in each place and went to Mr Hardy for three characters [references]; and there are numerous instances of a treacherous mind recited which we cannot afford space to detail.

While with Mr Hardy she imbibed an affection for a young man which seemed greatly to have unsettled her mind and perhaps to that may be attributed many of her subsequent follies.

Her last place was that of Mr Turner's, where her conduct, as appeared on her trial, soon exposed her to the reprehension of her mistress and she received warning to quit. It was after that warning, which she seemed to have taken so much to heart, that she committed the crime imputed to her.

In Mr Turner's service she had shewn a very amorous inclination which, while even under sentence of death, was more strongly manifested … For how does it appear she conducted herself [in the prison]? From the day of her trial she behaved in a manner so flippant and so unbecoming that she frequently called down the animal versions of the Reverend Mr Cotton, by whom she was attended, a gentleman of whom it is but justice to say, no man could fulfil the arduous functions of his office with a more exemplary spirit or a more pious zeal.

Her first act of impurity was that of writing a letter to Oldfield, who suffered with her, and who, it will be recollected, was convicted of a rape – the last man of all others with whom a virtuous mind would have communication.

This was followed by *billet-doux* [love letter] written to other prisoners and among others was a letter written to a prisoner in custody on a charge of forgery [possibly Edward Harland], couched in the most voluptuous language and inclosing [*sic*] a lock of her hair. To this man, who had been admitted to assist her in preparing a petition, she was heard to say, 'If she did not die otherwise she would in love of him.'

He felt a passion equally strong for her, short as had been their acquaintance.

The pamphlet continued with the suggestion that 'a few days before her execution she accused various persons of having committed the crime charged to her account'. Then she asked 'that a young man named King [Thomas King, the second apprentice] who had lived in Mr Turner's house, might be brought before her and confronted with her, observing that she was sure he would, by his confession, convince those who were witnesses to the scene that he alone was guilty.' The test 'which the prisoner required of his innocence was that he should go upon his knees and, placing his hand upon an open Bible, solemnly declare that he was not in the kitchen the day on which the dumplings were made.' Despite the 'most vehement and passionate' pleading:

> Thomas put his hand on the Bible in the most solemn manner, declaring he neither was in the kitchen nor knew anything of the mixing of the poison. Upon hearing this, she clapped her hand on the Bible and said, in the most passionate way, 'I am glad of it, you have sworn a lie'. Upon being reprimanded by Mr Cotton for expressing joy at conduct in a boy which would destroy his soul, she equivocated and said, 'She did not mean that, but that she was glad that she could contradict him.'[45]

The pamphlet continued:

> All the women who attended her declared their perfect conviction that she was guilty, as did every turnkey in the prison, and they all said they never saw a woman of a more malevolent disposition. She was heard to say, more than once, that she wished she could get leave to tear the heart out of her prosecutors; and to the woman who sat up with her for some nights before her execution, she admitted that there were two things which if they were to cut her in pieces she would not divulge. What these were could not be discovered although it may be inferred that she had made some mental reservation to avoid telling her guilt.

Further witnesses were called on to declare that 'her manners partook rather of a ranting and theatrical turn than of the serious

---

45   Eliza had said that, on the morning she made the dumplings, she left Thomas King in the kitchen while she attended to a delivery of coal. Both Charlotte Turner and Thomas King denied there was a delivery that day; however, when the coal merchant's order book was eventually checked, it appeared that there *was* coal delivered to the Turner household that day.

conduct of a person who is really innocent. She exhibited throughout an uncommon strength of mind and a degree of talent which was displayed in her letters, far above her situation in life.'

In 1829, a Penny Dreadful was published entitled *The Extraordinary Case of Eliza Fenning, who was executed in 1815: A Statement of Facts since developed, tending to prove HER INNOCENCE of THE CRIME.*[46]

It began:

> The Trial and Execution of Eliza Fenning in 1815, for an attempt to poison the family of Mr Turner, the Law-stationer, will be in the recollection of most of our readers. The event excited great attention and interest at the time on account of the conviction having taken place on circumstantial evidence only and the powerful asseverations of innocence on the part of the unhappy woman up to the very moment of her death.
>
> At that time a large portion of the public thought her wrongfully condemned and some of the newspapers espoused her cause warmly; but, after a patient and impartial trial and a subsequent investigation before the privy council, the evidence was considered too strong to leave a doubt of her guilt; she was executed.
>
> Years passed away without there appearing any reason to doubt the justice of the verdict; but fresh interest has been lately given to the subject by a report that has been circulated charging another with the dreadful deed; and it is, therefore, thought that a reprint of the trial will be acceptable as the first of a series of extraordinary Convictions on Circumstantial Evidence, intended to be given in the Universal Pamphleteer...

After giving details of the evidence given at the trial, the article continues:

> Within the last few weeks a paragraph has appeared in many of the newspapers stating that the son of Mr Turner had died lately in a

---

46   Published by Cowie and Strange, Paternoster Row, and Purkis, Wardour Street, Soho; and sold by 'all vendors of pamphlets [price ONE PENNY]'.

hospital after confessing that he had mixed the poison in the food prepared by Eliza Fenning and was consequently guilty of the offence for which she suffered. Upon this statement, the *Examiner* newspaper of 14 June 1829, remarks -

'We saw the paragraph alluded to but know not whether its statement to be correct. We think it very likely because this we do know that a son of the prosecutor, Turner, did on one occasion betray symptoms of insanity in the shop of Messrs. Corbyn, Holborn, where he went to purchase arsenic and was refused by a gentleman of the establishment.

This was not long previous to the affair of the alleged attempt to poison by Eliza Fenning; and when the unfortunate girl was so strangely found guilty by the jury, the gentleman alluded to thought it his duty to submit Mr Turner's situation and conduct to the consideration of the Recorder Silvester. That man, however, had made up his mind and nothing could move him.

We took considerable pains at the time to obtain all the testimony adduced and our firm conviction was that there was not sufficient evidence to convict. Arsenic was kept in the house and some of it certainly found its way into the flour that Eliza Fenning had made into a pudding. Of this she partook, as well as Mrs Turner (and the children)[47] and was extremely ill in consequence. She had occasionally quarrelled with her mistress upon common matters but there appeared no cause for anything like a feeling of revenge such as so deadly an attempt as that to poison a whole family would indicate.'

Despite the fact that forty-two years had passed since Eliza Fenning was hanged, during the trial of Madeleine Smith[48] in 1857, the case was again referred to in an article entitled 'Circumstantial Evidence' in *The Times* of 21 July 1857 which told of a supposed confession:

---

47   Clearly this was an error in the reporting: Robert and Charlotte didn't have any children in 1815.

48   Madeleine Smith was charged with poisoning her lover, Pierre L'Angelier, with arsenic. Her trial in Edinburgh, August 1857, caused a sensation. The jury returned a verdict of *not proven* and she was released. She married an artist, George Wardle, and had two children. She eventually moved to New York, changed her name to Lena Wardle Sheehy, and died in 1928, aged ninety-three.

Dr Fletcher, minister of Finsbury Chapel, London, narrates the following in regard to the case of Eliza Fenning, referred to by the Dean of Faculty in his defence of Miss Madeleine Smith:

'A considerable number of years ago I was sent to visit on a Sabbath-day Eliza Fenning in prison, who was sentenced to be executed on the following Monday [Wednesday] in the front of Newgate, and who was found afterwards – alas! Though too late – innocent of the crime. She was executed for a deed she never committed. In company with the Ordinary of Newgate I conversed and prayed with her. She was dressed in white, an emblem of her innocence. In the same garments she suffered death as a criminal on the following day. I had no opportunity of judging as to her innocence. The expression of her countenance will never be erased from my remembrance. It is literally stereotyped upon my heart. From what was communicated to me some years after the fatal and melancholy event I can now explain the expression of her countenance. It was the demonstration of injured innocence!

When the event of her execution was almost forgotten, a baker, dying in a workhouse in the vicinity of London, said to the matron of the ward, or some other individual, to the following effect:- 'My mind is heavily burdened. I cannot die until I make the following communication: – Eliza Fenning died innocent of the crime for which she suffered. I am the murderer of her mistress. I put the poison into the morsel which effected her death.'[49]

On the trial the jury concluded it must have been the cook who had administered the poison as they had not the slightest clue to suspect the baker. Yesterday, in the vestry of my own chapel, one of my elders stated to me that the baker was a relative of the deceased.[50] There is no doubt that he accomplished his murderous purpose to gratify some long-cherished passion of revenge from an offence given him, real or imaginary, by the fated victim of his malevolence.'

Confession was once more the subject of the following letter which appeared in *The Times* on 5 August 1857:

49 Charlotte Turner did not die from the poison: Eliza Fenning was charged with and convicted of 'attempted poisoning'.

50 It is not clear whether the writer is referring to the 'deceased' as Eliza Fenning or her supposed victim, Charlotte Turner; he seemed to think that Mrs Charlotte Turner had died.

Sir, – In the late trial at Edinburgh allusion was made by the Dean of Faculty to the case of Eliza Fenning. He mentioned it as illustrating the danger of trusting to circumstantial evidence and assumed that the verdict had been a wrongful one…

My late uncle, Mr William Brodie Gurney, shorthand writer to the Houses of Parliament, was well known to a wide circle of friends, and to many of our leading public men, as a man of strictest integrity. His accuracy all who were familiar with him can testify was perfectly unimpeachable. To dress up a story for effect, or to take a side and support it by doubtful statements, was as foreign to his character as robbery or murder.

I happened to be spending an evening with him a year or two before his death and he produced a little book of anecdotes and conversations in which things worth remembering had been jotted down for his own use, or for those who might come after him … but having the book in his hand, he said, 'Oh! Here is something that will interest you about Eliza Fenning. You have heard, I dare say, that a person of that name was executed for poisoning (or attempting to poison, I forget which) the family with whom she lived as a servant, and that a good deal of popular feeling was excited on the subject, many persons being persuaded that she was wrongfully convicted, because she maintained her innocence in prison and on her way to the scaffold.'

He then read the underwritten statement. I dare say Eliza Fenning will live in history as one unrighteously doomed to death … but, at any rate it is desirable that the candid and reasonable portion of the public, and especially men of influence and authority like the Dean of Faculty, should know how the case really stands,- namely, that Eliza Fenning did confess her guilt, in prison to a minister of the Gospel, who visited her as a friend; though afterwards, when persons came about her who doubted her guilt and gave her to understand that a reprieve might be hoped for, she changed her tone and, like Palmer and Patch and many others whose guilt no one doubts, went out of the world unconfessed.

The extract which follows is copied verbatim from my uncle's notebook, and has been supplied to me by his son, Mr Joseph Gurney, the present shorthand-writer to the Houses of Parliament:

'Doubts having been on several occasions expressed of the guilt of Eliza Fenning, I feel it my duty to record the facts with reference to her case which came within my knowledge.

... I heard that her strong asseverations of innocence had created a doubt and that many who visited her felt a strong interest in her case, believing her to be innocent and a petition to the King was sent in. The grounds of it were examined by the Secretary of State, the attention of the learned judge was called to the case, and, on his report that he felt no hesitation as to the propriety of the verdict, the law was directed to take its course, which it did. Still some people retained their doubts.

Shortly after her execution I heard that the Rev. James Upton, a Baptist minister, preaching in Church-street, Blackfriars-road, had visited her while under sentence of death, having been requested to do so in consequence of her having, when young, attended at his chapel, whether with her family or in the Sunday-school I am not aware. I knew him to be a very excellent man, – a man of great kindness of heart; I felt satisfied that he would not form a more unfavourable opinion than circumstances called for and I took an opportunity of seeing him. He informed me that on entering the cell Eliza Fenning, with great earnestness and tears, exclaimed that she was innocent of the crime imputed to her, – that it was a cruel charge, and so on. That he replied, 'Eliza, I have not come here to talk to you about that. I do not mean to ask you whether you are guilty of that crime or not, but I come to you as a minister of Jesus Christ, hearing that you are probably very shortly about to appear before your judge, to remind you that you are a sinner and that unless those sins which you are conscious you have committed are repented of and pardoned you have no good hope of eternity. I come to set before you Jesus as a Saviour able and willing to save.'

He said, 'I was somewhat affected, considering the situation of this poor girl about to suffer, and I talked to her earnestly, entreating her to seek mercy and avoiding altogether the subject of her conviction. Before I had done she was quite melted down and then it all came out.'

I said, 'Do you mean that she confessed the crime?'

'Oh, yes,' said he, 'there was no reserve then. She confessed that it was all true and I besought on her behalf the forgiveness of all her sins, and of that among the rest, and I hoped at the time that she had joined in that prayer, but I understand that after this she still persisted in assuring those who visited her of her innocence.'

I have felt it important to secure a wide circulation for this decisive refutation of a very current story while the recent trial is fresh in men's minds ...

But, having got upon the subject of reprieves and confessions, I should like, if you will allow me, to go on and speak of the fearful mischief often done within the walls of prisons by those who profess themselves the friends of the doomed criminals. The questionings which go on there, the repeated solicitations to confess, the importance attached to persevering denials of guilt, must necessarily have a blinding effect on those who are thus beset.

Numbers, I believe, will not confess just because so much is made of confession. 'They want me to confess that they may feel secure in hanging me,' is the natural feeling at such times. 'The verdict does not satisfy them unless I admit its justice. I won't do that. If I deny my guilt stoutly I shall perhaps be believed at last and escape.'

Thus, during the awful interval which is the murderer's brief preparation time for eternity, he is balancing probabilities of escape, demeaning himself so as to make a favourable impression on bystanders, heaping up lies which, by possibility, he thinks might gain him long time for repentance hereafter,- doing anything, in fact, but realising his position and opening his ears to the godly counsel of those who desire to save his soul alive. If a criminal wishes to confess there is no hindrance in his way. The penitent, without compulsion, will unlock the secrets of his heart to his spiritual adviser at any rate and to the world at large I do not know he is bound to proclaim his guilt.

… Alas! She [Eliza] had other advisers afterwards – persons who meant kindly but who did her fearful wrong. The confession was retracted. Hope was strong, doubtless, in that young bosom, and the efforts making on her behalf were sure to be reported to her.

Between her cell and the scaffold the Ordinary 'stopped her for a moment,' says the *Annual Register*, 'to ask her if in her last moments she had anything to communicate'…

She paused a moment and said, 'Before the just and Almighty God, and by the faith of the Holy Sacrament I have taken, I am innocent of the offence with which I am charged.'

By her own confession, at another time she was a murderess; dying thus with a lie upon her lips, she was no penitent. My fear is that the time of probation was lost, the faithful admonition forgotten, the course of repentance arrested, and the soul retained in the bondage of sin, because she was buoyed up with false hopes and her fatal gifts of youth and beauty, coupled with protestations of innocence made a party in her favour who hoped up to the last hour to extort a reprieve from Government.

I am, Sir, your obedient servant,

J.H.GURNEY, Rector of St Mary's, Gloucester-place, 31 July, Marylebone

Of course, the writer was mistaken when he assumed that Eliza had been charged with murder. How could she have been when no one in the Turner household had died? She had therefore been charged with attempted murder.

Invariably, in cases of poisoning, the evidence against the person accused is circumstantial; and so it was with the Eliza Fenning case. No one had seen her take the packet of arsenic from the drawer in the office or sprinkle it into the dumpling mixture. Unless we accept that Eliza had an irrational wish to take revenge on Mrs Turner by poisoning the whole family simply for reprimanding her for what she considered to be inappropriate behaviour, what motive for the crime is left?

So many factors in this case were never fully addressed. Why, for instance, wasn't the apprentice, Thomas King, called to give evidence? Why did Eliza insist on confronting him in her cell at Newgate? Where was he on that fateful day? His absence and subsequent avoidance of eating the dumplings could have been interpreted as fortuitous – suspicious, even. Likewise, the maid, Sarah, was also absent from the house that afternoon and didn't eat any of the dumplings. Did either of them have the motive or opportunity to poison the family, knowing that Eliza, the cook, would get the blame?

A rather farcical suggestion was made by those determined to point the finger at Eliza – Orlibar Turner and Dr John Marshall in particular – that she had eaten food containing arsenic in an attempt to divert suspicion from herself. Why on earth would Eliza risk her life by eating a dumpling if she knew it contained arsenic and would make her ill?

Why didn't her detractors ever consider that abstaining from eating food containing arsenic, as in the case of both Thomas King and Sarah Peer, was equally suspicious? Could Sarah have been the culprit? She admitted in court that she and Eliza had their differences: Eliza described Sarah as 'sly and cunning' and insinuated that she had put something in the milk that was used to make the sauce. Little wonder that she refused to drink the milk that the doctor, John Marshall, prescribed: she was convinced it was the milk that was contaminated. Was Sarah perhaps jealous of Eliza's looks and education and, moreover, envious of the fact that she was engaged to be married to, by all accounts, a caring and hard-working young man?

John Marshall was making a wild guess when he estimated that the residue in the dough pan contained half a teaspoon of arsenic. He had no way of ascertaining the precise amount of arsenic present. It was only after 1836, when the Marsh test was introduced – further refined in the Reinsch test, six years later – that the presence of an infinitesimal amount of arsenic could be accurately detected in food, body tissue and fluids. The investigative journalist John Watkins pointed out that, if Marshall's estimate was correct, this would mean that the four or six dumplings eaten that day had contained as much as 1,800 grains. It was generally accepted that just five grains of arsenic constitutes a fatal dose, though as little as four grains could sometimes kill. If Marshall's estimate was correct, between them Charlotte Turner and Orlibar Turner must have consumed enough arsenic to kill the whole household many times over. So why didn't it kill them outright?

Though products containing arsenic were, at the time, readily available for domestic use such as poison for killing rodents and fly papers – which ladies would soak to extract the arsenic to use as a face wash – how would Eliza Fenning know the correct dosage to use to ensure a bad attack of vomiting and diarrhoea, but not death?

It would seem that whoever put the arsenic in the dumplings that day didn't intend to kill the Turners – just to make them ill. Someone intent on killing them outright would have mixed a massive dose of arsenic to ensure death – as John Marshall had tried to indicate by over-estimating the amount in the dumplings, though he should have realised that the amount he had so wildly estimated would have, once ingested, resulted in a quick and agonising death. He was either an incompetent medic or absolutely determined to point the finger at Eliza.

Did it not occur to Marshall, Orlibar Turner and those who sat in judgement on Eliza during her trial to ask themselves this question – would an intelligent girl like Eliza, if she had poisoned the Turner family, leave the 'poisoned' remains of the dumplings in the pan? The principal concern of such a poisoner would be to remove all trace of the incriminating food as quickly and thoroughly as possible, not leave it around for the likes of Orlibar Turner and John Marshall to rake over and use as evidence against her.

There is no proof that Robert Turner had become so mentally unbalanced that he threatened to kill the whole family (besides the evidence of the chemist, Mr Corbyn), though it seems unlikely that a chemist would fabricate such a story. It is appalling that the group of powerful men – the Recorder, Sir John Silvester, the Home Secretary and others – were given this information on the eve of Eliza's execution and yet declined to question Mr Corbyn further, or interview Robert Turner regarding the allegations.

If Eliza had been afforded a committed defence counsel and Robert Turner had been questioned in court more stringently he might, under pressure, have displayed signs of the mental instability that the chemist, Mr Corbyn, evidently saw at his shop the previous September – signs which allegedly appeared as he tried to buy a quantity of arsenic and begged to be restrained in case he poisoned himself and the whole family.

Was Eliza a scapegoat, taking the blame for poisonings perpetrated by Robert Turner? Did Orlibar Turner suspect that his son had carried out his threat to poison his family and himself, as testified by Mr Corbyn? Realising this, did he persuade the doctor, John Marshall, to 'find' arsenic in the pan that Eliza had used? Or did he put it there himself? Why was Dr Ogilvy, the first doctor called to the house, not brought into court to give evidence? One cannot help wondering why the Turners waited so long to send for John Marshall – he arrived at a quarter to nine – when they had fallen ill shortly after three o'clock that afternoon. Why, after being attended to by the local doctor, Ogilvy, did they think it necessary to send for Marshall some four hours later – a doctor who moreover lived out of the area? Did the Turner family decide to call him that evening because, being unfamiliar with the neighbourhood, Marshall may not have been aware of any gossip relating to Robert Turner's odd behaviour and rants about poison only a few months before?

Further, why did John Marshall harbour such intense hostility towards Eliza, evident in his article pronouncing his conviction of her guilt? Was there some connection between Orlibar Turner and the doctor that would ensure his co-operation? A Masonic or business link, perhaps? It was noted by John Watkins in his pamphlet that they were both acquainted with the clerk of the court, who wrote down the original depositions, and the solicitor for the prosecuting barristers.

Whether or not the Fenning family and friends were aware that Mr Corbyn had voiced his concerns about the disturbed behaviour of Robert Turner, it seems evident that the huge crowds that attended Eliza's funeral were convinced that he was the poisoner. They surrounded his house, baying for blood, and were only prevented from burning the house to the ground – and possibly attacking him as well – by the police officers who were on crowd control duty that day. The most crucial omission in this case seems to have been the failure to confront Robert Turner with Mr Corbyn's evidence and question him, and his father, in more detail.

Alternatively, it has been suggested that Charlotte Turner, a few years older than Eliza and pregnant at the time, was jealous of Eliza's good looks and wanted to get rid of her, fearing her husband might be attracted to her. Eliza's father, William Fenning, had tried to testify in court that the Turner family were hostile to his daughter but the Recorder had refused to hear his testimony. Yet Charlotte Turner, of course, could have given Eliza notice to leave at any time – servants like her were two-a-penny and there were no 'unfair dismissal' tribunals or redundancy payments to worry about.

By the same token, why would Eliza risk everything by indulging in such a spiteful and dangerous act of poisoning when, if she had been given the sack, she could have found another job easily enough – she may not even have needed to work after her marriage, as her fiancé was described as 'much affected and industrious' – in other words, a decent and hard-working young man.

Some press reports referred to Eliza's behaviour as 'lewd' and 'salacious' both prior to, and during, her incarceration in Newgate Prison. It was even suggested that a book advocating abortion was found amongst her belongings (although, as mentioned, the

policeman who arrested her testified that he had found nothing
suspicious). He may, of course, have chosen not to mention such a
book out of decency. She may well have been a bit of a flirt – she
was, after all, young and pretty – but in the anguished letter she
wrote to her parents shortly before her execution she seems to
be desperate to assure them – without being explicit – that she
had not lost her virginity; to have done so was clearly considered
by her to be a sin, a notion instilled in her by her parents and her
religious upbringing.

In 1857, it was reported that Robert Turner had confessed, on
his deathbed, to poisoning the dumplings with arsenic. We have
no way of knowing the veracity of this confession, nor of that
of the baker quoted above. Likewise, we cannot know whether
Revd Upton's account of his meeting with Eliza in Newgate
Prison was the truth or a fabrication, the result of wishful
thinking. One must also wonder why this revelation was not
made public in 1815, instead of forty-two years later. Could it
be that Revd Upton's determination to prise out evidence of
contrition – or, the ultimate goal, a confession – from a terrified
and desperate girl, facing public humiliation and a truly horrible
death, might be considered extreme duress? Already distraught,
and primed since childhood in fearful and fervent religious
dogma, she was now called to task by the Reverend gentleman
who had taught her at Sunday school. Eliza may have seemed
ripe for last-minute redemption – but did she actually confess
to the attempted murders? Or, in the awful tension of a highly
emotive encounter, did she merely say what she knew he wanted
to hear, only to retract the 'confession' as soon as he had gone
away?[51]

Finally, the fact that the Reverend used the term murder when
recording his encounter with Eliza was highly suspect, for no
one died in the Turner household that day: if Revd Gurney's
notes were supposedly so accurate, why did he make such a
fundamental mistake?

In his notes, Revd Upton suggested that, encouraged by her
friends and advocates to believe she might get a last-minute

---

51 Was Revd Upton in fact the 'friend' who had written to Eliza in Newgate?
He certainly did his utmost to dissuade her from taking the sacrament unless she
confessed to *all* her sins – i.e. including the poisonings.

reprieve, Eliza had kept up the pretence of innocence. Yet surely, with her arms and legs pinioned and the hangman's noose already around her neck – she had to wait thus shackled while John Langley did the same to the other two convicts awaiting execution – she would have conceded that a reprieve was not going to happen and, as a girl with religious convictions, she would surely have confessed to the poisonings in that last moment? Unless, of course, she found it impossible to disappoint not only all the people who had tried so desperately hard to save her from the gallows, but also her distraught and traumatised parents and the heartbroken young man she had hoped to marry.

The scales of justice were definitely weighted against Eliza Fenning in the Regency era. Although she was a pretty young woman – so much so that her detractors accused her champions of being swayed by her prettiness – press reports referred to her, in derogatory terms, as a Roman Catholic, presumably because her mother was Irish. In 1780, only thirty-five years previously, the Gordon Riots had erupted in London – some estimates put the number of protesters at 50,000 – after the government had afforded Catholics more political equality. Catholics in the city were attacked and their property vandalised; Newgate and other London prisons were burned, and the Bank of England attacked. Such violent anarchy and lawlessness prompted King George III to send in the army, and several hundred people were killed during the skirmishes that ensued. Anti-Catholic prejudice was a real and powerful factor in Eliza's times.

Because Eliza could read and write very well, she may have been perceived as what today we might term being 'above her station', 'giving herself airs and graces' or 'too big for her boots'. She even owned several books, given to her by a previous employer – and she could actually read them! This combination of youth, looks and intelligence sat uncomfortably with the people who employed servants to work long hours, often for inadequate pay and, above all, to be their inferiors.

Surprisingly, it was never suggested that the sickness suffered by the Turner household that day was caused by food poisoning, a common cause of vomiting and diarrhoea in the pre-refrigeration days of the early nineteenth century. In addition, the primitive sanitary facilities and lack of personal hygiene may well have been to blame. There would also have been a number of other opportunities for contamination. The milk that Sarah Peer fetched after two o'clock that afternoon may well have been contaminated by the time it reached Chancery Lane – Eliza herself seemed to think it might have been the cause of the sickness. Likewise, the yeast or the flour from the bakery may have been stored close to arsenic put down to get rid of rats and mice.[52]

Furthermore, if Charlotte Turner had ingested arsenic whilst in an advanced stage of pregnancy, would she have been fit and well the following day? In fact, it was Eliza herself who seemed to have suffered sickness longer than anyone else in the household.

The fate of Eliza Fenning provides us with one of the most interesting and disturbing cases of the early nineteenth century. Although Charles Dickens was only three years old when Eliza Fenning was hanged, as an adult he was obviously familiar with the case and in later years wrote, 'I never was more convinced of anything in my life than the girl's innocence.' He was not against capital punishment *per se*, but against public executions. After visiting Newgate and witnessing hangings, including that of Courvoisier in 1840, he was so appalled at the behaviour of the mobs that attended them that he began to campaign vigorously, in letters to *The Times*, against public executions (a practice that finally ended in 1868, two years before his death). The following statement was issued in *The Times* on 27 May 1868: 'London yesterday witnessed the last of those hideous spectacles familiar enough to the hard eyes of our predecessors, but more and more repulsive to the taste of these days.'

Three years after Eliza's execution, Revd Cotton questioned the deterrent effect of public hangings when asked to give evidence at an inquiry into the conditions at prisons in the City of London:

---

52   On 17 April 1847, seventeen-year-old Catherine Foster was hanged at Bury St Edmunds for murdering her husband with a poisoned dumpling. Whereas Eliza Fenning went to the gallows proclaiming her innocence, Catherine Foster made a full confession. On 29 March 1961, *The Times* reported the death of a Mrs Alice Jones; arsenic was found in some dumplings she had eaten and traces of the poison were also found in the flour used to make them.

What effects are produced by such executions? They merely come to see an execution of that kind as a spectacle; they go away again and waste their time; and many of the spectators commit crimes … before the night closes, after witnessing such a scene; nay, we had a boy brought in some time ago, who had only a few days before been out of Newgate; he was brought in for picking pockets at the gallows; and when I spoke to him upon the subject, and said, 'How could you do such a thing at such an awful moment?' He said, 'Sir, that was the best moment in the world, for everybody's eyes were up when the drop was falling.'

We can never know whether Eliza was the tragic victim of a lax and prejudicial legal system, a revengeful little minx or a bit of a 'drama queen'. However, many would agree with the dean, who clearly believed that 'it is better that a hundred murderers should escape than that one innocent person should perish by "circumstantial evidence"'.

SARAH DRAKE

'The miserable creature in the dock'

The year was 1850, some thirteen years into the reign of Queen Victoria. The population of London had already reached an estimated 750,000 and, with the energy and innovation that defined the Victorian era, the lives of its inhabitants were made significantly more congenial with the advent of underground sewers, cleaner water supplies, railways and extensive building works – both domestic and municipal. The face of London was not only rapidly changing but the city was also expanding into the development of the suburbs.

The date was Thursday 10 January; the scene was the Central Criminal Court at the Old Bailey. The learned counsel had taken their places on the Bench; the jury was assembled and two judges, resplendent in full wigs and scarlet robes, prepared to sit in judgement. As always in a murder case, the public gallery was packed with eager spectators waiting impatiently for the drama to begin.

Sitting crouched down in the dock was a pathetically thin woman, her head lowered as she pressed a handkerchief to her face in an attempt to hide it from public view. Her name was Sarah Drake and she was charged with the wilful murder of her two-year-old son, Lewis, whose body she had packed in a box and sent to her parents.[53]

Some knowledge of the circumstances of Sarah Drake's troubled life prior to her presence in the dock of the Old Bailey that day might throw some light on her dreadful predicament.

---

53 Some reports give his name as Lewis whilst others call him Louis. To avoid confusion he will be referred to consistently as Lewis.

Members of the public were already familiar with the case as the newspapers had issued copious reports on the magistrates' hearing at Marylebone Police Court, in December the previous year; they had also furnished their readers with a great many prejudicial details relating to Sarah's life prior to the death of her son. Alongside these reports were descriptions of the inquest into the death being held concurrently at the Royal Oak, in North Leverton, the village a few miles from Nottingham, where Sarah was born in 1813, and where her parents still lived. The inquest was described in *The Sheffield Independent* on 15 December 1849:

> The investigation which has been going on at North Leverton, near Retford, touching the death of a male child, named Lewis Drake, aged two years, brought to a close on Monday last, at the sign of the Royal Oak, where the inquest was held before P.R. Falkner, Esq., Coroner, and a respectable jury. Sarah Drake, to whom there is no question the child belonged, from her confession, independent of most direct evidence of the fact, is charged as the murderer of her own offspring; but on account of legal difficulties [as the magistrates' hearing in London was still in progress], it was thought advisable for the jury to return an open verdict of 'wilful murder against some person unknown'.
>
> As will be seen from the report of the investigation before the magistrates at Clerkenwell Police Office [actually Marylebone Police Office], the prisoner stands remanded until Saturday (this day) when there is every reason to suppose that she will be fully committed to take her trial at the next Central Criminal Court, for the capital offence. The prisoner, as will be seen from the evidence, is a native of North Leverton, where her parents, who are respectable people, of humble circumstances, now reside, her father and only brother following the occupation of shoemakers.

The report offers some details of Sarah Drake's life to date, all of which would be reported *ad nauseam* during the subsequent Old Bailey trial. It did, however, proceed to inform its readers of a similarly shocking incident: 'it was given in evidence at the inquest that five years ago, [in 1844] the Burtons [Sarah's sister, Mary, had married into the Burton family] received a similar present – the dead body of a child in a box – but from whom or whence it came still remains a mystery.'

The following account in the *Morning Chronicle*, on Monday, 17 December 1849, describes the proceedings at the magistrates' hearing at Marylebone Police Office and also refers to the previous incident – now public knowledge due to press reports – of the dead baby, described as a 'new-born male', which had been sent to the Burtons in December of 1844:

> The numerous narrow avenues leading to the public entrance of Marylebone police-court on Saturday were completely blocked up by persons eager to see Sarah Drake, charged with the murder of her male child, named Lewis, or Louis, aged about two years. The appearance of the prisoner to-day was wretched in the extreme. She could not well stand, was nearly bent double, and during the whole of the proceedings completely hid her face in her handkerchief. Although stated to have been born in 1813, she looked as if she had been born thirteen years earlier. She is a woman of middle height, very thin, almost emaciated, and she could never have possessed even comely attractions.
>
> The police-court was crowded and among the gentlemen on the magistrates' bench were Lord Montford and Dr Mayo; Mr Long was the sitting magistrate. Mr Herring, a solicitor, appeared for the prisoner, who was led into court and allowed a seat in the dock, at the request of her solicitor, who stated that in the House of Detention she had been so much indisposed that she was transferred from the ward to the infirmary.[54]

The report then referred to the body of the baby sent to Thomas Burton, in 1844, and informed its readers that the coroner, Mr Falkland [sometimes called Mr Falkner], was of the opinion that 'the child had not been born alive, and also, from various appearances, he believed its mother had delivered herself'.

The jury consequently brought in a general verdict: 'That the child was sent, but did not appear by whom, and that whether it was alive before, at or after its birth, to them was unknown'.

The *Leominster Chronicle*, on 15 December 1849, went even further by drawing its readers' attention to yet another, earlier

---

54   During the magistrates' hearings, the gaoler, Mr Mitchel, was 'directed to see that she was closely watched prior to being conveyed away in the government [police] van'.

case of a dead child believed to have belonged to Sarah Drake.
This time, the body was sent in a box to a porter at the Knutsford
Workhouse, Cheshire, in 1842:

> At the inquest on that child's death, a surgeon, Mr Watson Baird, after
> finding a thumb mark on the right side of the baby's neck and finger
> marks on the left side, concluded that the child had been born alive.
>
> In this instance, Sarah had been brought to trial at the Old Bailey
> on 9th May 1842, and indicted 'for a misdemeanour'. [Some reports
> stated she was charged with the 'wilful murder of an illegitimate'.]
> At the time she had been working as a cook for three months in
> service to a Mr Catley, of Leyton, Essex. One of the other servants,
> a laundry maid called Ann Williams, told the court that she had seen
> Sarah about eight o'clock in the morning of 6th of April. She was in
> the kitchen and appeared to be very ill, so much so that the next day
> she took to her bed. The maid testified that she had 'examined her
> clothes and never saw clothes in such a state – unless a woman had
> been recently confined'.

On the 18 April, her suspicions were confirmed 'by seeing
discharges of milk on her under-linen'. It was this, she said, that
convinced her that childbirth had taken place.

Another witness, Mary Chapman, of Leyton, testified that
Sarah Drake's dirty clothing was given to her to wash on 12 April.
She agreed with the opinion of the previous witness – that the
underclothes were clearly those of a woman who had given birth.

One of the other servants, Mahala Clark, informed the court
that Sarah Drake was confined to her bed on 6, 7 and 8 April. She
lent her a box on the 13 April and later saw it tied up and sealed
with red [sealing wax]. It was, she said, heavier than when she
lent it to her. At this point the court was shown the box. Mahala
had no idea Sarah was pregnant, and there had been no such talk
amongst the other servants.

John Slade then entered the witness box and testified that he
had helped Sarah tie up the box and seal it. The address attached
to it was: 'Mr Tipley, Knutsford Union, Cheshire.' He had taken
the box to London and sent it by the Birmingham Railway. He
identified the box as the one in court but insisted that he didn't
know what the box contained. Mr Joseph Tipley, a porter at
the Union Workhouse in Knutsford, told the court that when

he opened it he found the body of a dead baby inside, wrapped in a ragged piece of shawl and some paper. Why the box was sent to Joseph Tipley was never explained, but no doubt, as a consequence, he was suspected of being the child's father. It was rumoured that there was a note in the box which read 'you will do your wife a favour by burying this'. Instead, he immediately informed the local police.

A Cheshire policeman, Constable William Harper, stated that he was sent to search Sarah Drake's room at the home of Mr Catley, in Leyton, by order of the coroner of Knutsford. He found there paper that corresponded with some similar paper found in the box by Mr Tipley; he also discovered a piece of fine linen and part of a shawl.

James M'Culloch, the policeman who had arrested Sarah Drake, was called next. When she was taken into custody, he said, she had cried out, 'What will become of me?' She later admitted that she had given birth to the child but that it had been still-born; she had sent it to the country, she said, because she didn't know what to do with the body.

The verdict at this first trial at the Old Bailey was 'guilty' [of a misdemeanour, that of concealing the birth of a still-born child] and Sarah Drake, then thirty-two years old, was imprisoned for six months.[55]

Prior to Sarah Drake's second appearance at the Old Bailey in 1850, the *Morning Chronicle* – and other newspapers – informed its readers of her antecedents:

Sarah Drake is the eldest daughter of a respectable cottager named Thomas, of North Leverton, at which place she was born in August, 1813. Her father and mother are still living but the latter is blind. She was the eldest of four children, three daughters (one of whom was dead) and a son. Having received a scanty education in the village, she was sent out to service and for two or three years was in the employ of the late Samuel Kay, of Sutton-cum-Lound, at the period when he was murdered on the 27th of December, 1831.

---

55 The crime of 'concealment of a birth' carried a maximum sentence of two years' imprisonment.

Shortly afterwards, she lived in the family of John Walker, Esq., of Lound; but after having, in order to avoid a prosecution, signed a paper acknowledging herself to be culpable [possibly of theft], she was discharged in disgrace.

We next find her in the service of the Rev. John Mickle, vicar of South Leverton, and soon afterwards in that of Mr F. Blagg, surgeon.

In the year 1836, she left Leverton, under the pretence of taking a situation at Manchester and was absent for several years, during which time her friends were in total ignorance as to whether she was living or dead. During her absence she said that she was in the East and West Indies and certainly passed part of the time on the Continent.

On the 26th of December, 1844, an inquest was held by Mr Falkland, coroner of Nottingham, on the body of a new-born male child which had been sent from Euston-square Station, London, to Nottingham, thence per Queen coach to Retford and by carrier to North Leverton, directed, 'Mr T. Burton, North Leverton, near Retford, Nottinghamshire.'

This circumstance, at the time, excited considerable interest and many were the surmises as to whence such a present could be sent and for what particular purpose.

After a post-mortem examination of the remains, however, the surgeon gave it as his opinion that child had not been born alive, and also that, from various appearances, he believed its mother had delivered herself.

The jury consequently brought in a general verdict – 'That the child was sent but it did not appear by whom, and that whether it was alive before, at, or after its birth, to them was unknown.'

After this investigation the body was interred and all the gossip which it had incited soon died away; and had not the recent dispatch of another dead child refreshed the memory of the past and pointed in a similar direction it would not have been thought necessary to notice the circumstance.

A few months after the burial of the child in question, Sarah Drake returned to Leverton but only stayed a short time. In 1848, she visited her father and mother for the second time and remained with them for nine or ten months; and it is believed that she would have continued to do so, had not her poor old mother continually teasing her about the other dead child with which she had previously troubled them.

Soon after her first visit to Retford she went to live as a servant with Mrs Ramsay, of Tosmore House, near Bicester, Oxfordshire, in

1845, with whom she remained until July, 1847, when she left that lady on account of being *enceinte* by, as she said, a person of the name of Lewis, or Louis, a Frenchman, who was butler in the same family and after whom the unfortunate child received his Christian name.

This child was born on the 9th of October, 1847, but by whom it was nursed until Mrs Johnson received it in January, 1848, there are no means of ascertaining.

Soon afterwards, Sarah Drake was known to be in the keeping of an officer in the army at Chatham; but they, not agreeing long, she then took a situation at the establishment of Lady Ann Gore Langton. On her leaving that lady, she was well recommended to Mrs Huth, in whose service she was when apprehended.

The fact that Sarah Drake had been tried once before, in 1842, over the death of a baby – and suspected of being responsible, but not tried or convicted, for another in 1844, was therefore common knowledge – and highly prejudicial – by the time of the 1850 trial at the Old Bailey, charged with killing a third child.

The following account of her second trial in the *Westmoreland Gazette*, dated 19 January 1850 – one of many in the contemporary press – will suffice to retrace the events that drew her once more in the dock of the Central Criminal Court. Much of the evidence in the report had already been heard at the magistrates' hearing at Marylebone Police Court, in December of the previous year, and further details were disclosed during the inquest on the body of Lewis, the child she stood accused of killing.

EXTRAORDINARY CASE OF CHILD-MURDER

Central Criminal Court, Thursday, Jan. 10.
(Before Mr Justice Patteson and Mr Justice Talfourd.)

Sarah Drake, aged 36, and described as a spinster, was placed at the bar, charged with the wilful murder of her illegitimate child, Louis Drake or Taverne, aged about two years.

The prisoner, who was attired like a respectable domestic servant, and wore a white cap with plain silk ribands, never raised her face from the moment she was placed in the dock, and concealed it in a handkerchief which she scarcely moved throughout the trial. She appeared very weak, sickly, and agitated, and was accommodated with a chair by desire of Mr Bodkin, who, with Mr Clarke, appeared for the prosecution. The prisoner was defended by Mr Collier, of the Western Circuit, and Mr Parry.

The features of this case are already partly well-known to the public. About three years ago the prisoner, who was then a domestic servant, bore a child, the father of which was not known to any of her acquaintance. This child, in January, 1848, she placed in the care of a woman named Johnson, at Peckham, the wife of a policeman, and agreed to give her 6s a week for the care of the infant. Gradually, she fell into arrears in her payments, and at last owed Mrs Johnson £9 or £10. The latter, upon the prisoner's earnest solicitations, agreed to nurse the child for 5s a week. In November, 1849, Mrs Johnson received the following letter from the prisoner:-

'Mrs Johnson – It is with a trembling hand and broken heart I write this letter to you. You will be sorry to hear that I have been obliged to sell the chief part of my clothes to pay my expenses. I am a poor creature, very weak and ill, and when walking in the park on Saturday for the benefit of the air, I accidentally met with Mrs -, whom I knew when I was living in a family at Manchester, and she told me she would take me to Madrid. I hope to see you before I go. I shall not write to you, for they are all strangers to me here, and I do not wish them to know my address. You say I am not true to the child. I hope you will never have the trouble I have had about him. I have suffered greatly on his account and I do not wish you to get more for him than I could pay for. It will take me some time to pay what I already owe. My wages are but £15 a year. Had I had my health and stayed in my place my wages would have paid you and have brought him up respectable; but I cannot do impossibilities. I have not heard from home since I saw you, nor is it in my power to do anything for him but what I now can earn. I wish you would let him go to the parish.[56]

If I am spared with life to return to my native land I will then take him and do all in my power for him. Should I die in going over I shall

---

56 The Bastardy Clause in the New Poor Law of 1834 stipulated that any illegitimate child should be the sole responsibility of its mother until it reached the age of sixteen years. If she and her family were unwilling or unable to support herself and her offspring, her only recourse was to enter the parish or union workhouse, a prospect dreaded by many who were so feeble and impoverished that they had no other choice. The putative fathers of illegitimate children were absolved from legal responsibility.

request that what few things I have left to be sold and the money sent to you, but you must say it is money I borrowed of you, for if it is known my parents will curse me in my grave.

My heart is broken at writing this but I know not what else to do. If I had not done this I must have been starved to death. If I am spared with life you will hear from me in a few months. It may be six months or it may be twelve before I return to England. If I live I leave London at six o'clock this evening. Kiss my dear child for me. I hope you are all well. Good night, God bless you.

Yours sincerely,

SARAH DRAKE

P.S. I leave London to-night.'

The statements in this letter turned out to be a fabrication, for upon Mrs Johnson proceeding to London she found Sarah Drake was in a situation as house-keeper to a Mrs Huth, in Upper Harley-street, where it was understood she was to receive £40 or £50 a year. Mrs Johnson proceeded thither on the morning of the 28th, with the child, and had an interview with her in her own (the housekeeper's) room where she told her that Mr Johnson had insisted upon her bringing the child to its mother and that he would not allow her to take it back.

Prisoner begged and prayed, but in vain, and Mrs Johnson left the prisoner and the child in the room and came away. A servant going to the room-door soon after, found it locked in the inside. The same day the prisoner got the butler to write a direction for one of her boxes – 'Mr Theophilus Burton, North Leverton, near Retford, Nottingham' – which box the footman conveyed for her to the Euston-square station. It was a heavy one.

On the 29th, a letter without signature reached Theophilus Burton, a blacksmith at North Leverton, who had married a sister of the prisoner, stating that there would be a box at East Retford on that day. The box was fetched and to the surprise and horror of the parties was found to contain the body of a child and some articles of dress. The box was handed over to the police. An extraordinary circumstance was that an apron in the box was found marked 'S. Drake, 18'. The connection of the prisoner with the box thus came out and she was apprehended on a charge of murder.

Although each report of the trial differed slightly in sequence and spelling, the evidence given by the witnesses was adequately covered by the following account, given by Mrs Johnson [some accounts use the name Jane, others Mary], the woman who had cared for the child. She was 'deeply distressed' when giving her evidence:

I went to 33, Upper Harley-street, the child being with me. [At this point the witness became violently agitated and sobbed aloud. Having recovered her composure, after a short time she continued.] When I saw the prisoner, I said, 'Good morning,' to which the prisoner replied, 'I thought it would be you, by my dream'. I said she was very cruel to cause me so much pain and trouble. She replied, that she could not help it, for she could not send me any more money. I said, 'Mrs Drake, I have not come for any money,' to which she answered that she did not know till the night before that she was not going abroad, but the family had put it off till the spring. I said, 'Don't say so, Mrs Drake; you have no intention of going abroad.'

She then asked me to go into the kitchen for a few minutes till she had seen her mistress in the housekeeper's room. I did so and on returning to the housekeeper's room again I told her that I must leave the child – that I was not to take it home any more if I found her.[57] She asked me to take it back for a week. I refused to do so. She remarked that the child was looking a great deal better and much stouter than when she had seen him last.[58] I told her he was quite well and had grown a hearty little fellow. I then told her she had better take his hat and pelisse off [a fur-trimmed jacket] or he would take cold when he went out. She did so. There was a little handkerchief round his neck and she said to me, 'This is yours, you had better take it.' I said, 'Yes, but keep it to put about him when he goes out to keep him warm.' (In saying this, the witness again wept bitterly.)

I also told her he would soon want something to eat – to which she replied, 'Very well; will he eat anything?' I said yes and left the house. As I was going up the area steps I told her my husband intended to

---

57   In her evidence given at Marylebone Police Court she said that her husband had forbidden her to care for the child any longer and insisted that she return the boy to his mother.

58   The magistrates at Marylebone heard that the child had been very ill in June – with *'water on the brain'* – and Mrs Johnson had him baptised. Sarah Drake insisted that, as the child's father was a Roman Catholic, the child should be baptised in that faith. As Lewis's father was French, Mrs Johnson called him Louis or 'Luey'.

summon her for the money and she called out and asked how much it was. I told her it was £9 10s, to which she made no answer. I then went home.

On Friday, the 30th Nov, I again called at Harley-street and saw the prisoner. She was alone and she told me she had got a friend to take the child and that she would send the money to pay us the first week of January. She asked me if I had received a letter from her to which I said 'No'. She then said she supposed my husband would get it at two o'clock. On that occasion I brought up the child's clothes which I gave to the prisoner, with a note inclosed [*sic*]. She said she would look at them by and by. I asked her to kiss the baby for me. She said, 'Yes, I will.' [Again the witness was overcome by her feelings.] She told me she had got him out of the house without any one knowing it. On my return home I found the letter which she spoke of.

The letter read as follows:

Mrs Johnson, I have got a friend who has taken him, and will lend me the money to pay you the first week in Jan.; their money is out, and they cannot get it before; I have none of my own till I have earned it, and if you summons me I cannot pay you now and I do not know what advantage you will have in depriving me of my place and character, as I shall then be forever prevented from earning my bread and at that time I will send you the full amount I owe you. Providence so provided for me that I have kept it from anyone in the house. I hope and trust you will not expose me.

Yours sincerely,

Sarah Drake,

33 Upper Harley-street, Cavendish-square. Nov. 29th, 1849

Mrs Johnson was then questioned about the inquest into the death of Lewis Drake; she testified that on Saturday 8 December she had gone to North Leverton, with the police, and was 'shown a coffin with the body of a child.'

When asked by Mr Bodkin the identity of the child, Mrs Johnson started to sob again, before replying: 'The child I had had to nurse. I also recognised its clothes, a red frock, and a black and flannel petticoat. The handkerchief which I left on his neck, the pelisse and the cap, were also there.'

Mary Ann Wigzell, a kitchen maid employed by Mr Huth and his family, at 33 Harley Street, was called to give evidence. She confirmed that Sarah Drake had started work as cook and housekeeper on Monday 26 November, the previous year. Two days later, Mrs Johnson had come to the house with the child, which she left with its mother. After that, the maid had not seen Lewis again.

Later that day Sarah had asked her for a box, saying she wished to send some clothes to her sister's children. Mary Ann gave her a box and Sarah said she was going to go upstairs to write a letter. She did not see Sarah again until about half past two, when she told her that she had packed, not the box she had borrowed, but one she had brought with her when she started work on the Monday.

Sarah and Mary Ann slept in the same room in the servants' quarters and the box, wrapped in cotton cloth and corded, remained in the room that night.

'I brought it downstairs the following morning,' the maid told the court.

> It was heavy, I could scarcely carry it down – there was no direction [address] on it – she told me to take it down and give it to Mr Glass, the butler; she would send a boy with it to the station, that she did not wish the other servants to see it because they might think she was sending things out of the house. I put it on the floor in the butler's room… I saw it again about an hour and a half afterwards, still in the pantry, and then lost sight of it.

In answer to questions put to her, Mary Ann said that Sarah Drake was unwell when she started work at the house, on Monday 26 November; she had a cold and 'was not in very good spirits – she kept very much to herself; she appeared rather low-spirited.'

According to the maid's evidence, Sarah Drake 'appeared to be remarkably serious and reserved and whenever an opportunity offered she employed her time in reading the Bible, the Prayer Book and other works of a religious and moral tendency'. She had seen her reading her Bible in the housekeeper's room and witnessed her praying in her bedroom for half an hour or more. She had seemed 'upset and distracted' after Mrs Johnson left the house without the child.

Sarah Powell, a housemaid at the same address, confirmed that about five minutes after Mrs Johnson had gone away she had tried the door of the housekeeper's room but found it locked.

The butler, George Glass, said that although Sarah Drake had started work on Monday 26 November, she had been hired a week before. On the Wednesday, after Mrs Johnson had left the house, Sarah asked him to send a box to the railway station at Euston Square. He agreed to send it with a footman but said it would have to wait until the morning. He wrote the address on the box: 'Mr Theophilus Burton, North Leverton, near Redford, Nottinghamshire.'

Sarah Drake did not dine with the other servants that day but she cooked dinner for the Huth family at half past six. The next morning, soon after seven, the maid, Mary Ann, brought the box into the pantry and the butler called Sarah to come and check the address, which he had sewn on to the cotton wrapping around the box. She checked the address and gave him two half-crowns to pay for the postage. Between nine and ten that morning, the butler ordered William Bryant, the footman, to take the box to the station. When told that the box had gone, Sarah said that, if there was any change from the 5*s* she had given him, he was to give the footman 6*d* for his trouble.

William Skelton Bryant confirmed that he had taken the box to the railway station as ordered, paid the carriage fee of 3*s* 6*d*, and was told that the box would be delivered that same night. When he got back to the house, Sarah gave him 6*d* as promised.

The court then heard the evidence of a coach driver, William Hall. On Friday 30 November, he had collected the box from the nearest station to North Leverton, which was at Newark. He then drove to The White Hart Inn, at East Retford, where he usually left parcels to be collected and left the box there at about half past four in the afternoon.

Sarah's brother, William Drake, a Nottingham shoe-maker, was next to enter the witness box. He confirmed that Drake was his sister's maiden name and, as far as he knew, she had never been married. His other sister [Mary] was married to Theophilus Burton and lived at North Leverton. She had asked him to collect the box from The White Hart Inn, in Retford, which he did and then carried it to his sister's house over his shoulder. On the way, he admitted the address label had come off and was dropped on Gringley Hill. This was later found by the police. When he reached his sister's house, he and Theophilus forced the lock on the box with a chisel and found inside the body of a child.

Sarah Drake's brother-in-law, Theophilus Burton, told the court that he was a blacksmith and lived in North Leverton. He remembered a letter arriving shortly before the box; it was not signed, but said, 'There will be a box at Retford, on Thursday; receive it as soon as possible.' Shocked at seeing the contents of the box, he handed it over to the police the following morning.

Edward Smith was called next and testified that he was a policeman for the county of Nottinghamshire. He confirmed that the previous witness had brought the box to him on Saturday 1 December and it contained the body of a male child; his evidence was as follows:

> The child was quite naked, except that there was a white pocket handkerchief round its neck, the underlap of which was tight and the two outer laps loose. He saw a bruise on the left temple and one on the left ear. They were round bruises, a little bigger than a halfpenny. They were severe bruises and quite black, as if inflicted by violent blows. He found in the box the white apron now produced, and marked, 'S. Drake, No. 18.' It was found near the face of the child and was stained with blood. All the clothes were shown to Mrs Johnson afterwards and recognised by her. They are the same clothes which have been produced here this day, and were all found in the box. The body of the child was in appearance quite fresh, and not in the least decomposed.

Further details of the condition of the body of the child were furnished by the next witness, a local surgeon, Francis Blagg, who was called upon to perform the post-mortem examination. In his opinion the child was between eighteen months and two years old and had been dead no longer than a week. The doctor informed the court of his findings:

> I observed a contusion on the left side of the forehead and also on the left ear; the face was swollen and the tongue was compressed between the teeth; there was a lividness about the face and particularly over the eyelids. The hands were clenched and the nails blue. There was a

1 Catherine Hayes as a young woman.

CATHERINE HAYES.

2 Catherine Hayes and her lovers pictured in the act of cutting off her husband's head.

3 The head of John Hayes displayed on a spike near St Margaret's church, Marylebone.

4 Catherine Hayes at Tyburn. The flames are here depicted just underneath the executioner's hands, and indeed would force him to let go of the rope, leaving Hayes alive inside the inferno.

5 Elizabeth Brownrigg.

6 A contemporary print showing scenes from the life of Elizabeth Brownrigg (from left to right): a naked Mary Clifford being whipped by her tormentor; Elizabeth in the condemned cell at Newgate; and Mary shivering in the coal-hole, her makeshift prison.

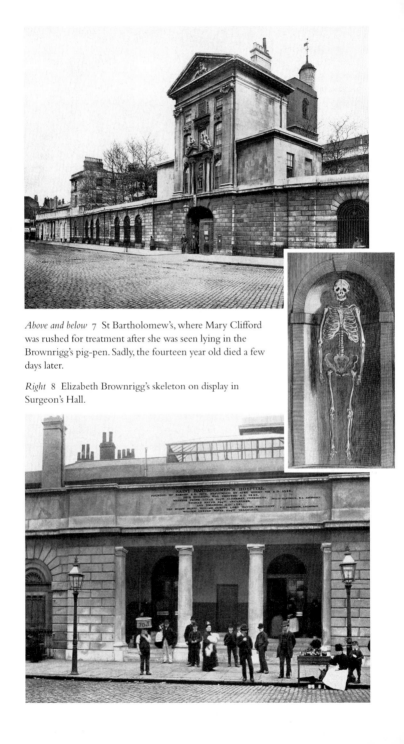

Above and below 7 St Bartholomew's, where Mary Clifford was rushed for treatment after she was seen lying in the Brownrigg's pig-pen. Sadly, the fourteen year old died a few days later.

Right 8 Elizabeth Brownrigg's skeleton on display in Surgeon's Hall.

9 A portrait of Eliza in Newgate Prison. Her detractors claimed that her attractiveness was the sole reason that so much interest was taken in her case.

AFFECTING

CASE

OF

ELIZA FENNING,

Who suffered the

SENTENCE OF THE LAW

July 26, 1815.

Unhappy maid! alas! thy awful doom
Consigns thee prematurely to the tomb;
Thou pleadest innocence—if just thy plea,
With endless bliss the Lord will welcome thee.

LONDON:

Published by JOHN FAIRBURN, 2, Broadway,
Ludgate-Hill.

Price Two Shillings

10 Frontispiece of John Fairburn's *Affecting Case of Eliza Fenning, who Suffered the Sentence of the Law.* It contained the news that Eliza 'wished she might drop down dead if she knew what arsenic was'.

THE IMPORTANT RESULTS

OF AN

ELABORATE INVESTIGATION

INTO THE

Mysterious Case

OF

ELIZABETH FENNING:

BEING A

DETAIL OF EXTRAORDINARY FACTS

DISCOVERED SINCE HER EXECUTION,

INCLUDING

THE OFFICIAL REPORT

OF HER

Singular Trial,

NOW FIRST PUBLISHED,

AND COPIOUS NOTES THEREON.

ALSO,

NUMEROUS AUTHENTIC DOCUMENTS; AN ARGUMENT ON
HER CASE; A MEMORIAL TO H. R. H. THE PRINCE
REGENT; & STRICTURES ON A LATE PAMPHLET
OF THE PROSECUTORS' APOTHECARY.

BY JOHN WATKINS, LL.D.

WITH

THIRTY ORIGINAL LETTERS, WRITTEN BY

11 The cover of John Watkin's rival pamphlet, *Important Results of an Elaborate Investigation into the Mysterious Case of Elizabeth Fenning*. This contains evidence not noted down by the shorthand writer at Eliza's trial.

CIRCUMSTANTIAL EVIDENCE.

THE EXTRAORDINARY CASE

OF

ELIZA FENNING,

WHO WAS EXECUTED IN 1815,

For Attempting to Poison the Family of Orlibar Turner, by Mixing Arsenic in Yeast Dumplings.

WITH

A STATEMENT OF FACTS,

SINCE DEVELOPED, TENDING TO PROVE

HER INNOCENCE OF THE CRIME.

LONDON:

PUBLISHED BY COWIE AND STRANGE, PATERNOSTER ROW;
PURKESS, WARDOUR STREET, SOHO;
AND SOLD BY ALL VENDERS OF PAMPHLETS.

[*Price ONE PENNY.*]

12 Cover of a pamphlet published by Cowie and Strange in 1829. It told its readers that the son of the Turner household had confessed to the crime for which Eliza was executed.

13 Bethlehem Hospital, better known as 'Bedlam', where Sarah Drake may have been held after she was found guilty of infanticide – though the records are sadly unclear.

14 Inside Euston Square Station in 1851. Sarah Drake packed up and sent the body of her son to this station in this year, and on from there towards her family home.

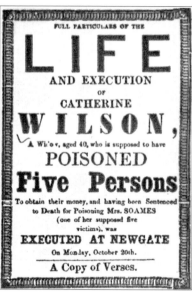

15 Catherine Wilson at the time of her trial, and a pamphlet published to mark her execution.

16 Guy's Hospital. Dr A.S. Taylor of Guy's was instrumental in the trial of Catherine Wilson, telling the court that a number of small doses rather than one large dose had most likely been ingested by her victims, of a poison now impossible for medical science to detect.

17 Kate Webster, from an effigy in Madame Tussaud's Waxworks.

THE MURDERED LADY Mrs THOMAS (From A Photo)

PUSHING THE BOX OVER THE BRIDGE

18 Mrs Thomas, and Kate pictured in the act of throwing the box containing her body over the parapet of Richmond Bridge.

19 Kate confronting Mrs Thomas, axe in hand. (This is rather a fanciful view as, according to her confession, she in fact strangled Mrs Thomas at the bottom of the stairs before dismembering her body.)

20 The execution of Kate Webster. (Courtesy of the British Library)

THE GRUESOME DISCOVERY AT BARNES BRIDGE.

21 The discovery of part of Julia Thomas, the unfortunate victim of Kate Webster; Henry Wheatly, a coal-man, was not at all pleased to find that the box he'd noticed contained not treasure but a mass of congealed flesh.

KATE WEBSTER TRIED FOR THE MURDER OF MRS. THOMAS.

22 Kate Webster, whose police description gave her as 'aged about 32, 5ft 5 or 6 inches high: complexion sallow: slightly freckled: teeth rather good and prominent', in the dock.

23 The outside of Newgate Prison as Catherine Hayes, Elizabeth Brownrigg and Eliza Fenning may have known it.

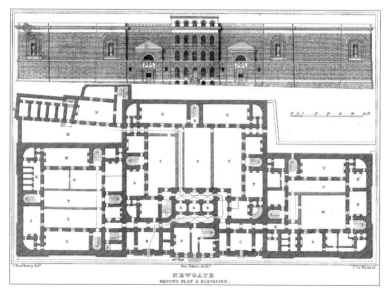

24 Plan of Newgate. M indicates the Press Yards, with the condemned cells to the east (O) and condemned room appearing as N. The letter Y indicates another condemned cell. The dotted line snaking from M to B shows the course by which condemned prisoners reached the gallows outside the prison.

25 Newgate Prison as it appeared just before it was demolished. (This scene may have been more familiar to Catherine Wilson and Kate Webster.)

26 Newgate Street at the turn of the twentieth century, just before the prison was demolished. The side of the prison can be seen on the right. Hundreds, and perhaps even thousands, of Londoners must have passed these walls each day.

27 The chaotic scene at a Tyburn hanging. A condemned man, atop the cart, may be seen making his mournful way to the gallows. He is leaning rather jauntily against his coffin as the Ordinary preaches, and reading some last words of biblical comfort as he goes. The stands, so prone to collapse, may be seen on the right.

28 A Newgate hanging outside the debtors' door. As can be seen, the gallows here could hang more than one person at a time.

29 Inside the court at the Old Bailey, at the start of the nineteenth century. Hopefully this trial does not feature a deaf juror, as did the Fenning case.

30 Newgate chapel, showing the condemned sitting around a coffin. Spectators were allowed in to scour the prisoners' faces for signs of terror.

31 For whom the bell tolls: St Sepulchre's-without-Newgate, whose great bell rang out for London executions. The execution bell, a hand bell rung by the clerk outside the prisoner's cell to let him (or her) know their last moments had arrived, may still be seen in the church.

bruise on the left side of the forehead and another on the lower part of the left ear.

In my opinion, the blows I observed on the head were sufficient to have caused death; they were caused by a blunt instrument or by the child's head being beaten against something, I cannot say which – a blunt instrument would have caused those appearances; a handkerchief was fastened round the neck – I untied the knot of the handkerchief and took it off. I then found a mark round the neck, caused by a ligature. There were decided appearances of strangulation about the child.

I think the handkerchief as I found it was not sufficiently tight to prevent respiration, unless it had been held or hung on some substance – the mark of the ligature round the neck indicated a sufficient compression of the throat to cause strangulation; in my opinion, death was caused by strangulation and the blows combined – either would have produced death…

I made an internal examination of the head – on removing the scalp I discovered extravasated blood on the left side of the head. The bruises were such as must have been caused by great violence from a blunt or obtuse instrument. There was a quantity of extra-vasated blood in the dura water of the left membrane of the brain and in the ventricles thereof were the same appearances. The brain was generally congested; on opening the chest I found the right lung collapsed and the left lung of the deceased infant was nearly in the same state; there was an abrasion of the skin about the neck which showed that much compression had been used.

The doctor was of the opinion that death might have been caused by either of the injuries of which he had spoken and these injuries had been caused while the child was alive.

Thomas Kinder, Superintendent of Nottingham police, was questioned next and told the court:

I went to 33, Harley-street, accompanied by Wicher[59], a metropolitan police officer, where I saw the prisoner. I asked her if her name was Sarah Drake, from Nottingham, to which she said 'Yes', and I then said

---

59 Detective Inspector Jonathan Whicher featured in several well-known cases, including that of Constance Kent, who was convicted of murdering her young brother, Savile, at Road House, Wiltshire, in 1860.

I apprehended her on suspicion of having murdered her son, Lewis Drake. She said, 'How do you know that?' I told her a box containing the dead body of a male child had been sent to North Leverton and that in it was an apron marked 'S. Drake.' She then sat down and began to cry. She said no more.

Police Sergeant Jonathan Whicher, of Scotland Yard, confirmed that he had accompanied Superintendent Kinder to arrest Sarah Drake and found three aprons marked 'S. Drake' in black ink, identical to the one found in the box with the body of the child. He also told the court that he was given a bunch of keys, one of which fitted the lock of the box. A large quantity of clothing, a gold watch and about £1 in silver was also found.

Next to testify was Mary Anne Bridge, employed as a searcher of female prisoners at the Marylebone station:

I remember the prisoner being brought there. I was called to search her. I asked her what she was charged with. She did not answer and I asked her a second time. She then asked me if I was a married woman. I told her I was and had a large family. She said, 'You can feel for me and I can tell you – it's all about a child.' I asked her was it a new-born baby? And she said, 'No, it was two years old and I hung it.'

She said the woman who had it to nurse brought it to her and she was afraid of losing her place through owing the woman some money and she had done it in a moment; that she packed it up and sent it to her sister in the country to be buried and she supposed it was her sister who made all the noise about it and she supposed she should be hung.

This testimony marked the end of the witness statements and proceedings were described in a detailed account in the *Westmoreland Chronicle*:

Mr Collier addressed the jury for the defence in a very able speech in which he contended that the prisoner must have committed the act in a sudden aberration of mind, caused by Mrs Johnston having come without any previous warning to expose her situation. It appeared, from the evidence of a fellow servant, that whenever the prisoner had an opportunity she read the Bible and in her bed-room she had been seen praying for half an hour together.

The learned counsel argued that her phase of mind was one of deep dejection, tinged with religious melancholy, a fearful state that was apt to terminate in frenzy and sudden acts of despair ... She appeared to him to be an object of compassion rather than anything else and if any man regarded her with indignation let him know that their verdict of guilty on the ground of temporary insanity would consign her to imprisonment for the remainder of her life.

He hoped that the result of their deliberations would not be the enactment of a still more fearful tragedy than that which they had been investigating ... He asked them to consider the deep affliction which she had endured, the mental torture she had suffered – greater than the greatest physical pain. The issues of life and death were in their hands and might God aid them to a just and merciful verdict.

During the greater part of the time occupied by the delivery of this address the miserable creature in the dock appeared to be undergoing the most intense anguish. She kept rocking her body to and fro and at short intervals her whole frame was convulsed with grief, but she never, even for a moment, raised her head or evinced the least curiosity as to what was going on around her.

Mr Justice Patteson summed up at great length ... was [it] clear the idea of destroying it [the child] occurred to her at the moment she did it? Was that sufficient to justify them in believing that she had lost her reason? It was for them to decide that question.

... If they were satisfied in their minds that she was not in her right mind at the moment, they must on their conscience, acquit her of the murder. If they were not satisfied, it was clearly and plainly a case of murder which had been committed, in consequence of the child's being thrown on her hands, and of her being in great difficulties when a sudden thought occurred to her to destroy it. If they found her not guilty on the grounds he had stated, they must tell him they had found her not guilty on the ground of insanity.

The Jury, after a few moments' consultation in the box, requested leave to retire. The prisoner, who never lifted her face from the handkerchief in which it was buried throughout the proceedings, was then removed from the front of the dock.

In about a quarter of an hour the jury returned to court and the prisoner was again placed at the bar. She was supported by a turnkey and female attendant and uncovered a portion of her face which was pale and sickly-looking; but she never once lifted her eyes and stood perfectly motionless.

The jury having been called over, the foreman handed in their verdict, – 'Not Guilty, on the ground of temporary insanity.'

Some slight applause followed the announcement; but the prisoner showed no emotion of joy and slowly fainted away in the arms of her attendants. Mr Justice Patteson signified that she would be 'confined to gaol during her Majesty's pleasure.'[60]

On 16 January 1850, a letter was published in the *Chelmsford Chronicle*:

Sir, – In your report of the trial of Sarah Drake at the Central Criminal Court, for the above offence, it is stated by Mr Collier, the prisoner's counsel, observed, 'rumours had found their way into the public papers without any authority, to prejudice the prisoner, and he had been informed and believed they were unfounded.'

Now Sir, I was the person who saw Sarah Drake when in the house of detention, before trial, and positively state and can swear she is the same person who was tried and convicted for a similar offence before the Common Sergeant, May session, 1842, and was sentenced to imprisonment in Ilford Gaol, six months: on that occasion the child was sent in a box directed to Mr Tipley, Knutsford Union, Cheshire.

I should not have addressed you only to convince the public my statement to Mr Long, the magistrate who committed Sarah Drake for trial, was correct.

I am, Sir, your obedient servant,

JNO. ANDERSON,

Governor, Ilford Gaol, 16th January, 1850.

Clearly, the verdict of 'temporary insanity' at the second Old Bailey trial did not sit easily in the minds of a number of newspaper reporters, as illustrated by this article in the *Worcestershire Chronicle*, Wednesday, 16 January 1850:

---

60   There was a similar case in 1860; Sarah Gough, a servant working in a house at Upper Seymour Street, sent the body of her newborn child in a box by rail to nuns at a convent at Clewer, near Windsor. It was unclear whether the infant had been killed, was still-born or had died shortly after birth, but Sarah was found guilty of 'concealment of a birth' and sentenced to one month's imprisonment in Newgate Prison.

...it was evident that the prisoner had been much alarmed by the nurse's suddenly leaving the boy with her at her master's house; she had previously exhibited affection for the child and there was no proof that the crime was premeditated. On these things Mr Collier built up a defence for the prisoner; urging that she had killed her boy in a sudden fit of delirium, induced on an ailing body and a mind oppressed by conscious poverty and by the leaving of the child with her.

But Mr Collier called no witnesses to support the plea of insanity. Mr Justice Patteson warned the jury not to acquit on this ground. They consulted together for a quarter of an hour and then returned a verdict of 'Not Guilty' on the ground of insanity. Some slight applause followed the verdict.[61]

(On the issue of this extraordinary case we offer no comment; but if the conclusion to which the jury came to just how many unfortunate persons have perished on the scaffold for whom a similar excuse might have been made?)

This article in the *Hereford Times*, on Saturday, 19 January 1850, addressed the subject of capital punishment:

A LESSON TO THE FRIENDS OF PUBLIC HANGING

Another jury has demonstrated the dislike to capital punishment, which is now fast spreading among the intelligent of all classes. The trial of Sarah Drake, the unfortunate woman who recently murdered her child, Lewis Drake, at the house of her employer, No 33, Upper Harley-street, has terminated in an acquittal on the ground of 'temporary insanity'.

This result is more extraordinary as no particle of evidence was produced to show the state of her mind, either before or subsequent to the fatal act. It was not asserted that she had at any former period been

---

61   Infanticide was common in the nineteenth century but, after the McNaghten Rule of 1843, courts would sometimes accept a plea of temporary insanity, often used as a euphemism for mental disturbance, 'puerperal psychosis', after childbirth. Generally, judges were surprisingly lenient regarding infanticide and, in some cases – Mr Justice Byles, for instance – contributed to petitions pleading for more moderate sentences. It must be said, however, that Sarah (suspected, if not proved, of killing three of her children), was fortunate in receiving a fairly brief custodial sentence and in a hospital rather than a prison.

affected with mental incapacity, or that there existed any hereditary predisposition to that fearful disease.

There was, in fact, nothing whatsoever to lead the jury to infer that she was labouring under any delusion sufficient to justify the commission, or rather to prevent the penal consequences of an offence of such magnitude, save the suggestion of counsel, who argued, from the circumstances of the case, the maternal affection which the wretched woman had previously exhibited towards her unfortunate offspring, her anxiety to bring it up with some degree of comfort and respectability, and the total absence of premeditation – that she must have been thrown into a state of sudden frenzy, which prevented her from being accountable for her acts. This view must have been adopted by the jury, who gave the benefit of the doubt, and thus preserved her from the extreme penalty of the law.

As a result of the Old Bailey jury's verdict, Sarah Drake was sent to 'a place of security at Her Majesty's pleasure'. It has been suggested that she was sent to the Royal Hospital of Bethlehem, and was recorded in the 1851 Census as 'a criminal lunatic' in residence, but the archives have no record of her. Asylums and similar charitable institutions at the time housed a number of inconvenient or embarrassingly eccentric relatives, predominantly female; of these, many were incarcerated, as in the case of Sarah Drake, on account of gynaecological factors radically affecting their behaviour.

However, ten years later, in 1861, records show that she was back in North Leverton, aged forty-six, and once more living with her parents. Her father, Thomas, now gave his occupation as 'farmer'. Also living with them was her brother, William, aged thirty-nine, and it seems that he was still unmarried.

Ten years later again, in 1871, Sarah was still living with her family. Her father, aged seventy-eight, was still alive, but her mother, Mary, had died. Her brother, William, was now fifty-two, and someone called George Moody, forty – possibly a lodger or a farm worker – had joined the household.

In 1881 Sarah was still living in the family home but, having taken over the household duties since her mother's death, she was now listed as 'housekeeper'. All three men – father, Thomas, brother, William, and George Moody – were also in residence.

Finally, in the 1891 census returns, Sarah's age is given as seventy-six; her father had since died and although her brother,

William, was still living at home, Fred M. Musgrave, aged twenty-one, had taken the place of George Moody.

In the spring of 1891, shortly after the census return that year, Sarah Drake died, at the age of seventy-seven.

During the nineteenth century many unwanted babies were either killed by their mothers or given over to 'baby-farmers' who were often known to starve them to death and dispose of their bodies amongst heaps of rubbish – or alternatively, if in London, throw them into the murky waters of the Thames.[62] During this period numerous young servant girls were brought before the courts charged with infanticide; most of the bodies of the murdered infants were found hidden in pig-sties, ash-pits, dung-heaps and privys, rivers, canals and ditches. Mary Anne Baines, writing on infanticide in the 1860s, stated that the police 'think no more of finding the dead body of a child in the street than of picking up a dead cat or dog.'

In 1834, when the Bastardy Clause was introduced into the New Poor Law, the fathers of illegitimate children were not expected to provide for them; this inferred that the mother alone was to blame. She was often depicted in the popular literature of the day as the 'fallen woman' – drunken, feckless and immoral – in sharp contrast to the sentimental ideal of her counterpart, the much revered 'angel in the house'. Even orphanages, often run by the Church, would sometimes turn away illegitimate children, accepting only those who had been 'lawfully begotten'.

Sarah Drake, however, did her best to support her son, Lewis, for the first two years of his life. Everything was against her – not only poverty but the difficulty of raising a child when employed as a live-in servant – yet she tried to provide him with a reasonable upbringing by paying Mrs Johnson 6s a week

---

62 In 1896 a notorious 'baby-farmer', Amelia Dyer, was caught in Reading, having thrown the bodies of infants she had strangled into a canal. She was hanged at Newgate. Some of these women would offer to 'adopt' and kill a child for a few pounds. In 1868, Mrs Jagger, of Tottenham, who advertised in the *Daily Telegraph*, was exposed by *The Pall Mall Gazette*, having starved to death between forty and sixty babies within three years. Another 'baby-farmer', Mrs Martin, was said to have disposed of some 555 babies in a period of ten months. In Brixton, Mary Hall, who ran a 'lying-in' establishment, was suspected of feeding aborted foetuses to neighbourhood cats.

(later reduced to 5s) to care for him, which was a fair amount of money at the time – her wage would probably have been less than £1 a week.

It is worth noting that Mrs Johnson, if her tears whilst giving evidence in court were genuine, had formed an attachment to young Lewis while he was in her care. The notorious practice of 'baby-farming' was widespread at the time, carried out by heartless women who would kill babies in their charge with impunity. They advertised their vile trade quite openly – using coded phrases that were easily understood – in newspapers, usually charging about 15s a month and no questions asked. Very young or sickly babies were especially welcome as their deaths would come as no surprise to anyone. They would be taken on for a set fee and then systematically poisoned, fed watered-down milk containing lime or given laudanum and other drugs. The usual cause of death was malnutrition and 'fluid on the brain' as a result of ingestion of strong narcotics. The bodies would then be wrapped in old newspapers or discarded clothing and dumped in an alleyway or simply thrown into a canal or river.

More robust infants ensured long-term fees extracted from their hard-pressed mothers; Lewis Drake did manage to stay alive for two years but Mrs Johnson was not prepared to care for him when the fee was not paid in full. Although she appeared to be fond of the boy and, as far as is known, didn't have any other charges, it was disclosed in her testimony that, at one stage, the child nearly died of 'water on the brain', a symptom, as mentioned, commonly found in the victims of 'baby-farmers'.

It is deplorable that the legislators and those in power chose for so long to ignore the plight of unmarried mothers and their unfortunate offspring, leaving them prey to unscrupulous characters, demanding money that these women could ill-afford and then cruelly killing the infants when they were no longer commercially viable.[63]

---

63   There were many who campaigned throughout the nineteenth century for legislation that provided protection for these children; Dr William Burke Ryan wrote extensively on infanticide and he, along with many others, lobbied the Home Secretary to address the problem. The Infant Life Protection Act was compiled in 1872 but this did not stop the practice of 'baby-farming', which remained widespread. It was not until 1889 that the Royal Society for the Prevention of Cruelty to Children was formed.

Having got behind with the payments, Sarah Drake was heading for disaster. Mrs Johnson's husband, Henry, had made it clear that he wanted rid of the child and was prepared to sue Sarah for the money owing. The fact that Sarah had only just started in her new job as cook/housekeeper to the Huth family – it was only her third day in the job – means one can easily imagine her distress when Mrs Johnson arrived at No. 33 Upper Harley Street and handed over the little boy.

A young, unmarried mother in the same predicament today would have a number of government and charitable agencies to offer help with accommodation, free medical attention and regular social security payments and, if eligible, she could be offered an abortion. In Sarah Drake's world, however, if a young woman had already failed to abort a foetus – using either the gin-bath or the knitting needle – what else could she do but give birth to the child? It is difficult for women today to imagine life without access to the contraceptive pill or legalised abortion.

No such options were available to the likes of Sarah Drake. As she pointed out in her letter to Mrs Johnson, with a young child in tow, how was she to find employers willing to give her work and accommodate the child as well? Once more she was well and truly cornered and, in a panic, made the fateful decision to solve the problem in the only way she could – to kill her own child. Most of the young women in this situation hid the bodies of their children in a variety of unsavoury places. Sarah Drake, however, chose not to do this, deciding instead to send all three bodies of her babies back to her home village, where she hoped her family would bury them.

If the evidence given by some of her fellow servants was true, Sarah was a religious woman, reserved and serious-minded, who read her Bible and prayed at every opportunity. For such a woman, the guilt she would have felt at killing her babies must have been heart-breaking. Indeed, after her release from the asylum she seems to have settled back home in North Leverton, content to stay there for the rest of her life, caring for her father in his old age and acting as housekeeper to the family.

The story of Sarah Drake is tragic, yet it was one that was echoed by hundreds of young women in the nineteenth century who found themselves in the same untenable situation; they were often from impoverished families who were unable or unwilling to support them (the condemnation of family members and neighbours was sometimes severe), a lack of any sort of job security and a reasonable living wage.

Above all, they lacked the education and attributes needed to change their circumstances, to resist being duped and humiliated, to climb from the lowest rung of society and thereby deflect the condemnation of their peers – steeped, as many were, in the hypocritical and sanctimonious tenets of Victorian society – whilst, at the same time, failing to condemn the fecklessness of the unnamed men who were morally responsible, in equal measure, for the birth of unwanted children.

CATHERINE WILSON

'A classic serial poisoner'

Twelve years after Sarah Drake's wretched figure left the dock of the Old Bailey, Catherine Wilson was indulging in a series of poisonings. No-one's fool and as tough as nails, Catherine Wilson murdered for money, even though she seems to have been perfectly well equipped to hold down positions in private houses as a cook, housekeeper, companion and nurse. Not content with her meagre wages, however, she was quite willing to kill to get more.

Catherine Wilson, *née* Crane, sometimes known as Constance Wilson or Catherine Taylor, was born in Surfleet, near the Lincolnshire town of Spalding, in 1817. Her father was a carpenter and in the latter part of his life was an inmate of one of the 'bede-houses' or almshouses of the town. There were two other children in the family, one of whom was disabled and died not long before Catherine's arrest for murder in 1862, by which time her parents had both been dead for some twelve years.

Catherine's life of crime began early. When she was fourteen she was involved in a theft whilst visiting the house of a friend. At first, on the false evidence given by Catherine, the family servant was charged with the offence. However, when Catherine was subsequently questioned about the robbery she confessed to the crime and admitted that she had fixed the blame on the servant. Soon after this disgrace she left home and went to live independently and, according to the subsequent newspaper reports, she 'openly lived a loose life'.

Progressing from petty theft and an erratic lifestyle, Catherine later made her way to the town of Boston, in Lincolnshire, and there, according to a posthumous report in the *Sheffield Independent*, dated Saturday, 18 October 1862:

> …she became acquainted with a master mariner trading from that port and by her plausibility and her apparent respectability she induced him to marry her and for some time they lived in comfort; but she returned to her old mode of living whilst her husband was at sea and he, upon his return, discovering it, left her to live with another woman.

About this time, the article stated, a son, born to Catherine Wilson before her marriage, was drowned at sea at the age of fifteen. By 1853, she had become the housekeeper for an eccentric, retired sea captain called Peter Mawer, probably her first victim, who 'died under very suspicious circumstances after a few hours' illness, it was said of cholera, leaving to the convict a good sum of money and property to the annual value of £50.'[64]

Two years later, in November 1855, Catherine Wilson made her way to London with a man called James Dixon. They found lodgings – taking the whole of the first floor, unfurnished – in the home of Mrs Maria Soames, at No. 27 Alfred Street, Bedford Square. Catherine initially described Dixon as her brother, but it was accepted by all in the house that this was not the case. The following July, 1856, James Dixon became violently ill, vomiting and retching and suffering acute pain. Dr George Ferris Whidborne, a surgeon who had a practice in nearby Russell Square, was called to the house but was unable to prevent his patient dying within a couple of days. The doctor at first thought that Dixon had been suffering from 'English cholera', but at a subsequent post-mortem examination it was established that Dixon's lungs were perfectly healthy and no poisons of any kind were found in the body. At the time, Catherine Wilson's circumstances were so dire she was unable to find the money to pay for the funeral.

---

64   During the police investigations prior to the murder trial of Catherine Wilson in 1862, a belated inquest was held into the death of Peter Mawer. Here it was established that Mawer had suffered from gout and rheumatism and was accustomed to taking small doses of colchicum to treat the condition. The drug is derived from the plant *Colchicum autumnale*. Although the leaves, corm and seeds are poisonous and there is no antidote, it is still widely used as a homeopathic remedy.

She did, however, continue to live in Maria Soames's house for a while, during which time she borrowed money from her landlady to buy expensive furniture for her first-floor apartment. Then, in the middle of October, 1856, Mrs Soames, with whom Catherine was on very friendly terms, became ill with similar symptoms to those suffered by Dixon. Once again, Dr Whidborne was summoned – one report states that when he arrived at the house he saw Catherine Wilson 'standing at the window, weeping' and he later said, when questioned in court, that he thought Catherine Wilson 'seemed very kind and very anxious about her condition'. The doctor's treatments, however, were unsuccessful and Maria Soames died on 18 October 1856. (Details of this case will be described in full later in the story of Catherine Wilson's murderous career when, six years later, she eventually stood trial for murder.)

Having seemingly got away with the murder of Peter Mawer, James Dixon and Maria Soames, Catherine Wilson went on to poison a Mrs Jackson, in Boston, Lincolnshire, in 1859, posing as a friend and confidante – and stole £120 from her. Again, her victim suffered similar symptoms to the previous three that Catherine Wilson had already dispatched – extreme vomiting and purging, rapidly ending in an agonising death.

A year later, in 1860, Wilson had found yet another victim – Mrs Ann Atkinson, a wealthy friend from Kirby, in Westmoreland, who came to stay with her in Kennington, East London, and soon succumbed to severe vomiting and purging. In fact, only four days after her arrival Mr Atkinson received a telegram from Catherine Wilson informing him that his wife had died suddenly after someone had robbed her of her money.

Catherine Wilson next attempted to poison her current paramour, a Mr Taylor, with whom she had lived for four years, but perhaps having a stronger constitution than her previous victims (and more effective medication), he recovered. His name was also mentioned at a later date in connection with two instances of theft at both houses belonging to Maria Soames.

It is possible that Taylor wisely decided to end his relationship with Catherine Wilson at this point for by the spring of 1862 Catherine had found employment with a Mr Carnell as a housekeeper and nurse to his wife, Sarah. Already in poor health, Sarah Carnell soon became very ill indeed and was tended most solicitously by the duplicitous Catherine Wilson. However, finding the medication she was given too revolting to swallow, Mrs Carnell immediately spat it out and refused to take any more. This instinctive reaction marked the beginning of the downfall of Catherine Wilson, and before long the heartless and manipulative serial poisoner was at last exposed – for the Carnells were horrified to see that the ejected liquid had burned a hole in the bedding. Some sort of corrosive poison was immediately suspected, and the police alerted. Catherine Wilson fled but was arrested six weeks later and subsequently stood trial for the attempted murder of Sarah Carnell.

The following announcement was issued in the *Lincoln Chronicle*, on Friday, 27 June 1862: 'Central Criminal Court, Old Bailey – Catherine Wilson/Constance – on Thursday 26th June, described in the calendar as being forty years of age and a widow, was indicted for feloniously administering to SARAH CARNELL oil of vitriol so as to end her life.'

On analysis it was found that the medication Catherine Wilson had given Sarah Carnell had contained enough sulphuric acid to kill fifty people, yet her defence attorney, Mr Montagu Williams, QC, successfully argued that the pharmacist must have given Mrs Carnell the wrong prescription and Catherine Wilson had, in all innocence, inadvertently administered it. The judge at the trial, Mr Baron Bramwell:

> …pointed out that the theory of the defence was an untenable one, as, had the bottle contained the poison when the prisoner received it, it would have become red-hot or would have burst before she arrived at the invalid's bedside. However, there is no accounting for juries and, at the end of the judge's summing up, to the astonishment probably of almost everybody in court, she was found 'not guilty'.

Although the jurors acquitted her, she was immediately re-arrested as she left the courtroom, for by this time the bodies of some of her previous victims had been exhumed, and the post-mortem examinations had confirmed that not all the deaths were from natural causes. Further charges against Catherine Wilson became imminent.

The *Nottingham Guardian* issued the following article on 1 August 1862, under the headline: 'The Adjourned Inquest on the Body of Mr Peter Mawer, of Boston, Supposed to have been Poisoned in 1834':

The jury again assembled at the Peacock Inn to receive Professor Taylor's report of the analysis of the viscera of the deceased.[65] Evidence was given to the effect that the body of the deceased was exhumed on the 3rd of July and that the lungs, heart, etc. were sent to Dr Taylor for analysis.

The Coroner then addressed the jury as follows:

'Gentlemen, several witnesses are in attendance who could give the most circumstantial evidence with reference to the death of Peter Mawer. I do not think it necessary to call them for this reason, that although their evidence aggravate previous suspicions, and prove almost to a certainty that Peter Mawer was poisoned, yet chemical analysis has entirely failed to prove the presence of poison in the remains.

It is now my duty to explain to you the circumstances which led to the exhumation of the body eight years after burial. Peter Mawer died on the 17th October, 1834, having previously made a will in favour of Mrs Wilson, his housekeeper: it is also known that he was paid a large sum of money in cash a few days before his death, which money has never yet in any way been accounted for. The whole neighbourhood believed that Peter Mawer was poisoned and that this suspicion had been a matter of conversation for eight years.

After the death of Mawer, the female, then called Catherine Wilson, but now called Constance Wilson, left the town for a time after disposing of her life interest in Mawer's estate. Two or three years afterwards, we find her in the house of a Mrs Jackson, near Bargate Bridge, Boston. She introduced herself as a nurse, companion, and confidential friend, Mr Jackson being from home in his business as a painter at Spalding.

In a few days Mrs Jackson died with all the symptoms of poisoning and it was then found that Mrs Wilson, in the name of the dead woman, had withdrawn money to the amount of nearly £300, from Mr Grant's bank, the hard earnings of the husband.

---

65 Dr Alfred Swaine Taylor (1806-1880) was a prolific writer and Professor of Medical Jurisprudence at Guy's Hospital. He specialised in forensic toxicology, and had over thirty years' experience of giving evidence in court in many poison cases, though his findings were sometimes controversial (as in the cases of Drs Palmer and Smethhurst).

With that money she got clear, bidding defiance to coroner, doctors and chemists. I pass over various rumours with reference to similar cases because they have not come, at present, before the public, but there need be no delicacy in reminding you that this woman was lately tried at the Central Criminal Court for administering oil of vitriol with intent to murder.

At the trial, Mrs Wilson's counsel objected that, as the vitriol had not been entirely swallowed, the proof of administration was incomplete!

The woman was acquitted only to be arrested on other charges and she is now under remand charged with having poisoned Mrs Atkinson and Mrs Soames. The body of Mrs Soames has been exhumed after six years' burial. It is possible that these cases may fail in the legal proof but they prove this fact – that wherever this woman introduced herself as a friend and a sister of mercy she proved a messenger of death. In every instance in which she succeeded in getting into a household, death occurred in a few days, the symptoms being always the same.

The press throughout the country soon took up the case. The *Bradford Observer*, on Thursday, 14 August 1862, informed its readers:

The Wholesale Poisoning Case – at the Lambeth police court on Thursday [7th August] Constance Wilson alias Catherine Taylor, was brought up for further examination on charges of having caused the deaths of certain persons by the administration of poison. A fresh charge was preferred in relation to the death by poison of a young gentleman named James Dixon, with whom it was proved the prisoner had co-habited and who had died two months before the late Mrs Soames, another supposed victim. The additional evidence taken on Thursday tended strongly to implicate the prisoner, who was again remanded.

The trial was fixed to take place at the next session to commence at the Old Bailey on Monday 22 September. By the end of the week a further and more ominous announcement was made in the *York Herald* on Saturday 13 September:

THE EXTRAORDINARY CASE OF
WHOLESALE POISONING

Sir George Grey, the Home Secretary, has at length determined that
the prosecution of Constance Wilson, alias Catherine Taylor, shall be
assisted by the Government ... It will be recollected that the prisoner
is strongly suspected of having caused the death of three other
individuals on whom she was in attendance at the time of their deaths
and whose death took place under precisely the same circumstances
and labouring under precisely the same symptoms as those of her
victims Mrs Atkinson and Mrs Soames. The prosecution, therefore,
being one of considerable importance, will be, it is said, conducted by
the Attorney General in person, with a sufficient staff of able assistants,
but it has not yet transpired who the counsel for the defence are to be.

The *Sheffield Independent* announced on Friday 26 September
that Catherine had been indicted for 'the wilful murder of Maria
Soames' by poison, and again on the same count. Mr Clark and
Mr Beasley formed the prosecution; Mr Oppenheim, Mr M.
Williams and Mr Warton the defence.

A brief summary of the facts were given to the court, as follows.
At the time of her death, Mrs Maria Soames was a widow who
owned two houses in Central London – she lived at No. 27, Alfred
Street, Bedford Square and also owned No. 13 in the same street.
She was about fifty years of age, gregarious by nature – she had
a number of close friends of long standing – and had previously
enjoyed very good health. She was later described by her doctor
as 'a good sized person, not very much one way or the other: I
should call her a middle-sized woman, florid and full and healthy'.

Whilst occupying the front parlour and kitchen of No. 27
she rented out some of the other rooms and her other house at
No. 13 was entirely occupied by paying tenants. Living with Mrs
Soames at that time were her two daughters – twenty-year-old
Anna, who the following year married a German watchmaker
called Herman Naacke, and nineteen-year-old Sarah.

Shortly before Christmas, 1855, the incorrigible Catherine
Wilson, probably already intent on finding another gullible
victim, came to lodge at No. 27, occupying the first floor with
a man named James Dixon, who Catherine referred to as her
brother but who the other residents of the house understood was
her lover. She immediately gave Mrs Soames a sob story about

having been mugged and robbed of £70 – a great deal of money at that time – maybe to attempt to either reduce the rent or delay paying it. Yet, practiced in the art of affecting friendship, Catherine Wilson and the landlady were soon on very familiar terms and, according to friends that visited the house regularly, they spent a great deal of time together chatting in the front parlour. Mrs Soames even lent Catherine the money to furnish their first-floor apartment with expensive items of furniture.

In July of the following year James Dixon died, at which time it appeared that Catherine Wilson was once again so short of money that she was unable to pay the funeral expenses. Although already behind with the rent, she remained in the house – no doubt already plotting to resolve her finances as soon as she could by employing the poisoner's craft in which she was now an expert.

On the afternoon of Wednesday 15 October, Maria Soames went to visit her half-brother – a draper, Mr Samuel Emery Barnes – at his home in Holloway. She had previously been left a legacy from her father, who had died two years before, and the arrangement with her brother was that he would give her the money in instalments. She went to him that afternoon to collect £10 owing to her but, for some reason, he gave her £9. When she left his home that afternoon she was in good health and cheerful spirits.

There was another lodger at No. 27, a Mrs Harriet Jane Stevenson, who lived on the second floor with her husband. She was pregnant at the time and the landlady had agreed to assist at the birth. After Maria Soames had taken tea with her two daughters in the front parlour, Catherine Wilson appeared and asked her to come to her room as she wished to speak to her. Maria readily agreed. Whilst there, she later told her daughters, Catherine had given her a piece of pork-pie and some brandy and water.

During that night Harriet Stevenson went into labour. Maria Soames went to assist her, as arranged, but by this time she was vomiting persistently and was obliged to go back to bed immediately.

She was even worse the following morning, and during the whole of that Thursday she was unable to get up and suffered from severe pain in the chest and repeated attacks of nausea. She had often suffered short bilious attacks in the past, however, and assumed this was again the case. But she continued to get worse and the next day, Friday, a Dr Whidborne was sent for. Thinking that she was suffering from another bilious attack he gave her some chalk mixture – an aromatic confection – and Batley's sedative – a mild preparation of opium – to stem the diarrhoea.

It appeared that, in the course of that day, a friend and lodger at No. 13, a seamstress called Mrs Emma Rowe, came to see Maria. Catherine Wilson told her that Mrs Soames was very ill and she had better not see her as she must be kept quiet. Another visitor was Maria's cousin, Mrs Hawkeshead, but she was allowed to see Maria and had sat up with her for most of the Thursday night.

When Maria's condition continued to worsen, despite the medicine he had prescribed, Dr Whidborne was again called and he asked her what she had eaten. Catherine Wilson informed him that her landlady had eaten some pork-pie but that she, Catherine, had also eaten some without any ill-effects.

Dr Whidborne sent for a much stronger mixture from the pharmacy. As soon as it arrived, Catherine Wilson took it up to her own room. She locked the door, and then, after a short time, took it downstairs to Maria Soames and administered a dose. She appeared to be extremely sympathetic and anxious about her sick friend and took it upon herself to wait on her, doing all she could to alleviate her suffering, and frequently plying her with brandy and eggs. However, whenever Maria was given a dose of medicine, extreme pain and vomiting was sure to follow.

Maria Soames continued to get worse throughout that Friday evening. Her friend, Mrs Emma Rowe, was a constant visitor. Passing Catherine Wilson's room and seeing her inside, Emma went in. She noticed two bottles on the mantel – one, a large one, containing a dark yellow liquid, and a second phial containing a light liquid. Mrs Rowe asked Catherine what the bottles contained: the large one contained Mrs Soames's mixture, Catherine replied. When Emma asked Catherine why she locked it up, Catherine replied that it was 'particular stuff and the doctor had told her to administer it herself'. Mrs Rowe asked if either of the daughters could do it; 'No,' Catherine said, 'the doctor had told her to and she would.' The doctor later denied, however, that any such instruction had been given.

During that same evening, while Maria's daughters were in the room, the invalid said she felt a little better. Hearing this,

Catherine Wilson said it was 'time she took her medicine'. She went up to her room and brought her a dose. After taking it Maria Soames was stricken with terrible pains in the chest and violent retching and said it was 'that horrid physic' which did it – and that she would take no more of it. Catherine Wilson, however, said she must take it, 'for her own good'. As usual, she then took the bottle of medicine back up to her room, which she kept locked at all times.

Catherine's next move was a classic ploy to plant the idea of suicide into the mind of the doctor. She took him aside and suggested that Mrs Soames was 'in great distress of mind'. She had met a man, she told him, on a bus in Islington, to whom she was engaged to be married, and had lent him £80; but he had turned out to be untrustworthy and had not repaid the debt, and this had caused her landlady great distress.

On the morning of Saturday 18 October, between two and three o'clock, Maria Soames died. Shortly after her death Catherine Wilson called Emma Rowe to her room and said that she had a great secret to tell her and asked her not to tell anyone. When Emma Rowe agreed, Catherine Wilson told her that Maria Soames had taken poison and that she had been acquainted with a man to whom she had become engaged. She had corresponded with him and his letters to her were always addressed to her, Catherine, so that Mrs Soames's daughters were unaware of the liaison. She then suggested that the fact that this man still owed Maria £80 had caused her great distress. She further stated that a letter would come from him on Monday. A letter did come without date or signature, the writer stating that he was 'sorry he could not meet her as promised but he could not pay the £80 but if she would lend him another £10 he would be able to pay the whole soon'.

Another witness, Mrs Eliza Matthews, the wife of a grocer and oilman, had been on very friendly terms with Maria Soames for more than sixteen years. On the day of her friend's death she had called at No. 27, but did not see Catherine Wilson there. On the following day, Sunday, however, she called again and spoke to Catherine Wilson – who then took her to see Maria Soames's body, laid out ready for burial.

'I was very much surprised at the appearance of my friend; her hands were clenched and her face was dreadfully distorted.'

(This is often a sign of death from an irritant poison.) She said to Catherine, 'Her's must have been a bad death.' And Catherine shook her head and said, 'Poor dear, poor dear, ah! You don't know all.'

When asked for an explanation for this remark, Catherine repeated the story about the man on the bus, Maria's engagement and the loan of the money which remained unpaid. She insisted that neither Maria's half-brother nor her two daughters knew anything about the whole affair.

Another visitor that Sunday after Mrs Soames's death was one of her close friends, Sarah Allen. She was also shown the body by Catherine Wilson and, noticing the distorted features and clenched fingers of the 'dreadful corpse', asked the cause of death. She was told: 'I know all her secrets and I am the only one who does but I want to keep it a secret for the sake of the daughters: she has taken poison.'

When Sarah Allen was asked later why she hadn't mentioned this conversation to either of the daughters, she said that 'they were so grief-stricken that they could hardly speak to me'.

By the time of the inquest, Catherine Wilson was already living with another man, referred to simply as Taylor. She even had the gall, straight after the funeral, to demand £10 from Mrs Soames's daughters, saying that she had lent their late mother the money; she even produced a fake IOU note signed 'A.M. Soames'.

The fact that Maria Soames's death followed so soon after that of James Dixon – and they had both suffered similar symptoms – soon set the rumours, in the words of Dr Whidborne, 'buzzing', and there was already talk of both victims having been poisoned by the time of the inquest into the death of Maria Soames.

Perhaps mindful of the rumours that were rife in the area, Dr Whidborne felt unable to issue a certificate unless a post-mortem examination was made. This was done on Wednesday 22 October, and the contents of the stomach were sent to University College Hospital for analysis. No traces of poison were found; but it appeared from the scientific evidence given by Professor Taylor at the trial that there were many vegetable poisons which would leave no perceptible trace forty-eight hours after death. It was suggested that the poison administered had been colchicum. Professor Taylor suggested that a number of small doses rather than one large dose had been ingested, as a large dose was more likely to be expelled from the body by violent vomiting and purging. Nor would he expect to find evidence of poison in the remains of Mrs Soames, now nearly six years after internment.

This was an opinion welcomed by the prosecution as Dr Whidborne, who had also attended James Dixon before his death, had found a bottle in Catherine Wilson's room which contained colchicum. When asked its purpose, she said she was in the habit of giving it to Dixon as a treatment for rheumatism and gout. She was told it was 'a very dangerous poison and required great care and she said she knew all about that and knew how to administer it.'

During the lengthy evidence given by Dr Whidborne and Dr Swaine Taylor, both agreed that, if an irritant vegetable poison had been administered to Mrs Soames, much of it would have been expelled from the body through vomiting and purging – it would not be surprising, therefore, to find no evidence of poison at the post mortem even though it was carried out within two days of death. It was suggested that, rather than one large dose of colchicum being given to the victim (if that was the poison that killed her), it was more likely that a succession of small doses were the cause of death. The anxious expression and contorted features of Mrs Soames's body were consistent with death from an irritant poison. After the court had heard the lengthy evidence of the medical men, the trial was adjourned until the following day.

The *Sheffield Independent*, on Monday, 29 September 1862, kept its readers informed of the developments:

The trial of Catherine Wilson for the murder of Maria Soames was resumed at the Central Criminal Court on Saturday [27th Sept]. Mr Justice Byles proceeded to sum up. In reference to the evidence of one of the deceased's daughters he remarked that 'it was not likely that she had committed suicide as when she called her up she said she had a bilious attack and if she had taken anything she must have known better than that and would have known that she was likely to die, whereas she had no idea'.

He likewise drew the attention of the jury to a remark which the deceased made after having taken a dose of the medicine which the prisoner had administered. After taking the medicine she was seized with a fresh attack of vomiting and pain in the chest and she said it was 'that horrid mixture and she would have none of it'.

With regard to the £9 which deceased had had from her half-brother, Mr Barnes, there could be little doubt from the evidence of that witness that she had it in her pocket at the time she left his house; it was never seen afterwards and it would be an important question for the jury to consider what had become of that money.

There was one circumstance in favour of the prisoner and that was that she continued to reside in the same house after the death of Mrs Soames; but then again, the prisoner had stated that she saw the deceased take the poison in brandy and water. Could the prisoner, queried the judge, stand quietly by and see her in such excruciating agony, in the presence of her own children, and not mention the fact?

The jury retired at one o'clock to consider their verdict. They did not return until nearly three. They then returned a verdict of 'guilty of wilful murder' and the learned judge passed sentence of death without holding out the slightest hope of mercy.

The prisoner heard the verdict and sentence 'without exhibiting the least emotion.'

The trial had ended on Saturday, 27 September 1862, and it was covered extensively in the newspapers in the days that followed. This appeared in the *Sheffield Independent* on Monday, 29 September 1862:

> The trial of Catherine Wilson terminated on Saturday in a verdict of guilty and she was sentenced to death in the usual form, the judge holding out no hope of mercy. The charges against this woman rival the number those against the notorious Palmer[66] and, if true, show how a crafty person may evade suspicion and defy the law through a long course of crime.

---

66 Dr William Palmer (1824-1856), a compulsive gambler and ruthless serial poisoner. He was convicted at the Old Bailey, in 1855, of poisoning his friend, John Cook, with strychnine, and suspected of poisoning others – including his brother, mother-in-law and four of his own infants within weeks of their birth. He was publicly hanged by George Smith at Stafford Prison before a crowd of some 30,000 spectators.

Sheffield and Rotherham Independent on Tuesday, 30 September 1862 went into great detail regarding the speech of Mr Justice Byles as he passed sentence:

> Catherine Wilson, after a long trial, and a most patient and anxious consideration of every circumstance of your case, the Jury have come to the conclusion that you were guilty of this most atrocious crime. It is very seldom that I think it any part of my duty, in a case of this or any other description, to express either concurrence or dissent with the verdict of the Jury; but, upon the present occasion I am bound to say that in my opinion the Jury could not have arrived at any other conclusion than they have done, consistently with the facts that were set before them.
>
> I never heard a case where it was so clearly proved that a murder was committed and where the excruciating pain and agony of the victim were watched with so much deliberation by the murderer.
>
> The greatest care was taken during the progress of the trial that nothing should be improperly introduced into the inquiry and that you should not be prejudiced in anything that had happened before; but, now the Jury have delivered their verdict and there can no longer be any fear that their decision should be in any way improperly influenced, I think it right that the Jury should know, and that the public should also know, what sort of person it is that the avenging arm of the law has at length overtaken.
>
> I find, then, that about the year 1853 or 1854, you were employed in the capacity of a servant or housekeeper to a person named Mawer, who lived in Boston, in Lincolnshire, and that person was in the habit of taking colchicum. He made his will in the month of April and by that will he left to you the whole of the little property he possessed.
>
> He died in the month of October following. I will say no more about this case except that it is quite clear that at this time you were perfectly well-acquainted with the nature and effects of colchicum.
>
> In the year 1856, I find that you are living with a young man named Dixon and that you came to London and went to lodge with him at the house of the deceased and Dr Whidborne was called in to attend him. He was not allowed upon the present trial to state any of the circumstances connected with the illness of this person; but I may now state that it appears by his deposition that Dixon, after eating, was suddenly taken ill with violent vomiting and purging; that his symptoms were exactly the same as those exhibited by the

unfortunate woman, Mrs Soames; and that he died very speedily afterwards – you, yourself, representing that he had died of galloping consumption but upon his body being opened his lungs were found perfectly healthy.

About the year 1859, I find that you were in habit of visiting a Mrs Jackson, who also resided at Boston, and that you were aware that she drew from a bank in that town a sum of £120 and that this sum was in her possession. She was taken ill with the same symptoms and died in four days and after her death the money was nowhere to be found. It appeared that upon this occasion you produced a promissory note apparently signed by two persons residing at Boston, for the amount that was missing; but it was proved that both these signatures were forged.

In the month of October, 1860, I find that you were connected with a Mrs Atkinson, who resided at Kirby Lonsdale, and that she came to live with you at your residence at Kennington; and it appears that you were aware that she was in possession of a considerable sum of money. On the 19th of that month, Mrs Atkinson was taken ill. Again the same symptoms – retching, violent purging, vomiting and great agony, and in four days she was dead.

If the jury had acquitted you on the present charge you would have been immediately put upon your trial for this murder. I have read the depositions in the case, most carefully and anxiously, and the result upon my mind is that I have no doubt that you committed that crime than if I had seen it committed with my own eyes.

In 1861, I find you living with a man named Taylor and that he was attacked in the same manner as the others to whom I have alluded but that, fortunately for him, remedies were immediately resorted to, and he recovered.

Again I find that, only in the present year, [1862] you were tried in this court for an attempt to murder, by the administration of sulphuric acid, a woman in whose house you were dwelling [Mrs Sarah Carnell]. You were acquitted upon that charge but although this was the case there is too much reason to believe that you were guilty of this crime also.

I am informed that the learned judge who tried you felt it his duty to sum up the case most unfavourably to you. These facts, I regret to say, rendered it extremely probable that the startling statement made by Dr Taylor, in the course of his evidence, is correct, and that, in the midst of apparent prosperity and obedience to the law, dreadful crime and vice are rife in this metropolis – the destruction of life by secret poisoning.

Your life is in the hands of the Crown and I think it right to inform you that, if I am consulted in reference to your case, I shall not feel justified in interfering [in case of an appeal] and that I cannot hold out to you the slightest hope of any commutation of your sentence.

The learned judge then passed the awful sentence of death in the usual form. The prisoner was then asked, as is customary in all cases in which women are sentence to capital punishment, whether she had anything to say in stay of execution (i.e. was she pregnant). The meaning of this was explained to her by one of the warders and she merely shook her head.

'During the whole of the trial,' the article concluded, 'the prisoner exhibited the greatest coolness and self-possession and she was not the slightest degree affected at any portion of the learned judge's address to her: and when he had concluded, she walked firmly away from the bar.'

Catherine Wilson's sentence of death was, in fact, the first for a woman at Newgate in fourteen years, and she would become the last woman to be hanged in public in London. She received no sympathy whatsoever from the newspaper reporters, as shown by the following in the *Sheffield Independent*, on Tuesday, 30 September 1862:

Secret Poisoning – In the conviction and sentence of Catherine Wilson for the poisoning of Maria Soames there is a moral certainty that justice has at length stopped the career of a person who for several years has moved about in society, appearing to be amiable, friendly, and useful, but constantly engaged in a series of dark intrigues, each ending in murder. In an intensely depraved state of society, such as formerly existed in France and Italy, the art of poisoning was carried to its highest perfection, but even then there was nothing in its operations more horrible than this case, which is only one of several cases, disclose.

Catherine Wilson is a widow, about 40 years old, stout, not bad looking, with a countenance indicative of great spirit and determination, and having a degree of coolness and self-possession enabling her to go through a trial for her life with perfect composure, and even to hear the verdict of guilty and the sentence of death without so much as a change of colour. Her demeanour at the trial renders it easy to understand how she can have committed the crimes imputed to her.

The charge that has resulted in her conviction is one about which she may long have congratulated herself that it would never arise to trouble her. Probably she has thought she went rather near the wind at the time but that her tact baffled suspicion and an enquiry having taken place [the first trial] ending in nothing, she may have concluded she was safe. And yet now that years are gone by, within a few weeks of the sixth anniversary of the death of her victim, Mrs Wilson finds herself called to answer for the murder of Maria Soames, and ere the year be complete she will have suffered death on the scaffold...

The case against the prisoner derived no support from post-mortem examination or chemical analysis. No traces of poison could be found, either before the inquest or after the recent exhumation of the body and the scientific evidence to account for this defect was very startling. The celebrated Dr A.S. Taylor, of Guy's Hospital, expressed the opinion that vegetable poison administered in a fluid state would not be discoverable a few days after death and that colchicum is not discoverable when once absorbed in the blood. The symptoms, however, were precisely those of poisoning by colchicum and could not be accounted for by any natural disease.

The *Morning Post*, dated Tuesday, 30 September 1862, had this to say:

The *Morning Post* deprecates any attempt to obtain a mitigation of the sentence on this prisoner. Surely it is needless to throw out any such hint. One cannot believe that a woman who has run such a career of crime will find any persons to interpose on her behalf. It would be worse than labour wasted for it would show that their efforts are not attributable to any candid consideration of circumstances but to a desire to save from the gallows, right or wrong, all criminals.

It is one thing to advocate the abolition of the punishment of death. It is a very different thing to plead for mercy to convicts irrespective of evidence. In the case of this wholesale and systematic murderess whose crimes are attended with the aggravation of foul deceit under the mask of friendship and the horrible cruelty of inflicting death by prolonged tortures while she pretended to be soothing the sufferings and administering to the wants of her victims, it is hard to believe that even if her sentence were to die as she has made others die, a single voice would be raised to spare her.

Whilst awaiting execution, Catherine Wilson wrote the following letter to her uncle and aunt. It was printed in the *Kentish Chronicle*, on Saturday, 25 October 1862, along with the following comment: 'The handwriting is neat and good, but common-place, presenting no peculiarity. There are only three words spelt incorrectly and three or four slight grammatical errors. With these exceptions, it might be taken for the letter of an educated person':

Gaol at Newgate, 8th October, 1862

My dear Uncle and Aunt, – with great pain I received your letter and with greater pain I sit down to answer it: for it recalls to my mind past scenes too painful to dwell upon.

My dear friends – all of you – I must decline your very kind offer of visiting me. I could not bear an interview; it would be too painful for us all. You must think of me as you last saw me: that is the best for you to do. Twelve months ago who could have thought of my being here? Six months today I have been in prison. How much better it was for me when I feared God and thought of pleasing Him more than man! Although innocent of this dreadful crime with which I am charged, I am a great sinner, and I have lived in wickedness and sin. Though I could deceive the world I could not deceive the Almighty. May He be more merciful to me than man has been is my earnest prayer. During my imprisonment I have received many letters and seen many friends: one lady from Boston has visited me and written too … but I got a lady to answer it for me. I felt I would answer this to you myself and I dare say it is the last letter I shall write; at least I think so. I am in ill-health, and cannot bear much. I do not receive visits from anyone now. I have this morning seen a solicitor; he is a very kind gentleman: I have received great kindness from him and his wife. I felt the interview very painfully this morning. I have received a letter from a gentleman in Lincoln, wishing for an interview, which I declined. I cannot see any one excepting the pious ladies who visit the prison.

My time upon Earth is very short. I shall be executed on the morning of the 20th inst. At eight o'clock in the morning, I suppose.

May God in his mercy receive my soul! Jesus is a present help in the time of trouble: on Him I cast my burden. It matters little how the body dies; may I be found right before the judgement-seat of God. I am not what man thinks of me; it avails nothing now to me.

My dear relatives – all of you – I take it as a great kindness you sending me this letter. You once thought much of me. This letter has cost me many tears. I have often thought of you all. And now, dear friends, I give you my dying love. Farewell.

From your unfortunate relative,

Catherine Wilson.

The *Manchester Guardian* carried the following on 31 October 1862:

It will be remembered that Catherine Wilson was some years ago housekeeper to a person named Peter Mawer, at Boston, who died under most suspicious circumstances, shortly after he had made a will, leaving his property, which was worth £50 a year, to Wilson, thus setting aside the will he had previously made in favour of his brother, John Mawer, a bricklayer.

It was suspected that he had been poisoned by Wilson, and immediately after his death John Mawer consulted a solicitor, with reference to taking steps to set aside the will; but as it was properly drawn up and attested, the matter was allowed to drop.

After the conviction of Wilson, however, John Mawer stated these facts to his employer, Mr Ward, and the latter, thinking it possible to obtain an admission from the condemned murderess, that coercion and undue influence was used to induce Peter Mawer to sign the last will, endeavoured to obtain an interview with her. He accordingly wrote to the Sheriff for permission to visit the condemned, at the same time stating that Catherine Wilson refused to see him. Mr Ward then advised John Mawer to write to Wilson with reference to the will. A letter was accordingly written by Mawer's wife and the following reply, in the handwriting of the prisoner, was received:

Gaol of Newgate,-13th day of October, 1862

Sir – I received your letter this morning. I must decline your visit, with thanks. You say you sincerely forgive the past. You never had anything to forgive me of. I always treated you well, and should of treated you the same had you of come to my house 8 years the 17th of this month. Then your visit might have been beneficial to us both. You know the advice of a friend in need is a friend indeed seldom to be found.

I never had any malice towards you, and now I have none towards those that have falsely swore my life away, for I most solemnly declare I am innocent of those dreadful charges. There has not been any poison traced to my possession or satisfactorily proved that anyone had died of poison. At the same time how much better to be innocent than guilty.

I have been in prison 6 months, my time has been spent in seeking my Saviour who alone can save my soul. It matters little what way the poor body is disposed of, as long as the soul is all wright [*sic*] with its Maker.

Next Monday by this time I shall be in Eternity there to give account of deeds done. I am not afraid to die. I care not what man say of me or what they think, I will only ask mercy of an offended God and there … [sue?] … for pardon. I shall die in peace with all.

I have had a few lines from George Kent [a young man who resides in Lincoln] but I was too ill to write and of course I declined to see him if he comes. I will not see any of my own relatives who have begged for an interview. I saw all the friends that I wish to see before my trial, then I never asked any to come to speak for me and since my trial I have refused to see any.

I have been very kindly treated by all since I have been in prison. I have plenty of sympathies from ladies who visit the prison, and all my wants supplied here.

I know this letter I received is not written by you. I hope you have these sentiments that I read in it is my earnest prayer, and believe me to be your well-wisher [*sic*].

Enclosed in the letter was a copy of verses headed 'the Question of Questions' and 'What think you of Christ?' on which the following words were written by the condemned: 'To the writer of this letter from Catherine Wilson, 1862.'

It will be seen from the letter that Wilson entirely shirked the question put to her.

According to an article in the *Caledonian Mercury*:

Only one person had visited the convict since her trial. This was a Mrs Williams, who resides in Loughborough Road, Brixton, and who was a neighbour of Catherine Wilson when she resided at Boston. The interview lasted only about ten minutes and it was very evident that the convict had no desire to prolong it. On Saturday last two women called and desired to see her but on their names being taken in she said she had no desire to see them.

The *Dunfermline Press* informed its readers of a reporter's attempt to gain access to Wilson:

…Yesterday morning, at four o'clock, a special messenger arrived at the Governor's house from the Post-office, with a letter addressed to Catherine Wilson. The Governor at once opened it and found it to contain two tracts on religious subjects – a species of literature which has been freely offered to her by well-meaning people out of doors. On Sunday a clergyman called upon the Governor and requested to see the convict in order [that] he might afford her spiritual consolation. The Governor introduced the rev. gentleman to the Ordinary who did not seem disposed to allow his spiritual duties to be interfered with. After some conversation the rev. gentleman admitted that his main object in wishing to see the prisoner was to obtain some information on which to write an article for a periodical with which he was connected and upon this admission, his services were declined.

The *London Standard* printed a copy of the letter Catherine Wilson sent to Queen Victoria a couple of days before her execution:

The following is a copy of the statement of her case, drawn up by the prisoner herself a few days before her execution and transmitted to the Home Secretary to be laid before her Majesty, imploring the clemency of the Crown. The expressions made use of are the prisoner's own and the document was written in a firm, legible hand, and there were merely a few errors in the spelling:

To her Most Gracious Majesty – I most humbly beg your Majesty's pardon for the liberty I have taken in sending this paper and crave your Majesty's most merciful consideration of my case. I am now lying under sentence of death for the dreadful crime of poisoning, which I solemnly declare I am innocent of. I am very deaf and was unable to hear any of the evidence upon my trial, therefore could not contradict anything that was said.

I have been in prison six months and unable to get the evidence to come forward on my behalf for want of means, my means being all exhausted; and yet, without one witness, there has never been proved one person or place I had ever poison of, nor that I had ever had poison in my possession. One witness says I told her the day of the death of Mrs Soames the death was not a natural one for Mrs Soames had taken poison in my room on the Wednesday night before; yet this witness, though a friend of the family for six years before, living with the daughters two years afterwards, never named it to anybody till now, six years afterwards, when I am tried for my life, then comes forward to say I told her this, which I never did.

Then comes another witness and friend of the family for 20 years who declares I told her there would be a letter come to the house on the Monday. She says I told her this on the Sunday before the letter came yet before this letter did come it was never told to Mr Barnes, Mrs Soames's brother, nor her two daughters, nor anyone else until my trial. I never did tell either of those witnesses anything of the kind. How strange those two women should be friends of the family both before and after death.

When the inquest was held not a word was ever said by either of the parties what I had said. No, because I had never said anything of the kind to them. Mrs Hawkshaw, a niece of Mrs Soames, was in attendance upon her most all the time on the Thursday and Thursday night she attended her alone; not until Friday and Friday night did I attend and sit up with the daughter until she died. Mrs Hawkshaw was sent to her aunt to buy the penny stamp paper to give me for to show that I had sent Mrs Soames 10/-; it was wrote every word by Mrs Soames herself. It was never disputed by the family or said one word against until now, six years afterwards; yet this witness was not called.

Mrs Soames's circumstances were not good and she could not meet her tradesmen's bills. She belonged to a building society. She had a certain sum of money to pay every week and to pay that with she always had to pledge her property. The two daughters say they never knew their mother to lend me any money, and I always paid my rent every week, 8s 6d. I could have no motive for taking the poor woman's life.

It was known by the witnesses that Mrs Soames thought of marrying again to better her circumstances to a man I had frequently heard her talk of, but I never saw. The letter produced in court a day or two after the death of Mrs Soames came to the house. Two people is [*sic*] called to say they believe it to be wrote by me, although in a disguised hand. When asked if they ever saw me write, one says he never saw me write, the other says he saw me write seven years ago. Neither of these men never saw me write in their lives. I am sure I did not write that letter. A part of it was torn away.

A false report has been circulated in the papers that I understood the nature of medicine, for I had lived with a Dr Mower, of Boston, which I never did, nor was there a Dr Mower living there at any time. All this proved very injurious to me. Every person that I have attended upon and done my best for, those that have died, has been exhumed and nothing found in them like poison or any poison traced to my possession or any doctor says anything against me except one, whose evidence is false, and yet I am condemned to die. I, therefore, through [throw] myself on your Majesty's most merciful consideration and pray to God to be more merciful than man.

I remain, your Majesty's most humble servant,
CATHERINE WILSON

Needless to say, this rather garbled plea did not move the Queen to mercy and no reprieve was considered. It would seem that Catherine Wilson didn't really expect any other result, for she seemed 'unconcerned'.

The *Manchester Guardian*, of Saturday 25 October, was one of numerous newspapers that described the execution:

It is 14 years since a similar exhibition was witnessed in London to that which took place on Monday at the execution of Catherine Wilson for poisoning Maria Soames. There was an immense crowd of men, women and children in Smithfield, great numbers of whom assembled on Sunday evening, in spite of the storm, so as to secure 'a good place' at the gallows. To the last, this woman protested her innocence. Her appeal to the Home Secretary produced no effect and no petition on her behalf emanated from the public. The convict was either friendless, or in her extremity was deserted by nearly all who had been on terms of intimacy with her. No relative, if any she had, applied to see her in prison either before or after her conviction.

One acquaintance only saw her while under sentence and that was a woman who had once been her neighbour, and whom a feeling of commiseration on that account had induced to visit her. Two other women applied for admission from a similar motive, but she declined to see them.

When Catherine Wilson stood pinioned in her long, loose gown on that ghastly stage: when the hangman fastened a cord or strap round the skirt of her dress, a little below the knee, so as to keep the folds together, and to prevent her struggling in the last agony – when he drew a long white cap over her head, the mob at once saw, recognised, and laughed at an image exactly resembling a figure with which the walls and hoardings of London are placarded. It was a low, stifled laugh that ran through the brutal concourse: and in the tone of its deep cynicism there was, as we fancied, a rough, harsh kind of pity. When the hangman had bound his victim after the manner we have detailed, he hastened from the scaffold with senile agility, his gait being between a skip and a totter. It was a fearful pause which then ensued. While it lasted there were a few faint screams in the crowd, and lads were seen to faint, though women did not. A cry, too, was raised that the barriers were giving way: and a rush was made in one quarter, very likely by thieves.

Gazing all this time at the fearful object beneath the beam, with the rope hanging loose between her neck and the iron chain above, it seems an age before the drop will fall. A horrible fascination prevents you from turning aside your face, though you would give all you possess to be able to do so: and then, at the moment when you seem to have overcome the spell, and are in the act of turning your eyes away, the form shakes, and plunges straight down with a dreadful shock: the rope is tightened to a rigid line: and the quivering body turns slowly round with a fearful mockery of life.

If any sort of compassion had been felt by the multitude at the very moment of their savage mirth, it was soon forgotten. The crowd broke up with loud yells and whoops of laughter.

In the afternoon the body was buried within the prison.

According to another article in the *Sherborne Mercury*, although Catherine had listened to the sermon on the Sunday before her execution, 'she had been respectful in her conduct and attentive to the religious instruction which had been afforded to her, but she had shown no further sign of contrition.' The article continued: 'Nothing has been said by her which can be construed into an acknowledgement of her guilt; indeed, her last words were a declaration of her innocence. The body, after hanging an hour, was cut down, and buried within the precincts of the gaol.' The sheriffs had conducted the proceedings 'with proper solemnity'.

Another version of the same ghastly scenario was published by the *Chester Chronicle* on the same day:

> The wretched woman Catherine Wilson, who was convicted at the last session of the Central Criminal Court of the crime of murder by poisoning, was executed on Monday morning at eight o'clock in front of Newgate, in the presence of an immense crowd.
>
> Notwithstanding the apparent conclusiveness of the evidence against her, the prisoner has all along maintained her innocence. Only a few days before her execution she herself prepared a statement in writing to be transmitted to the Secretary of State, in which she entered into a detail of the circumstances connected with the death of her supposed victim and declared most positively that she never administered any poison and she was entirely innocent of the crime of which she was convicted.
>
> It would seem that there was such a strong feeling in the mind of the public as to the guilt of the prisoner that no effort was made by any section of it to procure a remission of the capital punishment; even the Society for the Abolition of Capital Punishment appeared to feel that it was a case that would not justify them in interposing; the prisoner's own memorial (petition) and a statement of her case by her attorney, were the only steps taken to induce the Home Secretary to interfere. Mr Under-Sheriff Mackrell, as is customary upon these occasions, went to the Home Office on Saturday and had an interview with the Chief Secretary, in reference to the prisoner's case, receiving a communication in writing to the effect that, upon careful consideration of all the circumstances, the Home Secretary did not feel himself justified in interfering with the courses of the law. The prisoner was informed of this very soon afterwards and she heard the announcement without exhibiting the least concern.
>
> Since her conviction the prisoner has been constantly attended by two female warders and it appears that to them she has repeatedly stated that she was innocent of the crime for which she was to suffer. Her demeanour, however, was such as not to create any belief in the

minds of the officials of the gaol that she was speaking the truth. The prisoner was evidently a woman of the most firm and determined spirit, and it was the opinion of all those who have been about her that she had resolved from the first to pursue this course; her indomitable will enabled her, as will be seen, to carry it out to the last moment.

The prisoner attended the prison service in the chapel twice on Sunday and she appeared to pay great attention to the discourse of the Rev. Mr Davis, the Ordinary of the prison. She took her meals as usual and did not seem at all dismayed at the near approach of death. After she retired to rest on Sunday evening she slept soundly for several hours, undisturbed by the fury of the elements, it being a most tempestuous night, or the noise of the workmen erecting the scaffold which can be plainly heard within the prison.

She was visited at an early hour by Mr Davis, who prayed with her for some time, but he forbore from making any allusion to her crime or pressing her to make any statement upon the subject.

Mr Alderman and Sheriff Lawrence and Mr Sheriff Jones arrived at the gaol shortly after seven o'clock, accompanied by the under-sheriffs, Messrs Farrer and Mackrell, and a few minutes before eight they were joined by Mr Jones, the Governor of Newgate, Mr Humphreys, the principal warder, and several other of the prison officials, who escorted them into the gaol to the room where the process of pinioning was to be performed. Here the prisoner was introduced, after a short interval, accompanied by one of the female warders. She walked across the room to a seat that was pointed out to her with a firm step, apparently as unconcerned, indeed even more so, than any of the spectators.

The female warder kissed the prisoner and shook hands with her and then retired. After a short interval, Calcraft[67], the executioner, commenced placing round the prisoner's arms and body the leathern straps and apparatus by which unhappy criminals are secured. During all this the prisoner did not exhibit the least emotion; she only once raised her handkerchief to her eyes, and appeared to press it to her forehead, as though she had felt some sudden pang, but she

---

67 William Calcraft (1800-1879) was appointed executioner in 1829; he had been previously employed to flog juveniles held at Newgate prison. Over forty-five years he carried out at least 450 executions and had a brutal record of botched hangings. One of his successors, James Berry, devised a system of drops according to weight that ensured, as far as possible, a quick and merciful death, a practice perfected by Albert Pierrepoint, executioner from 1932 to 1956.

quickly withdrew it and resumed her composure, which never again abandoned her to the last moment.

The fatal moment having by this time nearly arrived, Mr Jones, the Governor of the prison, went up to the culprit and, in an impressive manner, said that her time was now very short and he inquired whether she had anything to say to the sheriffs. Prisoner (in a firm, calm tone): 'I am innocent.' Nothing more was said to her. The melancholy cortège then proceeded to the scaffold, the prisoner walking without the least assistance the whole of the way, also up the steps to the drop. Her appearance was the signal for a loud murmur among the crowd but there was no other manifestation of feeling. During the time that Calcraft was adjusting the rope and pulling the cap over her face the wretched woman stood firm and unconcerned. She did not appear to exhibit the slightest emotion and when the drop fell she seemed to be dead almost instantaneously.

The crowd assembled was immense, the number of persons present being variously estimated at from twenty to thirty thousand. They were, however, certainly much more orderly than usual on these occasions.

Additional details can be found in various newspapers, including the following from the *Caledonian Mercury*:

…from Smithfields to Ludgate Hill there was a dense mass of human beings and at all the windows in the Old Bailey from which a view of the scaffold could be obtained were well-dressed people, many of whom had provided themselves with opera-glasses, which were levelled at the miserable woman when she came forth from the prison to die.

The crowd began to assemble on Sunday evening but as it rained incessantly until past midnight they took up their positions in the courts with which the neighbourhood abounds and in any other place in which they could procure shelter from the storm.

When the morning began to clear they came out of their retreats and took up their position by the gallows. At a quarter before eight o'clock a procession consisting of the Sheriff, Under-Sheriffs, the Ordinary of Newgate, the Governor, and the surgeon, went to the bedroom of the convict and then brought her to the room in which the pinioning was to be performed. There she met Calcraft, who commenced the operation of strapping her arms. While this was being done she sat on a form, and was slightly agitated. The female warder, who accompanied her, asked her whether she could do anything more for her and having been told that she could not, she kissed her and left.

Mr Jones, the Governor, than asked her whether she would have some brandy but she declined. He held a glass of water to her lips and she drank a little, after which he said to her: 'The last moment has arrived, do you wish to say anything?' She replied, feebly: 'No, I am innocent.' She then rose from her seat and followed with unfaltering step the Ordinary, who, as the procession moved across the yard, read the burial service. From the prison she ascended the steps leading to the gallows, without betraying any emotion. The white cap was drawn over her eyes, the rope was put around her neck, her legs were tied, and the bolt having been withdrawn, she fell heavily, and died apparently without a struggle. There was very little groaning or noise on the part of the mob.

The *Reading Mercury* offered further details: 'The culprit got up and dressed herself shortly after six o'clock on Monday morning and when she had partaken of breakfast she was visited by the Ordinary and joined with him for some time in apparently earnest prayer. About half-past seven o'clock, the Sheriffs arrived at the prison.' As the group walked out of the prison towards the waiting gallows:

...the prison bell tolled out at the same moment and every circumstance of the painful scene was well calculated to create awe in the beholder; all, however, apparently failed to strike any terror to the unhappy culprit; not a muscle quivered, not a limb trembled. She walked without the slightest assistance and when she came to the scaffold she tripped quickly up the steps of the ladder and placed herself under the beam from which the rope was suspended and did not appear in the lest dismayed at the sight of the thousands of upturned faces that were straining their sight to gaze at her.... In a few seconds the drop fell and the wretched culprit was dangling in the air, a corpse, her death appearing to take place almost instantaneously.

Catherine Wilson, whose wretched fate has been thus recorded, was a well-proportioned and muscular woman, forty-three years of age and about five feet five inches high. When she was cut down it was observed that her eyes were closed as if in sleep and her features were not at all distorted, and no-one would have imagined, from her appearance, that she had died a violent death.

The crowd, formed chiefly in a dense mass in the large open space in the front of the prison, stretched away as far as Smithfield on the one hand and Ludgate-hill on the other. Scores of people, men and woman, sat at open windows commanding a view of the spectacle, or stood on the housetops. The moment the convict appeared on the scaffold the huge concourse of people surged to and fro and raised that indescribable murmur characteristic on such occasions; but no expressions of popular feeling could be distinguished in the uproar.

There were a great number of women in the crowd. The people began to assemble shortly after midnight and by four o'clock in the morning many hundreds had taken places in front of the gaol. In the height of the prevailing excitement, as the convict appeared on the drop, an iron *chevaux-de-frise*, running along the top of the wall connecting the Court-house with the prison and against which many people had leant for support, suddenly gave way, but with what result is not known. Fourteen years have elapsed since a woman had been executed at the Old Bailey.

At nine o'clock the body, after hanging the usual time, was taken down and removed in a shell to an adjoining room. At three o'clock in the afternoon it was buried within the precinct of the prison.

In *Harper's Weekly*, a particularly damning article was published after Wilson's execution:

From the age of fourteen to that of forty-three her career was one of undeviating yet complex vice… She was foul in life and bloody in hand, and she seems not to have spared the poison draught even to the partners of her adultery and sensuality. Hers was an undeviating career of the foulest personal vices and the most cold-blooded and systematic murder, as well as deliberate and treacherous robberies…

We speak without hesitation of her crimes as plural, because, adopting the language of Mr Justice Byles with reference to the death of Mrs Soames, we not only 'never heard of a case in which it was more clearly proved that murder had been committed and where the excruciating pain and agony of the victim were watched with so much deliberation by the murderer' but also because the same high judicial authority, having access to the depositions in another case, pronounced, in words of unexampled gravity and significance 'that he had no more doubt but that Mrs Atkinson was also murdered by Catherine Wilson than if he had seen the crime committed with his own eyes.'

Seven murders known, if not judicially proved, do not after all, perhaps, complete Catherine Wilson's evil career. And if anything were wanted to add to the magnitude of these crimes it would be found, not only in the artful and devilish facility with which she slid herself into the confidence of the widow and the unprotected – not only in the slow, gradual way in which she first sucked out the substance of her victims before she administered, with fiendish coolness, the successive cups of death under the sacred character of friend and nurse – but in the atrocious malignity by which she sought to destroy the character and reputation of the poor creatures and to fix the ignominy of suicide on the objects of her own robbery and murder.

We are lacking a clear understanding of the nature of Catherine Wilson. She doesn't seem to have been a sexual free spirit like Catherine Hayes or possess the alcohol-induced bonhomie of Kate Webster (the final case in this volume). Yet she was an accomplished actress able to play the part of a comforting nurse or special friend with ease and plausibility. She was also able, it seems, to attract a succession of men with whom she could cohabit and she met her fate, one might say, with courage, incredibly steadfast even as she mounted to steps to the gallows, exhibiting quite extraordinary self-control.

The motives for poisoning are usually jealousy, revenge or sheer hatred, and in many cases the animus is directed at a family member, lover or close acquaintance. Yet Catherine Wilson seems to have killed people purely for money and expedience. She exhibited the classic manifestations of the poisoner's craft that she had perfected over a number of years. Poisoners are always secretive, devious and determined. It was with extreme cunning that she somehow managed to poison Mrs Soames under the very noses of her two grown-up daughters and several visiting friends – they were all living together in close proximity – even when 'buzzing' rumours were circulating in the neighbourhood after the unexpected death of James Dixon two months before.

Furthermore, the prosecution at her trial failed to produce any evidence that Wilson had acquired any poison by subterfuge or devious means. She frankly admitted that she kept a supply of colchicum in her room and volunteered the information that she had regularly given doses of the potentially lethal drug to both Peter Mawer and James Dixon to treat their rheumatism and gout.

In her killing of Maria Soames she shared the classic actions of other poisoners such as Adelaide Bartlett,[68] Jane Cox[69] and Louisa Merrifield. As with Adelaide Bartlett, she did her best to isolate her victim by restricting visitors and kept all medications well out of view in a separate room. Affecting deep concern, they both suggested to doctors, friends and family members that their victim was extremely distressed, anxious and therefore possibly suicidal. Jane Cox even went as far as to actually tell a doctor called to the bedside of Charles Bravo that 'he had taken poison'. Catherine Wilson did much the same and she also shared the ploy of Louisa Merrifield who plied her victim with brandy and eggs to disguise the taste and smell of the poison she was callously administering. After she had poisoned Maria Soames, Catherine Wilson told one of her victim's closest friends that she had lent Maria 10s, to which she added: 'Poor dear, I would have lent her anything if I had had it; I had such love for her.'

In all these cases, the poisoner, heartless enough to stand by and watch their victims suffer terrible agonies, sometimes for days on end, gave the impression to loved ones and friends that they were doing their utmost to treat the patient and affect a cure, whilst being both solicitous and cruelly duplicitous in equal measure.

---

68   At the Old Bailey, in 1886, Adelaide Bartlett was acquitted of poisoning her husband, Edwin, with liquid chloroform – see the author's book, *The Pimlico Murder*. revised edition.

69   Jane Cox, Florence Bravo's companion, was never charged with the poisoning of Charles Bravo though some writers, myself included, have suggested she was guilty – see *Murder At The Priory: The Mysterious Poisoning of Charles Bravo*. The case of Louisa Merrifield is featured in the author's book, *Deadly Service*.

KATE WEBSTER

'A truly appalling crime'

Undoubtedly, one of London's wickedest women was the hard-drinking, ill-tempered maid servant Kate Webster. Seventeen years after Catherine Wilson's execution, Kate Webster found herself in a corner – and retaliated with extreme violence.

Between four and five o'clock on the afternoon of Tuesday, 4 March 1879, a tall, gaunt woman turned the corner into Rose Gardens, Hammersmith – a street in West London that was at the time little more than a rough track flanked by rows of two-up, two-down working men's cottages. Though poor and grossly overcrowded, the district was, nevertheless, a respectable one, and its inhabitants formed a close-knit community, bound by a shared struggle for survival.

Kate Webster was no stranger to the street, for she too had once lived there. Now, some six years later, she had come back to the area to visit old friends, Henry Porter and his wife, Ann, at No. 10. She was carrying a black canvas bag, the sort of bag a woman might use to carry vegetables back from the market.

Only Mrs Porter was at home, and at first she failed to recognise her visitor for the woman standing on her doorstep was wearing a finely-cut dress of black silk, a fur-trimmed jacket and a fancy bonnet with a feather in it. Around her neck was a gold watch and chain and on her fingers several expensive rings. It was not until the woman greeted her warmly with a familiar, 'How are you, mother?' that she realised who she was – a woman she once knew simply as Kate, a next-door neighbour and drinking companion. Though both Mrs Porter and her husband were later to deny that they knew about Kate's busy criminal life, this claim seems doubtful. Living so closely together, without the luxury of privacy, they must have been aware that Kate was, even in her mid-twenties when they knew her, a seasoned jail-bird with a string of convictions behind her for fraud and theft.

She was born Katherine Lawler, in Killane, near Enniscorthy, Ireland, in 1847. Raised in a Catholic farming family, she had married a sea-captain called Webster whilst still in her teens and they had four children, all of whom died in infancy. She said later that when her husband also died, she had turned to crime in order to survive. It is as well to remember, however, as subsequent events will show, that Kate was a habitual liar, changing the details of her life many times to suit her current circumstances. She was sentenced to a brief term of imprisonment for theft in Ireland and on her release made her way to Liverpool to continue with her criminal activities.

During her subsequent career as a thief, she adopted a number of aliases – Webb, Shannon, Gibbs, Gibbons or Lawless – and occasionally reverted to her maiden name of Lawler. Her criminal speciality was robbing lodging houses. She seemed to have found no difficulty in finding rooms, having first presented herself as an honest and respectable woman in need of lodging. Once installed, she would wait her chance to rob the occupants before disappearing, only to turn up in another district to repeat the offence, time and time again. Her mode of life, therefore, made her a rolling stone, forever changing her territory once she became known to the local police.

In 1867, she served a four-year prison sentence for larceny and a number of other charges, including prostitution. On her subsequent release, she headed for London and – according to a statement she made later – she attempted to make an honest living by taking work as a domestic servant whenever she could. It was in 1873 that she had first turned up at Rose Gardens, Hammersmith, taking lodgings next door to the Porters. They said later that, when they knew her, she was an out-of-work domestic and they believed her when, after five or six weeks, she said she was leaving to take up a position as a maid in a house in Norland Crescent, Notting Hill.

However, she was soon to return to her criminal ways and on 4 May 1875, at the Surrey Sessions, she was convicted of thirty-six charges of larceny, all committed in the Kingston area, and sentenced to eighteen months' imprisonment at Wandsworth

Gaol. Two years later, on 6 February, she was again convicted of felony and served a further twelve months' imprisonment.

After leaving the area, Kate had occasionally gone back to see Annie Porter, but when these visits eventually stopped they lost contact altogether. Until, that is, there came that knock on the door. Remembering Kate as rather shabbily dressed and generally down-at-heel, it was little wonder that Mrs Porter barely recognised her. Not only was she now well-dressed, she seemed much more self-assured, almost proud in her carriage, and although she was a strong, big-boned woman, the cut of her new clothes suited her well. She even spoke differently, although her Irish accent was still strong.

Keen to hear what had brought about such a remarkable change in her fortunes, Mrs Porter invited her in for tea. Kate had come prepared – from a pocket deep in the folds of her skirt she pulled a bottle of whiskey and the two women settled down to bridge the gap of the intervening years over a glass or two.

Shortly after six o'clock, Henry Porter – or Harry, as Kate liked to call him – came home from work and joined them. He was also intrigued by the change in Kate and the story she had to tell. Since they had last seen her, she told him, she had married again: her name was now Mrs Thomas, and she had a young son called Johnny. But, she confided, although she was a widow once more she had been more than fortunate, for an aunt had recently died and left her a respectable house, one of a pair known as Vine Cottages, in Park Road, Richmond.

Harry Porter and his wife were impressed. My goodness, Kate, what a stroke of luck! To celebrate her good fortune, the lodger's daughter was sent out for half a pint of gin – all the characters in this story, Kate included, seem to have drunk copious amounts at every opportunity – and the friends settled down to chat in the tiny back parlour.

Little did they know that inside the innocuous-looking shopping bag their guest had placed so carefully under the table by her feet was the recently severed head of Mrs Julia Martha Thomas, neatly wrapped in brown paper...

By the time Kate rose to take her leave that evening it was nearly seven-thirty and dark outside. Annie Porter, already the worse for drink when Kate arrived that afternoon, had gone upstairs to lie down and Harry Porter, feeling especially magnanimous towards Kate after all the whiskey, gin and talk of old times, offered to accompany her to the railway station at Hammersmith, taking his fifteen-year-old son, Robert, to carry the bag. Despite her errant ways, Kate had been well-liked in the area and was remembered as a kindly neighbour. So it was with a camaraderie fuelled by alcohol that Kate and Harry Porter set off for the station, with young Robert trailing behind with the canvas bag, which he found surprisingly heavy. So heavy, in fact, that his father took it from him when they reached the Angel public house. Outside, they met twenty-two-year-old William, the Porters' other son, who worked close by. This was as good an excuse as any to have a glass of beer in the Angel before resuming their journey.

It didn't take them long to reach their next port of call, a public house called the Oxford and Cambridge, close to Hammersmith Bridge. Naturally, the trio found it impossible to pass its doors without popping in for another drink. Whilst in the bar, Kate told Porter that she had arranged to take the bag to a friend in Barnes. She suggested that he wait for her there as she wouldn't be gone more than half an hour. Declining his offer to go with her to carry the bag, she disappeared into the murky blackness of Hammersmith Bridge.

Twenty minutes later, she was back in the pub – minus the bag – showing Harry Porter and his son five gold rings. They were family heirlooms, she told them, a legacy from her sister who had recently died. She went on to show them some photographs – one, she said, was a picture of her father and another, a likeness of her dead sister. As for the house at Richmond, she assured Harry, it was full of nice pieces of furniture, not rubbish but good quality stuff. But she had been unlucky with her lodgers and, as her father was very frail and on his last legs, she had decided to sell the house and its contents and go home to look after him. She would like Porter to find her an honest broker to deal with the sale. (Rather a hypocritical proviso, one would have thought, for someone like Kate to stipulate.) However, when Harry suggested she find someone in the Richmond area, which would make the transaction more convenient for everyone concerned, she dismissed the idea.

She didn't know anybody in Richmond, she said, and would much prefer a broker recommended by Porter.

Despite Kate's reputation as a thief, the Porters seemed to believe her – or, perhaps, more to the point, they simply chose to accept her story and enquire no further. Harry Porter promised to sort something out and when Kate asked if young Robert could accompany her back to Richmond, Porter agreed on one condition – that the lad was back in Hammersmith in time to get to work at half past five the next morning.

After finishing their drinks, Harry Porter walked as far as the railway station at Hammersmith and Kate and Robert boarded a train for Richmond, arriving at the newly-built station by the bridge. When they reached Vine Cottage they entered the house by the side door and Kate asked Robert to go inside ahead of her and light the gas lamps.

Once inside she showed him into the drawing room, gave him a glass of rum and had one herself. Clearly thrilled to be the possessor of such an elegantly furnished home, she ran her fingers along the keys of the piano declaring that it was a very fine instrument indeed. She also showed him two £5 notes, a Building Society Book and a Post Office Savings Book, all left to her, she said, by her sister. She asked him to count up the figures, presumably because, despite being innumerate, she was anxious to impress the boy with her newly-acquired assets.

A little later, she went upstairs and came back dragging a wooden box, bound with strong cord. She also fetched a carpet-bag full of meat, vegetables, tea and sugar from the kitchen, saying that, as she thought she might come back to Rose Gardens for the night, the food would come in handy. But the first priority, she said, was to deliver the wooden box to a friend who would be waiting for her at the far end of Richmond Bridge.

By this time it was nearly eleven o'clock – yet, with the apparent complacency that marked the attitude of all Kate's familiars, Robert took the bag of provisions in one hand and helped her carry the heavy box with the other. Unfortunately, the handle on his side was broken so he had to grip the cord instead; this caused his knuckles to rub against the rough side of the box, making them quite raw. He was no doubt extremely thankful, therefore, when, once on Richmond Bridge, Kate made him put the box down on a bench in one of the five pedestrian recesses. Then she abruptly told him to go back the way they had come, towards the railway station, and wait for her there.

The boy instinctively did as he was told and began to walk away but, perhaps because it was so late, the night was particularly dark and there were few people about, he hovered apprehensively in the next recess. Almost at once, he heard a splash as something hit the water below. A gentleman, who happened to be passing at the time, also heard it and stopped to peer over the parapet for a moment before hurrying on his way.

Almost immediately, Kate emerged from the darkness and joined Robert, telling him that she had met her friend at the far end of the bridge as arranged and had handed over the box. Together, they hurried to the railway station – only to find that the last train to Hammersmith had already gone. The boy tried to persuade a cabbie to take him home for 2*s* but the fare was 3*s* and neither he nor Kate had the extra 12*d*. Robert had no alternative but to go back with Kate to the house in Park Road, Richmond. They sat up drinking rum until well past midnight, when Kate made him a makeshift bed on the floor of her bedroom.

The following morning, Wednesday 5 March, while the lad no doubt nursed a bad head, Kate was up bright and early to make his breakfast. Once he had eaten, Robert, carrying the provisions in the carpet-bag, hurried to catch the morning train, at five past seven, to Hammersmith, already more than an hour and a half late for work.

At about the same time, less than a mile downstream, a coalman called Henry Wheatly was driving his cart along the banks of the Thames, near Barnes Bridge, when he spotted a wooden box that had been washed up by the tide and become stuck in the mud. Perhaps hoping he might find something of value he hauled it clear of the mud and cut the cords. Curious to see inside he gave the box, which had a hinged lid, a good kick. He was horrified, however, when the box burst open to reveal a mass of congealed flesh.

Convinced the meat was human in origin and not animal meat he hurried to the police station at Barnes where he reported his find to the officer on duty. A local surgeon, Dr Adams, was immediately called. He was able to confirm that the contents of the box were, indeed, portions of human flesh, and, when pieced together at the mortuary, it formed almost the complete body of a woman. He estimated that the woman was probably in her thirties. The head and one foot, however, were missing. The colour and texture of the flesh, the doctor concluded, seemed to indicate that it had been boiled – except, that is, for part of the woman's thigh, which had been left in its raw state.

This horrendous find, dubbed 'the Barnes Mystery', was soon the subject of some sensational newspaper reports, and during the days following the gruesome discovery several theories were proposed – one being that the body in the box was some sort of practical joke played out by medical students. But this was soon discounted as the dismemberment of the body had been so amateurishly done and with such disregard for any underlying anatomical structure. Another suggestion was that the whole thing was merely a macabre hoax thought up by an enterprising journalist. Some newspapers dwelt on a number of similar cases where dismembered bodies had been washed up on the banks of the Thames.[70]

Young Robert Porter, however, his knuckles still sore from the night before, didn't read about the grisly find until the following Sunday 9 March. Nor had he mentioned helping Kate carry a box to anyone, not even to members of his family – it was, he thought, of no consequence and the incident had completely slipped his mind.

Meanwhile, later that morning, as the doctor probed the disgusting remains, Kate, neatly dressed in her fashionable clothes and a fancy bonnet, made her way to Rose Gardens to spend the day with her old crony, Annie Porter. Husband Harry was at work; he had been a painter and decorator with the same firm for twenty-five years and worked from five thirty in the morning to six o'clock in the evening each day, with a half day on Saturdays.

Kate seemed to be unwilling to spend the night alone in the house in Richmond and, probably worse for drink by the evening, she decided to stay the night with the Porters. She settled down to sleep on the sofa in the front parlour – in fact,

---

70 There was a similar case in 1827 of a man's headless remains, also boiled, found near Waterloo Bridge. And in 1873, the remains of a woman were found scattered on the foreshore at Battersea – other parts of the same body were later found downstream at Greenwich and Rotherhide.

she had little choice for, incredibly, the rest of the tiny cottage was jam-packed with the Porter family – Annie, Harry, their two full-grown sons, William and Robert – and the lodger, Emma Clark, her husband, and their young daughter – all these people squashed into four very small, shabby, candle-lit rooms.

The following day, Thursday 6 March, Kate reminded Harry Porter about his promise to find her a broker to buy the furniture at Richmond. About nine o'clock that evening he took Kate to the shop of a local greengrocer, Mr Brook, who had a sideline in moving furniture, but it was closed. Kate, again not wishing to spend the night alone at Richmond, asked Harry to come back with her so that she could show him the furniture. But Porter declined, promising to make the journey on the following Saturday, when he finished work at midday.

Sometime during the remainder of the evening with the Porters, during which there can be little doubt that a great deal of alcohol was consumed, Kate managed to persuade their son, William, to accompany her back to Richmond, although the exact purpose of the visit was never fully explained. What is known is that Kate, probably inebriated and unaccustomed to owning keys to property, left her purse and latch-key at the Porters' house. When they reached Vine Cottage she had to ask William to fetch a ladder and climb in through a window.

Whether or not young William spent the night with Kate was never fully established, but there is evidence that she, at least, was in residence early the next morning. Confirmation of this came from Annie Porter, who, finding the purse with the key inside, had brought it over to Richmond. It seems rather an unnecessary journey on Mrs Porter's part – unless, of course, she used the key as an excuse to check up on young William's whereabouts. Whatever her real reason, by the time she arrived, according to her recollection, between eight and nine o'clock in the morning, Kate alone was there to welcome her. There was no sign of William. Kate gave her friend some breakfast and proudly showed her around the house. Whilst Mrs Porter was there, a paper-boy passed the house, calling out a headline from the *Daily News*: 'Supposed murder; shocking discovery of human remains in a box found in the Thames.'

Hearing this, Kate said: 'I expect that's only a catch penny, but we might as well have a paper.'

With that, she went to the front gate and bought a copy. Later that day, the two friends returned to Hammersmith together and Kate spent the night on the Porters' sofa once more.

The following day, Saturday 8 March, Kate arranged to meet Harry Porter at the house in Richmond at two-thirty so he could assess the value of the furniture. She then went to see her friend, Sarah Crease, who lived in Richmond, the wife of a boot-black. She worked as a Saturday cleaner for a Miss Loder and was also looking after Kate's young son, Johnny, for 3*s* a week. Kate and the child's father, a man called Strong, had brought him to her on 13 January. Kate was, in fact, extremely fond of the boy and, despite her miscreant ways, she always ensured that he was well-cared for during her frequent terms of imprisonment. But for Mrs Crease she changed her story. There was no mention of an ailing father when she told Sarah she would come to fetch the child on 12 March – she said she would be sending him to her parents in Glasgow.

From there she hurried back to Vine Cottage where Harry Porter joined her. After a quick look at the furniture, he stayed in the house for more than three hours, drinking and gossiping with Kate. There was certainly something about her that men, and women for that matter, found compelling, for she seemed to find little difficulty in persuading her friends to fall in with her various schemes.

Whilst not exactly pretty, the effigy of Kate Webster that appeared in the 'Chamber of Horrors' at Madame Tussaud's Waxworks was misleading for, according to the *Penny Illustrated Newspaper*, she was 'not as ill-favoured as she has been described. The obliquity of her eyes, however, gives her a sinister appearance; the mouth is very determined'.[71]

Another description of Kate, in *Lloyd's Newspaper*, indicates that she was 'rather above medium height, strongly, though not

---

71   It was a deplorable fact that the effigy of Kate Webster, depicting such a sinister and thoroughly evil looking woman, was on display on the Easter Monday, shortly after the magistrates' hearing and before she was sent for trial.

stoutly built, dark complexioned, with sharp, darkish eyes and a palish sallow face, the features being tolerably regular, neither showing refinement or absolute coarseness'.

Whatever it was that attracted Harry Porter, it was not until late in the afternoon that he accompanied Kate back to Hammersmith, where she again commandeered the sofa in the front parlour.

The next morning, Sunday 9 March, Kate continued to nag Harry Porter into finding her a broker. As a result he took her a few doors along the road to the Rising Sun, a small, two-roomed beer-house run by a Mr John Church and his wife, Maria. Kate said later that she knew 'Jack' Church very well when she lived in Rose Gardens six years before, but he always denied this. It is possible that Kate was still operating as a part-time prostitute, which would explain Church's reluctance to admit a past liaison – yet, at the same time, in the days following their introduction that Sunday, she soon had him dancing attendance on her and he spent a great deal of time in her company.

The next day, Monday 10 March, a human foot, recently severed at the ankle, was found in a dung heap on some allotments in Twickenham. It was also the day on which Mr Hull, the coroner for West Surrey, opened the inquest on the remains in the wooden box. The enquiry was held at the Red Lion Hotel, in Barnes. Dr Adams was called to give evidence concerning his findings but the identification of the body remained a mystery. After hearing the doctor's evidence, the enquiry was adjourned pending further investigations.

On Tuesday 11 March, Kate finally managed to get Jack Church over to Vine Cottage to look at the furniture. Needless to say, he admitted later that he, too, spent several hours alone with Kate, drinking and smoking. He was about forty-one at the time, sporting a sandy-coloured beard and whiskers. His hair, according to one newspaper report, was piled up high in a quiff at the front and he liked to wear tweed suits and a deerstalker hat.

Jack Church was an ex-soldier who, after buying himself out of the army in 1866, took a job as a coachman before buying the Rising Sun. He was considered to be a man of some means – he had at least £500 in a bank account – despite a weakness for brandy (which he didn't sell at his own hostelry), hard-drinking women and betting on horses. Whilst he was out gallivanting, it appears that his wife was quite happy to run the beer-house single-handed, for she made no complaint and spoke highly of her husband.

As for Kate, she entertained Jack Church at her house in Richmond, revelling in her impersonation of Mrs Thomas, showing off her fine furniture to Church and even telling him that a portrait hanging over the mantelpiece in the drawing room was a likeness of her deceased husband, a Scottish solicitor. Church so enjoyed her company he was back at Vine Cottage on 12, 13, 14 and 15 March. Kate did find time, however, to collect her young son from Sarah Crease on the 12 March and take him to Hammersmith, where Annie Porter had promised to look after him. On Sunday 16 March, Jack Church, his wife and their seven-year-old daughter, accompanied by William Porter and a friend, went for a boat trip on the river. Kate also joined the party, although Church later said that she had not been invited. Yet the following day, Monday 17 March, he was back at Vine Cottage, helping Kate to pack her belongings. He valued the furniture and effects at £68 and, as Kate said she had some pressing bills to pay, he gave her an £18 deposit to tide her over. Later that day Church splashed out £1 on a pair of earrings for Kate. His wife, Maria, had a similar pair and Kate had expressed a wish to have the same.

On Tuesday 18 March the inquest at Barnes was resumed and Dr Bond, a surgeon and lecturer in forensic medicine, who had examined the remains, was called to give evidence. He produced the severed foot found on the dung heap in Twickenham and confirmed that, in his opinion, it belonged to the other portions found in the box at Barnes. Unfortunately, as the headless body had still not been identified and no arrest had been made in connection with the case, the jurors had little option but to record an open verdict.

That same evening, shortly before seven, Jack Church and Harry Porter arrived to supervise the removal men. Whilst they were loading up one of the vans, the next-door neighbour, Miss Elizabeth Ives, was watching them closely. In fact, she had spent a great deal of time recently peering from behind her lace curtains at all the comings and goings next door. She wasn't just being nosy – she owned both cottages and had rented the other to a Mrs Julia Martha Thomas. She had last seen her neighbour planting flowers in the garden on the afternoon of Saturday 1 March – which was more than two weeks ago. It was all very odd. She knew that Kate, who she knew to be Mrs Thomas' surly-looking and uncommunicative maid, was still there and, moreover, much to her disgust, she knew for a fact that several different men had been coming to the house at all hours. What on earth was going on? And where was Mrs Thomas?

Determined to find out, Miss Ives hastened down the garden path and spoke to one of the men. She demanded to know where the furniture was going and who had ordered its removal. She then asked for Mrs Thomas's new address. Seeing her and the man in conversation, Kate panicked, sure that her impersonation was about to be discovered. She hurried round to Miss Ives's front door and spoke to her. When Miss Ives demanded to know the whereabouts of Mrs Thomas, Kate seemed momentarily lost for words. She simply said, 'I don't know' – and then ran back into the house, her face flushed and agitated. As she did so, Miss Ives declared that she would enquire further and angrily slammed the door.

A few minutes later Kate had pulled on her coat, grabbed her bonnet and run out of the house (carrying several dresses and a hat box, which she flung into the back of one of the vans). Then she hastily retrieved one of the dresses, made of black silk, before running towards the station at Richmond, leaving the men without a word of explanation.

As soon as Jack Church realised something was wrong, he quickly removed all the items of furniture already loaded into the vans and returned them to the house. The removal men objected strongly to this sudden change of plan and demanded the £4 removal fee, though they eventually settled for £3 for their trouble.

Arriving at the railway station, Kate straightway hailed a cab to Hammersmith and from there headed for the Rising Sun where she borrowed a sovereign from Mrs Church. This done, she ran to the Porters' house but found only young Robert at home and her child in bed. She ordered Robert to go upstairs and fetch the little boy so that she could take him to her relatives as planned. Robert dressed the sleepy child in his best knickerbocker trousers and pea-jacket and then carried him to the end of the street where the cab was waiting. Kate leaned over and whispered something to the cabbie; Robert waved and said goodbye to the boy as the cab moved off in the direction of Hammersmith railway station.

From there, Kate caught a train to Kings Cross, where she and the boy boarded a train for Liverpool. Once there, she managed to secure a passage to Ireland on a coal-boat and on arrival in Enniscorthy, she sought out, not her mother, who was apparently still in the area, but her uncle, Mr Lawless, at his farm in Killane.

Meanwhile, back in London, Jack Church was in a quandary. Having dismissed the removal men and returned home, the whole business continued to bother him. The deal had gone badly wrong and now Kate had disappeared. He had, moreover, lost his £18 deposit. Perhaps it was this that propelled him – with Harry Porter in tow – to Richmond the following evening, hoping to talk to Miss Ives. She was growing decidedly worried about the whereabouts of Mrs Thomas and, probably suspecting that, as friends of Kate, the men had been party to the dubious furniture transaction, she refused to speak to them and slammed the door in their faces.

All the next day Mr Church worried and schemed. There was still no sign of Kate. She hadn't even bothered to get touch with the Porters and the dresses from the van were still in his wife's wardrobe. It was whilst Mrs Church was looking through the pockets on Friday 21 March that she found various bits and pieces belonging to Mrs Julia Thomas. Amongst these was a letter from a lady called Mrs Menhennick, of Finsbury Park.[72]

Realising that Kate had fooled them all by masquerading as Mrs Thomas, Jack Church and Harry Porter decided to call on Mr Menhennick that same evening. Once the Menhennicks had described the lady they knew as Mrs Thomas – a religious, middle-aged woman who was petite, genteel and fastidious – they were left in no doubt that she and Kate Webster were quite different women. The sinister aspect of Kate's impersonation was just beginning to dawn on Church and Porter. Mr Menhennick

---

72   Her daughter, thirteen-year-old Edith Menhennick, had been staying with Mrs Julia Thomas for the four months prior to her employment of Kate Webster.

was also worried about the whereabouts of the real Mrs Thomas and immediately dispatched a letter to her solicitor, Mr Hughes, which he received the following morning. Being unwell at the time, Hughes sent his brother over to Hammersmith to interview John Church.

After hearing the whole saga of Kate's sudden reappearance in Rose Gardens on 4 March, her assertion that her name was Mrs Thomas and that the house and its contents had been left to her, followed by her sudden flight when challenged, Mr Hughes decided to investigate. He visited the Rising Sun on Saturday 22 March and sent for Harry Porter. After hearing further revelations about Kate and her supposed inheritance – and, perhaps, a little of her criminal past – the three men went straight to Richmond Police Station. Concerned by the story they had to tell, Inspector Pearman accompanied them to Vine Cottage and a cursory search was made.

It was at this point that one aspect of Jack Church's behaviour became extremely suspect. Once inside Vine Cottage he went straight to a cupboard in the front parlour and opened it. Still with his back to Inspector Pearman, he said: 'Here's her gold watch and chain.' There was no way of seeing whether the items came from the cupboard or from Church's pocket. It seems most likely that Kate had given him the watch, either as a gift or to sell for her, and he couldn't wait to get rid of it, lest it implicate him still further in what was now clearly, at the very least, a serious case of fraud.

Nothing else of interest was found on this first visit but the next day, Sunday 23 March, Inspector Pearman called for a further interview with Jack Church at the Rising Sun. He subsequently sent for young Robert Porter and it was at this interview that he told the police about helping Kate with the wooden box on 4 March. He hadn't, he said, given it a thought until he'd heard his father reading about the inquest in the newspaper. He proceeded to tell the policeman everything that had happened that night concerning both the bag at Hammersmith Bridge and the box at Richmond Bridge.

He was taken later in the day to the mortuary where he identified the box in which the human remains had been found as the same one that he had helped Kate Webster carry across Richmond Bridge. The side without the handle (it was later found at Vine Cottage), which had caused his knuckles to bleed, made this a simple task.[73]

This evidence, the mysterious disappearance of Mrs Thomas and the finding of some charred bones in her house – a further search on 27 March revealed some bloodstains and a 'fatty substance' – led the police to finally issue a warrant for Kate Webster's arrest. The following description of her was circulated throughout the country:

> Wanted, for stealing plate &c, and supposed murder of mistress: Kate ----, aged about 32, 5ft 5 or 6 inches high: complexion sallow: slightly freckled: teeth rather good and prominent. Usually dressed in dark dress, jacket rather long, and trimmed with dark fur round pockets: light brown satin bonnet: speaks with an Irish accent and was accompanied by boy, aged 5, complexion rather dark, dark hair. Was last seen in Hammersmith.

With her criminal record it didn't take the authorities long to trace Kate to her family home in Killane. She was arrested on Friday 28 March, at her uncle's house and taken to the jail at Enniscorthy. In the presence of two police officers from Scotland Yard, she was charged with the murder of Mrs Julia Martha Thomas, on or about 2 March 1879, and in addition, with stealing Mrs Thomas's furniture and effects.

Several newspapers carried articles describing her arrest, informing their readers that Kate did not panic or become violent when taken into custody. On the contrary, she offered no resistance whatsoever and appeared to be 'a most reticent and determined character'.

However, no sooner had Kate and the two London policemen boarded a train to Dublin than she asked: 'Is there any other person in custody for the murder? There ought to be; the innocent should not suffer for the guilty.'

Kate was taken to Dublin and later that evening transported to London. During the journey by steam-boat from Holyhead she insisted that it was Jack Church, the landlord of the Rising Sun,

---

73 Young Edith Menhennick and Julia Thomas's friend, Mrs Mary Ann Kent, both identified the box as the one that was in a bedroom at Vine Cottage and used by Mrs Thomas to store her best bonnets.

who had killed Julia Thomas and should have been arrested in her place.

When they reached Richmond Police Station, Kate repeated her allegation in a formal statement which was taken down in writing. On Sunday 30 March, Church was called in, ostensibly to identify Kate Webster, and her statement was read to him – at the end of which, to his 'absolute amazement', he was arrested on a charge of murdering Mrs Thomas in conjunction with Kate. His initial reaction was to burst out laughing as though the idea that he was a murderer was preposterous and he later admitted to being 'utterly dumbfounded'. Both prisoners were locked in the cells and appeared before the Magistrates' Court the following day, 31 March.

Brought into the court by the two Scotland Yard detectives, both Kate and Church were charged with the wilful murder of Mrs Julia Thomas. The *Penny Illustrated Paper* described Kate's appearance in some detail, saying she was dressed in a:

> …plum-coloured dress, black cloth jacket, edged with fur, and hat of French grey and brown, with feather. She carried on her arm the grey waterproof cloak she put on at the time of her arrest. The woman, though not of pleasant features, is decidedly not so coarse or ill-favoured as she has been described; but a certain obliquity of the eyes gives her at times a rather sinister appearance, which is not decreased by an expression about the mouth denoting great firmness and determination.[74]

Throughout the proceedings she 'scarcely moved a muscle' and appeared 'calm and indifferent'. She was 'pallid and somewhat haggard but there was no nervousness or physical prostration'.

The atmosphere was tense, however, for although Jack Church and Kate stood side by side in the dock she deliberately kept her head turned away from him. For his part, he showed no emotion as Kate's statement was read to the court. In it, she insisted that she had known Jack Church on an intimate level for some seven years during which time he had often taken her out drinking in various public houses. And, said Kate, Church had killed her mistress, Mrs Thomas, on the evening of Monday 3 March.

---

74 There was a possibility that Kate was only partially sighted in one eye.

The previous day, according to Kate, he had been drinking heavily at Vine Cottage and had suggested they rob and 'do away' with Julia Thomas. Kate had told him she would have none of this, and anyway, Mrs Thomas didn't keep any money in the house. He had then said: 'We would have her things, and go off to America together and enjoy it, as I am getting tired of my old woman.' She claimed that he did not leave until late that night. Furthermore, according to Kate, Jack Church had come to the house again on Monday 3 March and, masquerading as her brother, had taken tea with Mrs Thomas. Soon after, Kate expressed a wish to go and see her little boy – which, incidentally, she usually did on a Sunday afternoon – leaving, as far as she was concerned, the potentially murderous Church alone with her mistress.

'When I returned,' her statement went on, 'I noticed the light was turned down. I knocked three times at the door, and, at the third knock, Church opened the door, when I saw Mrs Thomas lying on the mat in the passage, struggling and groaning.'

Jack Church, Kate said, had beckoned her in but she had been too frightened. Despite the fact that there was a policeman standing on the opposite side of the road, she allowed Church to grab her arm and pull her through the doorway. At this point, he had then threatened her with a knife if she told anyone that he had killed Mrs Thomas.

Her statement detailed the days that followed: her handing over the corded box without knowing its contents; finding blood on a carving knife in the kitchen at Vine Cottage. When Miss Ives became suspicious, Kate went on, and confronted the removal men, Church had given her his photograph and address (which were, in fact, found on her when she was arrested) and told her to go back to Ireland and wait for him while he 'brazened it out' – then they would go off to America together. Finally, Kate said this:

I never laid a hand on Mrs Thomas, and had nothing to do with murdering her, but I knew Church had done it. All the money left in the house belonging to Mrs Thomas was a £5 note and 30s. This note I changed at a fishmonger's in Richmond. Church and Porter were with me at the time. I intend to tell the whole truth, as I don't see why I should be blamed for what Church has done. I wouldn't accuse my greatest enemy of anything wrong, let alone a friend, which Church has been to me up till now.

When the proceedings were resumed on Wednesday 9 April, Church vehemently denied that he had known Kate before Harry Porter had introduced her on 9 March. This was confirmed by Porter himself. He also produced a cast-iron alibi for 3 March, the date on which Kate said he had killed Mrs Thomas. As luck would have it, there were several witnesses able to swear that Church was in an upstairs room at the Rising Sun all that evening; there was no way he could have been in Richmond that night. Church, the gambler was, indeed, a lucky man, for his imprudent attendance on Kate Webster had already led him to stand charged with murder – it could have also cost him his life.

Thrown into confusion when the lies she had told in her first statement were so clearly disproved, Kate made another statement on 10 April, which was subsequently read at the magistrates' hearing that day. This time, she tried to incriminate Harry Porter as well and changed the date of the supposed murder of her mistress from Monday 3 March to Sunday 2 March. But Church was able to produce an equally sound alibi for that day as well and, after a further two days of rigorous questioning, the magistrates withdrew the murder charge against him and he was released on 17 April.

As for Harry Porter, he, too, was able to produce an alibi for both days and, whilst no charge was ever made against him, he spoke bitterly about being implicated in the first place. For some reason, when he was giving evidence at the Magistrates' Court on 17 April and recalled how Kate had greeted him when he came home from work – and how he had found her drinking in his back parlour – she burst out laughing. Two weeks earlier, seeing the vast crowds gathered outside the courtroom – despite the fact that she was mercilessly hissed and booed whenever she appeared in public – her somewhat dour expression softened into a smile.

The public, however, reserved their venom for Kate Webster only – the subsequent release of Jack Church was a popular one and there were scenes of great jubilation when Church returned to the Rising Sun. One newspaper said that the place was 'crammed up to the time of closing and hundreds of persons visited Rose Gardens during the evening without being able to gain admittance to the house.' Church had to scale the counter and push his way through the crowd several times to receive the congratulations of his friends in the road outside.

He was still not entirely off the hook, however, for when the magistrates' hearing was resumed, Church was called to give evidence. When questioned about the nature of his relationship with Kate Webster, he implied that he had gone to Vine Cottage for business purposes only – nothing else. At this, he was subjected to a torrent of verbal abuse from Kate.

'It is false, you scoundrel!' she screamed. 'You had me up stairs in bed, and took the brandy to make me drunk. Seven years ago you took my character. You know more about me than you do about your wife. You scoundrel, you.'

She said this 'in a most indignant manner' and turned to face Church, glaring at him with those fierce black eyes.

'Her voice,' one journalist noticed, 'was interrupted by sobs and trembled with excitement: and the witness seemed to quail before this sudden attack.'

A great many witnesses were examined in the weeks that followed and it was not until 16 May that Kate was finally committed to stand trial for the murder of Julia Thomas at the Central Criminal Court of the Old Bailey on Wednesday, 2 July 1879.

The judge who presided over Kate Webster's trial was the Hon. Justice Denman. The Prosecution was led by the Solicitor General, Sir Hardinge Gifford KC, on behalf of the Crown; he was assisted by Messrs Harry Poland and A.L. Smith. Defending Kate Webster, who pleaded not guilty to the charge of killing Julia Thomas, 'feloniously and willfully, and with malice aforethought', were Messrs Warner Sleigh and Keith Frith, whilst Mr Brindley watched the case on behalf of Jack Church, who was to appear as a prosecution witness.

Kate Webster was brought up from the cells beneath the Old Bailey to stand in the dock of Court Number One, the scene of so many great criminal trials – Drs Crippen, Pritchard and Palmer, Reginald Christie, Edith Thompson and Frank Bywaters, Ruth Ellis – and many more.

According to the *Daily Telegraph*:

...the prisoner was quite pale. She wore a black cloth jacket, which was thrown open at the top, disclosing a white knitted woollen small shawl. Her hair was neatly and carefully arranged. During the reading of the indictment she stood at the Bar, but afterwards, at the suggestion of the learned judge, a chair was handed to her, and she sat during the remainder of the day. She listened attentively to the opening speech of the Solicitor-General and subsequently scrutinised every witness before the court. Though occasionally her face wore an anxious expression, her demeanour throughout was one of 'perfect composure'.

The Solicitor General began by outlining the details of the case and describing the main characters involved. The court was told that Kate Webster had been recommended to Mrs Thomas as a general maid by a Mrs Loder and began work at Vine Cottage in January of that year. Mrs Thomas was a lively, middle-aged widow, considered a little eccentric by her neighbours (though this judgement was not supported by any incidence of eccentricity).

At about six-thirty on the evening of Sunday 2 March, she had attended church as usual at the Presbyterian Church in Richmond. On arrival, she seemed agitated, so much so that her face was flushed and at one stage her bonnet fell off. She sat, not in her usual seat at the front, near the pulpit, but at the back of the church, near the door. She left ten minutes before the end of the service and was never seen again. However, as local tradespeople continued to receive orders for meat and vegetables to be delivered to 2 Vine Cottages, the alarm was not raised. Only her landlady and next-door neighbour, Miss Ives, seemed to suspect that something had happened to her.

There was no doubt whatever, the Solicitor General suggested, that Mrs Thomas was murdered and that the person responsible was the prisoner in the dock, and, moreover, he would produce a witness to testify that the crime was one of premeditation.

One of the first witnesses to take the stand was Miss Ives's mother, who lived at No. 2 Vine Cottages with her daughter. She was at home that Sunday evening (while Elizabeth Ives was at church) and recalled hearing a noise 'like the fall of a heavy chair' between eight and nine o'clock. It sounded as if it came from the hallway next door.

The following morning, shortly before six o'clock, she went out to the back of the house to turn on the water tap. Looking up, she noticed a light in one of the bedrooms of Mrs Thomas's house. About an hour later she heard the sounds of washing or scrubbing coming from the scullery next door. She also heard someone poking the fire under the copper, which lay behind her own kitchen range.

At eleven o'clock that morning, she noticed various items of household linen hanging on Mrs Thomas's washing line. Asked by Mr Sleigh, for the defence, why she had not mentioned hearing any noises next door when she was questioned at the Magistrates' Court, Mrs Ives said she had been unwell at the time and was confused.

William Thomas Deane, a coal merchant, was called next. He had gone to No. 2 Vine Cottages at about twelve thirty on Monday 3 March, expecting Mrs Thomas to settle her bill. The door was opened slightly by Kate Webster; she looked distraught and answered his queries abruptly, saying that her mistress was not at home, nor did she know when she would be in. The door was slammed shut.

Questioned by Mr Poland, Emma Roberts, a friend of Mrs Thomas, said that she also called at Vine Cottage the day after the alleged murder. She received no answer but noticed lights in the hall, basement and drawing room.

She was followed into the witness box by Mary Roberts, a young woman who worked for Miss Ives. Between nine and ten on the morning of Tuesday 4 March, she called at Vine Cottage with a message from Miss Ives (that some workmen would come round to fix the leak in the roof). Kate Webster spoke to her from a bedroom window and told her not to bother as the leak had been caused by melting snow and was now perfectly dry. Miss Roberts went on to say that at about eight o'clock that evening she had heard someone playing the piano next door and, a little later, poking the fire. Later that week she saw Kate Webster walking arm-in-arm with a man who was dark-haired like her but slightly shorter and wearing an Ulster coat.

The landlady, Elizabeth Ives, was called next and questioned by the Solicitor General. She said she last saw Mrs Thomas planting flowers in the garden between three and four on Saturday 1 March, the day before the alleged murder. She, too, heard the sound of the boiler being stoked early on Monday 3 March, and saw the washing on the line before eight o'clock. She also noticed a very unpleasant smell which she thought at first was gas. Between eleven and eight o'clock that day the house was quiet but, in the evening, the noises had started again – the sound of chopping wood, of fires being stoked and furniture being moved.

On the Tuesday evening, Miss Ives remembered hearing voices and people going into the house. The sound of someone tinkling on the piano followed, though she realised it was not Mrs Thomas, who played well. On one occasion, the landlady's gimlet eye noticed Kate leaving the house in a cab; it was late at night and she was in the company of two women, two or three men and a small child.

'During the ten days or fortnight (after the alleged murder) people were continually coming to the house at all sorts of odd hours,' announced Miss Ives, primly, 'and taking things away in cabs'.

In the evening of Wednesday 5 March, Miss Ives – no doubt with her ear firmly pressed to the party wall – recalled hearing a filing sound coming from the kitchen next door. She seemed to think there was a man and a child in the house at the time, for she could hear a man's voice breaking into song every now and then.

By the 18th, Miss Ives realised that something was wrong and watched with alarm as the men began to load Mrs Thomas's furniture into the vans. She confirmed that when she asked about Mrs Thomas's whereabouts, Kate seemed very 'frightened' but did not take flight immediately. Miss Ives went off to find the land agent and when she got back, half an hour later, Kate was still there, standing in the road with Church and Porter and several removal men.

Young Robert Porter followed Miss Ives into the witness box, to be questioned by Harry Poland. He told the court that he was nearly sixteen and lived with his family at 10 Rose Gardens, Hammersmith. He then proceeded to relate the whole story of Kate's sudden appearance and the disposal of the black bag and the wooden box on the night of 4 March. He confirmed that he stayed that night with Kate at Richmond and that, when he went back on the following Saturday afternoon, his father was already there with a Mr Ricketts, who had a small removal van. He saw some old chairs, an India rubber plant and six flower pots being loaded into a van. These items were taken to the Porters' house in Rose Gardens but were of little worth – the family kept the plant, and the pots, he said, but broke up the chairs – the cane seats were missing – and used them as fire-wood.

On the second day of the trial, Robert Porter was recalled and cross-examined by Mr Sleigh, for the defence. He told the court how kind the prisoner had been to his young sister when she was alive – how, when Kate lived next door, she would lift the child over the wall and spent hours playing with her. In answer to further questions, he said that the first time he heard about a box being found in the Thames was 6 March but, he added: '…the first time I spoke about it was when I told Inspector Jones on Sunday 23 March. From the night it happened until the 23rd I never mentioned a word about the box to anybody.'

The next witness was the boy's father, Henry Porter, questioned by the Solicitor General. Describing himself as a painter and decorator, he said that the prisoner always called him Harry. He confirmed his son's account of 4 March and admitted that he and Jack Church were at Kate's house on 13, 14 and 15 March, 'looking over the furniture'. In addition, he said, to the chairs and plant already mentioned by his son, some linen Kate wanted to keep was brought to his house in Ricketts's van on Saturday 15 March. She also left a basket of silver plate at Church's residence, the Rising Sun, until she went back to Ireland. Harry Porter went on to admit that Kate had given him a set of artificial teeth, set in gold, from the house in Richmond. He had sold them to Mr Nibblett, a jeweller in Hammersmith, for 6s. He gave the money to Kate and she gave him 1s for his trouble.[75]

Recalling the day the removal men arrived at the house in Richmond, Porter said that, after talking to Miss Ives next door, Kate had asked him to go upstairs and fetch some dresses and a fur jacket. He handed them to her and she went out of the front door – that was the last he saw of her until she was under arrest at Richmond Police Station on 30 March.

Regarding his alibi for the time of the murder, the evening of Sunday 2 March, Porter said he was drinking in the Rising Sun

---

75 A local dentist, George Henry Rudd, identified the false teeth as those he had made for Mrs Julia Thomas in February of that year, a month before she died.

until eleven o'clock – he was also there, he assured the court, the following night. In fact, he drank in Church's beer-house every night after he'd finished work, had his 'tea and a wash' – he never normally left Hammersmith at all.

Questioned about his knowledge of his son's part in disposing of the wooden box, he said that Robert had told him all about it when he heard his mother reading about the Barnes Mystery in *Lloyd's Newspaper* about 9 March, whereas Robert had said that the first time he mentioned it was 23 March, at the police station.

The next witness to be called was Harry Porter's wife, Annie. Questioned by Harry Poland, she told the court that she had looked after Kate's little boy since 12 March – until, that is, she had taken him back to Ireland. At this point, Kate started to cry – which she did throughout the trial whenever her son was mentioned. Seeing this, Annie Porter immediately burst into tears as well. Still upset, she said that, in return for the boy's keep, Kate had provided a generous supply of meat and vegetables and went on to describe her as a 'kind, good-natured girl'.

Having established that Mrs Porter knew about her son carrying a box for Kate Webster long before he told the police, the judge asked her why, after reading about the remains found in the river, she had said nothing. He seemed annoyed by her response and remonstrated with her quite mercilessly. *The Times* made a special reference to their confrontation and described Annie Porter's whole demeanour whilst giving evidence:

> The witness's behaviour was extraordinary. She laughed, cried, muttered, shook her head inexplicably, and she repeatedly spoke in so low a tone that at last the learned judge made her come and stand beside him to give evidence. At the end of her examination he asked if she was in the habit of drinking too much and on her owning the impeachment with a titter, severely cautioned her, saying that the habit was a peculiarly disgraceful one in a mother of a family, and it was a miserable vice, which made her a terrible spectacle.

The *Daily Telegraph* noted that, when the judge asked the poor woman, who was standing close by, if she was 'not above taking a drop too much gin', she had laughed, causing him to snap: 'Do not laugh. It is a disgraceful and a melancholy thing. You stink of drink today.'

A painter and decorator, James Thurlow, who lived at 42 Rose Gardens, testified that he called at the Porters' house shortly before seven on 4 March and saw the prisoner drinking in the back parlour. He also confirmed that both Harry Porter and Jack Church were in the Rising Sun on the nights of Sunday 2 March and Monday 3 March; he knew, he told the court, because he drank there himself every night of the week.

The Porters' eldest son, twenty-two-year-old William, was called next. He had worked at a bakery in King Street, Hammersmith, for seven years. Tuesday 4 March had been his birthday and he remembered meeting his father, carrying the black bag, with his younger brother Robert and Kate Webster outside the Angel, in Hammersmith. He admitted that he went over to Richmond with Kate on the evening of Thursday 6 March but, he insisted, he only stayed a couple of hours. He went back again with a friend early on the morning of Saturday 15th. Jack Church was already there, but he, William, had left before the arrival of his father and Ricketts with the van.

It was with some eagerness that the crowds in the public gallery watched Jack Church take the stand on the third day of the trial – Friday 4 July. He was questioned by the Solicitor General and said that he was at his home, the Rising Sun, all day on Sunday 2 March. For most of the time he was serving behind the bar – they opened from one to three on Sunday lunchtimes and again from six to eleven.

On the Monday evening there was the monthly meeting of 'The Oak Slate Club', which he described as a 'sick and burial' insurance club. This was a popular way for the poor to put aside a little money by monthly instalments to cover loss of earnings through sickness and to pay their funeral expenses. Jack Church was the treasurer and he, and two stewards, held keys to the box containing the funds. A number of subscriptions were paid that evening requiring Church's signature, and there was no question whatever that he was, in fact, on the premises the whole evening.

The following day, Tuesday 4 March, he had gone to the Vestry Hall, in Kensington, to renew his billiard and bagatelle licence, after which he went to the races at Sandown Park. He was first introduced to Kate Webster by Harry Porter, in the bar of the Rising Sun, on Sunday 9 March. After renewing his beer and wine licence the next day, he went over to see Kate in the evening. Although her little boy was there on that occasion, they left him alone in the house while they went for a drink in the Railway Tavern in Richmond, after which Jack Church returned to Hammersmith by train.

The witness then recalled his various visits to Vine Cottage during the days that followed. Besides Church, a number of other men went to see Kate on Saturday 15 March – including William Porter, one of his friends and at least two greengrocers with their vans. They all had a good rummage through the furniture and effects looking for anything worth having. And all the while Miss Ives watched from her window – and did nothing. Anxious to convince the court that, as far as he was concerned, his visits to Vine Cottage were not personal but strictly business, Church insisted that he did not buy Kate the expensive earrings already mentioned but had lent her the money to buy them. Asked to explain the presence of his photograph and address amongst Kate's possessions when she was arrested in Ireland, Church said that she must have stolen them from a pile of photographs that his young daughter was showing her one day in the bar of the Rising Sun.

What a sanctimonious picture Church must have made, wriggling out of his licentious liaison with Kate, filled with righteous indignation, with his carefully arranged, bouffant hairstyle, pipe and deer-stalker hat! Who can blame Kate for shouting, 'You scoundrel!' during the magistrates' hearing?

When questioned by Mr Sleigh, for the defence, Church reacted defensively. He repeatedly refused to say what he did for a living before enlisting in the army, nor would he say where he had lived as a child – or even the name of the school he attended. The reason for his reticence was never made clear – he may, for instance, have been defensive about being raised in a workhouse or charitable institution or, although he later denied it, he may have served a prison sentence whilst still in his teens.

Jack Church was followed into the witness box by his wife, Maria. They had been married for eleven years, she said, and had kept the Rising Sun for nine. Kate Webster had come there on Thursday 13 March with a basket full of silver plate, which she asked them to keep for her. The following day she brought some tablecloths, curtains, mats and lustres for a chandelier and the day after that she presented Mrs Church with two glass vases and a carving knife and fork.

The following Monday Kate came to the house and gave her a pair of boots that she said she couldn't wear because they hurt her feet. In one of Kate's subsequent statements she said that she gave Maria two pairs of boots – one pair, she insisted, Jack Church had bought for her.

Questioned further, Mrs Church described finding a purse in the pocket of one of the dresses brought in the van from Vine Cottage – inside were five rings, some stamps, a pencil and a small comb. She also found a diary, two pocket handkerchiefs with the name 'J. Thomas' embroidered on them, a pair of gloves and a letter to Mrs Menhennick. She gave all these items to her husband who, she added, never wanted them left at his house in the first place. But, said Maria Church, she took them in lieu of the sovereign she'd given Kate the day she took flight.

It is worth noting that, like her husband before her, Maria Church did not mention the fur jacket that Harry Porter said was taken to the Rising Sun with the dresses. She insisted that she had never even set foot in the house at Richmond, and only knew the prisoner as Mrs Thomas. She knew nothing about her husband buying Kate a pair of earrings, nor had she realised he'd spent so much time alone with her, drinking brandy and smoking cigars.

Henry Weston, another greengrocer and removal man, was called to testify that he had taken two vans to Vine Cottage on 18 March. He said that Church and the prisoner seemed to be on very familiar terms, she calling him 'Jack' and he addressing her, not as Mrs Thomas at all, but as 'Kate'.

Mrs Lucy Loder, the lady who recommended Kate Webster to Mrs Thomas, was called next. She told the court that Kate had been lodging with one of her friends, Mrs Sarah Crease, who lived about a mile from Vine Cottage. Kate had done some laundering for her and she thought she would make an excellent live-in maid for Julia Thomas. Leaving her little boy with Sarah, Kate started work at Vine Cottage on 29 January.

Six days after the alleged murder, Mrs Loder called to see Julia but was told by Kate Webster that her mistress was out looking for a replacement for her as she was going to live with a 'very well to-do aunt' in Glasgow. Mrs Loder was pleased for her as, in her opinion, Kate was 'a very obliging girl, and did her work well'. Kate, said the witness, spoke highly of Julia Thomas, saying she was a 'very good-living woman' and as far as she knew 'there was no animosity between her and Mrs Thomas'.

Called as the next witness, Mrs Sarah Crease also spoke well of Kate Webster:

> She has always been a kind-hearted, good sort of girl so far as I know, and affectionate and grateful for kindness done to her. My husband had an illness for four months, during which time she nursed him and waited on him all day, and did all she could for him. She was then in a situation at Mr Mitchell's and came backwards and forwards simply for the purpose of being kind to my husband and bringing him things ... I never heard her say or do anything unkind to anybody. She came to my house every Sunday night but one to see the child.

But, said the witness, she always had to get back by six-thirty so her mistress could go to church. Kate had told Sarah that Mrs Thomas was a 'very nice lady, very kind and good-hearted' and she seemed 'very fond of her as a mistress.'

Later that day, Charles Menhennick described the murder victim as an 'amiable, good-natured sort of lady, about fifty years of age and very animated in her manner'.

A total of fifty-three witnesses were called to give evidence during the trial, including William Hughes, Mrs Thomas's solicitor and Inspector John Dowdell, the officer from Scotland Yard, who went over to Ireland to arrest Kate Webster.

Questioned at some length, he said that Kate was 'very calm on the voyage, except when she was sick. She had a very good supper on the steamboat, and appeared an amiable, pleasant sort of woman, as far as I could judge. She gave no trouble, and came back quite quietly and calmly.'

Police Inspector John Pearman was then asked to describe his various visits to Vine Cottage. After his initial search in the company of Jack Church and Harry Porter, he made a further visit on Monday 24 March. On that occasion, he told the court, he found 'a quantity of charred bones' and some dress buttons under the kitchen grate. In the coal cellar in the basement,' he continued:

I found a chopper and in the room next to the scullery I found a razor. In the area I found a nightdress which appeared to be burned. I put these things into a carpet bag and took them to the station.

On the 27th I went again and found a quantity of charred bones under the copper grate. The outside of the copper, the brickwork, was well whitened and clean. I took out the copper from the brickwork and about halfway down I found a fatty substance, which I scraped off and placed in a small earthen pot.[76]

He also found traces of blood on the skirting board in the back bedroom, on a wall near the hallway and by the pantry door. Under the sink in the scullery, Pearman had found the missing handle to the wooden box in which the alleged remains of Mrs Thomas were found. He also discovered some cord identical to that used to bind the box.

Later that day, various members of the 'Oak Slate Club' – a Hammersmith bricklayer, a cabinet maker from Notting Hill, a watch and clockmaker, and a couple of labourers from Rose Gardens – were called to testify that John Church was present at the Rising Sun on the evening of 3 March, bringing to a close the fourth day of the trial.

On the fifth day of the trial, Monday 7 July, after hearing similar testimony from yet more labourers, the court saw Mary Durden, a straw bonnet and hat-maker from Kingston, take the stand. 'I have known the accused for four years,' she said:

I saw her on Shrove Tuesday 25th February, at my house. She told me she was going to Birmingham to see about some property which her aunt had left her. She told me she had had a letter from her aunt telling her where to find her gold watch and her chain and her jewels; and everything the aunt had was to come to her. During the interview she told me that she was going to sell the furniture.

---

76 This was probably the source of a rumour spread by Mrs Hayhoe, the landlady of the Hole in the Wall tavern, a few doors from Vine Cottage. She always maintained that shortly after the murder Kate Webster had been hawking two jars of 'best dripping' around the pubs in the area. Mrs Hayhoe was reported to have said: 'I little thought when Kate came in and I chatted with her that she had left her mistress boiling in the copper.'

Mary Durden further informed the court that Kate Webster had laughed a lot during this conversation and seemed excited at the prospect and had spent more than an hour talking about it.

This was damning evidence indeed: the implication was that Kate Webster had planned to rob – and possibly kill – Mrs Thomas as early as 25 February, less than a month after going to work for her. It was an implication not lost on the jury. However, during his cross examination Mr Sleigh sought to establish that Mary Durden might be considered a hostile witness, in that it was rumoured that there was ill-feeling between her and Kate Webster – so much so that they had been involved in a public slanging match over whether Mary's husband had been 'consorting' with Kate in the Three Tons. Mary, of course, denied this – though it seems likely, with Kate's propensity for drink and her liking for male company, that there was some truth in the rumour.

The next witness was Dr Thomas Bond, assistant surgeon and lecturer on forensic medicine at the Westminster Hospital. He described piecing together the grisly jigsaw of boiled flesh found in the box. The body was, in fact, incomplete – the head, several ribs, a thigh and a foot were missing.

He was followed into the witness box by Dr James Adams, the local surgeon who first examined the remains by the river at Barnes. Although he had initially suggested that the body was that of a woman of about thirty, he was prepared to concede to Dr Bond's view that it was of a woman of fifty years or more and was that of a woman approximately 5ft 3in in height.

John Church was further recalled as the last witness in the trial. He was questioned by Mr Sleigh, who tried once more to get to the truth about the publican's life before enlisting in the army – whether, for instance, he had worked as a barman – but his answers remained non-committal. At one stage, Mr Justice Denman, clearly exasperated at the number of times Church replied with the words 'I might have been', intervened by saying: 'Don't say that any more. Now, upon your oath, were you a barman or not?'

To which Church replied: 'I was in a public house before I entered the service.'

Asked if he had ever been in prison, he said, 'Not to my knowledge.'

'Not to your knowledge?' the judge exclaimed, impatiently. 'Have you or have you not been in prison before you were arrested on this charge?'

'No,' replied Church.

After this irritatingly truculent performance, the various statements made by the prisoner since her arrest were read to the court by the Solicitor General. At this juncture, Mr Warner Sleigh rose to deliver his speech on behalf of the accused. It was, he said, a puzzling and difficult case. If a murder had, indeed, been committed – and there was no proof whatever that it had – any evidence against his client was purely circumstantial; no one had seen the crime committed.

'Are you sure,' he went on, 'that the bones found are the bones of Mrs Thomas; and, if they be, are you sure that she died by violence?'

Was it not possible, he argued, that the lady had died of natural causes – a heart attack, a burst blood vessel or apoplexy? There had been witnesses, he reminded the court, to testify that, shortly before she disappeared, Mrs Thomas was showing all the signs of extreme stress, sufficient perhaps, to precipitate an attack of this sort – a flushed face, confusion and nervous agitation.

Turning now to the character and disposition of his client, Kate Webster, Sleigh pointed out that, despite the hardness of her looks, several witnesses had described her 'as kind and good-hearted a creature as ever lived'. Could they really believe that she had 'committed one of the most foul and horrible murders ever alleged to have been committed?'

Sleigh then proceeded to question the integrity of John Church, who clearly had something to hide. 'Church was such an unmitigated scoundrel,' he told the court, 'and the whole transaction with regard to Vine Cottage was so tainted with nefariousness, from beginning to end, that it really was not safe to act upon such testimony.'

Moreover, he suggested, it was surely naïve to believe for one moment that Church and Porter did not know about the body found in Kate's box until Robert told the police about it on 23 March. There had been 'so much talk about the Barnes Mystery – the papers teeming with it, and all the neighbourhood being alive with the sensation'. They must have heard about it, so why didn't they say anything to the police about Kate's strange behaviour on the night of 4 March and her subsequent plans for the disposal of furniture and effects?

Finally, he reminded the jurors that they were 'the bulwarks of safety between the accused and an unjust conviction. Upon them lay the power of sending a woman to the gallows or preventing a miscarriage of justice.'

On the last day of Kate Webster's trial, Tuesday 8 July, the Solicitor General rose to address the jurors on behalf of the Crown. He urged them to 'apply their common sense and ordinary reasoning powers to the facts before them and arrive at the conclusion which conscience dictated'. With regard to the defence counsel's assertion that the identity of the remains in the box were not legally proved to be those of Mrs Thomas, he pointed out that Robert Porter had positively identified the box as the one he had helped the prisoner carry from Vine Cottage. Surely their common sense must tell them that, in all probability, the body inside belonged to the missing mistress of the house? And in the kitchen, despite its freshly scrubbed condition, a fatty deposit was found in the copper and traces of blood and some charred human bones were found in the fireplace – these bore 'dumb testimony' to the fact that Julia Thomas had been murdered in that house and her body dismembered, boiled and burned in that kitchen.

He suggested that the head, which had never been found, had been disposed of separately in an attempt to prevent identification. From the evidence of Miss Ives and her mother, the 'sound of a heavy fall' on the night of Sunday 2 March, the repeated stoking of the boiler and the dreadful smell the following day must surely coincide with the process of disposing of the body.

As to the suggestion that Mrs Thomas had died of a heart attack or something similar – why then had no doctor been called to notify the death in the usual way? What need was there, if this were the case, to mutilate and dismember the body and attempt to prevent its discovery? 'These facts,' said the Solicitor General, 'put together rendered the conclusion of murder having been committed absolutely irresistible.' Kate Webster, the wretched woman in the dock, was guilty.

It was now Mr Justice Denman's turn to address the jury. He carefully summed up all the evidence heard in court for and against the prisoner, during what had been, he said, a 'long, laborious and important case'. This was made even more complicated, he added, by the prisoner having made several contradictory statements about those present at Vine Cottage when Mrs Thomas died. The jury must therefore consider 'whether it was established beyond reasonable doubt that the accused was there – whether she was alone or one of several persons who committed the murder'. He went on to say that, 'if they were convinced beyond all doubt that the accused was concerned as one of several in doing the act, then she would be guilty of murder.'

Regarding the defence counsel's argument that there was no evidence to prove that the remains found in the box at Barnes were those of Julia Thomas, he said that it was not necessary to have legal proof but 'if a multitude of circumstances so combined that to hold otherwise would be contrary to common sense' then they must conclude that they were. Especially, he emphasised, as Kate Webster herself, in one of her statements, had confirmed that a murder had been committed – by Church – and had admitted to carrying the box, later found to contain human remains, from the house.

The judge then proceeded to remind the jury of all the characters involved in the case and to detail with meticulous care the evidence each had given as to the events subsequent to the death of Mrs Thomas. Some witnesses had made conflicting statements, he said, as to exact times and places, but such was the nature of memory and the jury should not interpret falsehood where none existed.

He reminded them that the prisoner had said she was in Hammersmith with Jack Church on the evening of 3 March, yet when Emma Roberts had called at Vine Cottage in Richmond there were lights on all over the house, although no one answered her knock on the door. Furthermore, Kate Webster was certainly there at midday for she answered the door to Mr Deane, the coalman. It was also during that morning that Miss Ives noticed the horrible smell and heard the sound of the copper boiling.

All these facts, went on Mr Justice Denman, 'were perfectly consistent with the accused, or whoever it was in the house, being employed in getting rid of any traces of mischief, if the murder had been committed on the previous evening'.

The judge next dwelt on the part that Jack Church and Harry Porter played in the discovery of the fraud and, ultimately, in the murder. As to the prisoner's accusation that it was Church who killed Julia Thomas, if the jurors entertained 'any reasonable doubt as to whether the real fact is that Church committed the murder, and she [Kate] was a mere accessory after the fact, helping him to get rid of the body, and so forth, she would not be guilty of murder…'

Finally, he said this:

> Gentlemen, the case has been conducted most admirably by the counsel on both sides; it has been conducted impartially and fairly and mercifully by the counsel for the prosecution, and ably and efficiently by the defence. The witnesses have been examined with great elaboration and with great care. If you are satisfied beyond all reasonable doubt that the accused is guilty of this murder, you will say so. If you entertain any reasonable doubt about it, you will then acquit her and say she is not guilty.

The jury retired at twelve minutes past five that afternoon and returned to the court shortly before half past six. As the foreman stood to deliver the verdict, the tension in the court was high. Kate Webster's life was at stake.

Then came the verdict: guilty. On hearing the word, Kate 'still showed scarcely any emotion, beyond what was expressed by a slight increase of previous pallor and a tight compression of the lips'.

Her solicitor, Mr O'Brien, was permitted to enter the dock to talk to her, and 'for about two minutes he appeared to be engaged in earnest conversation with her, not a syllable, however, being audible in court'.

When asked whether she had anything to say before being sentenced, Kate, in an unusually quiet voice, replied:

> I am not guilty, my lord, of the murder. I have never done it, my lord. When I was taken into custody I was in a hurry, and I made a statement against Church and Porter. I am very sorry for doing so, and I want to clear them out of it. And another thing, I was led to this, my lord. The man who is guilty of all this is not in the case at all, nor never was. Therefore, I do not see why I should suffer for what other people have done. There was a child put in my hands in 1874. I had to thieve for that child, and go to prison for it. Anybody can tell it round

Kingston or Richmond, too. Therefore, the father of the child is the ruin of me since 1873 up to this moment, and he is the instigation of this; he was never taken into custody. I have cherished him up to this minute, but I do not see why I should suffer for a scoundrel who has left me after what he has done.

There was a profound silence in the court as Mr Justice Denman placed the black cap on his head.

'Prisoner at the bar,' he began, his words delivered in sombre, measured tones:

After a very long and painful inquiry, and after a powerful advocacy on your behalf you have been found guilty upon what, even in the absence of what you have now told us, I should have ventured to say was irresistible testimony of the crime of wilful murder. You tell us now, for the first time, that you were instigated to that crime by some one who is not in custody, and whose name is not before us, and you have made some reparation at this moment by exonerating from all charge two persons, who, it was not impossible, might have been sent to the scaffold upon the statement that you made against them, coupled with circumstances which it was hard for them to explain. So far, I think, all will feel that the result of this trial is in one respect satisfactory; but though you put it to me that you ought not to suffer because another instigated you to this crime, that is a consideration which will not warrant me one moment from hesitating to pass upon you the sentence of the law. Indeed, I have no option. My duty imperatively demands it, and I must do it. Whether your statement now be true or not, God only can tell. After so many false statements as you have made, it must not be assumed to be true as a matter of course. If it be so, it is no excuse for you, because, in point of law, you have been proved to be guilty of the crime of murder, and indeed that very statement shows the justice of the verdict of the jury. I say no more. I do not wish to hurt your feelings by saying a single unnecessary word, but it is my duty to pass upon you the sentence of the law.

The judge thereupon passed the sentence of death.

Kate, in a firm voice that was heard throughout the courtroom, then said: 'I am not guilty, my Lord.'

Whereupon, the Clerk of Arraigns, declared: 'Prisoner at the bar, you have been convicted of the crime of murder. Have you anything to say in stay of execution of your sentence?'

'Yes,' said Kate. 'I am pregnant.'

There were gasps from the public gallery, where a great many women had gathered throughout the trial. The judge, who admitted that such a plea had never been proposed during the whole of his court experience – though under English law a pregnant woman may not hang – ordered that the prisoner be examined.[77] A jury of matrons was selected from married women in the gallery, the previous jury having been dismissed. The prison matron, Thirza Belcher, denied that Webster was pregnant. After examining her in the jury-room, Dr Bond and the jury of matrons also declared that she was not 'quick with child'. This decision meant, of course, that the death sentence remained.

'The prisoner,' the court report went on, 'who was in a prostrate condition, was then raised by the attendants, and almost borne by them to the steps which led from the dock to the cells below.'

It was half past seven when the court finally rose. As it was a pleasantly warm evening, a huge crowd had gathered outside to hear the result of the trial and to see the prisoner driven away to Wandsworth Gaol to await execution. As there were no special facilities for condemned prisoners at Wandsworth at the time, Kate Webster was confined in a fairly comfortable cell and assigned, by the sympathetic intervention of the prison Governor, Captain Colville, a sister of compassion from a convent in Hammersmith to watch over her. She also received several visits from the prison chaplain, Revd Father McEnery.

She made two more statements, one on 10 July and the other on 17 July, which were both lengthy, conflicting and sanctimonious in tone. Still hoping for a last-minute reprieve, Kate swore she knew nothing about the murder, never saw the body of Julia Thomas and blamed the father of her child – a man presumed to be Strong, although she did not divulge his name – for the murder. Two of his friends, a man and a woman, were also

---

77   Charlotte Harris was sentenced to death at the Somerset Assizes in 1849 but, being pregnant at the time of her sentencing, her execution was postponed until after the birth of the child. More than 40,000 women petitioned Queen Victoria for mercy on Charlotte's behalf and the sentence of death was commuted to one of life imprisonment.

involved, she said, but she was entirely under Strong's influence and it was he who made her incriminate Church and Porter. She also insisted that Church knew perfectly well she was not Mrs Thomas and that the furniture was not hers to sell.

In the statements, she repeatedly threw herself on God's mercy 'in the last moments of her mortal existence' and forgave 'those who have been ready to condemn' her and all those people who had directed 'harsh and unkind remarks' against her. She finished by hoping that her 'miseries, troubles, trials and awful fate' will 'serve as a warning to young girls never to be led away from the path of virtue and honesty.' The statement ended with a phrase chosen to tug at the heart-strings of the Home Secretary: 'These are the dying words of the unhappy and unfortunate – Katherine Webster.'

Although it was noted that she behaved herself remarkably well at Wandsworth, her fierce reputation as a foul-mouthed trouble-maker had preceded her from Newgate, where she had previously been confined. The *Chronicles of Newgate* contain this note: 'Kate Webster … is remembered as a defiant, brutal creature, who showed no remorse, but was subject to fits of ungovernable passion, when she broke into language the most appalling.' Yet the authorities at Wandsworth described her as 'remarkably submissive and docile'. This was probably due, in part at least, to the pacifying effect of the sister of compassion; she was also sustained by the possibility of a reprieve. She was said to be relatively cheerful – until, that is, the 26 July, when the appeal presented to the Home Secretary on her behalf was rejected. Naturally, she was 'greatly affected'.

The time of her execution was set for nine o'clock, on Tuesday, 29 July 1879. The barbaric and sickening practice of public hanging had been abolished in 1868 and the county sheriff went further by depriving members of the press access to the spectacle. Although Kate received several visits from her spiritual adviser, Father McEnery, and was comforted by the sister of compassion, she was said to be 'heartbroken at not seeing any of her friends.'

On the Saturday before her execution, she had hoped to see her little boy for the last time and was said to be 'inconsolable' when the visit was cancelled. Then, late on the night before she was to hang, Kate Webster made this final confession to her

spiritual adviser, Father McEnery, aiming to 'clear every one' of
the people she had falsely accused of complicity in the murder:

> In the first place I heartily beg God's forgiveness and mercy for
> numerous falsehoods I have told throughout this unfortunate case,
> especially because they affected the character and reputation of
> persons whose names are mentioned [Mr Strong, for one], and
> secondly, because of the injury they have done to myself in the sight
> of Almighty God, whose mercy and forgiveness I have no doubt of
> having obtained.
>
> Since I was arrested I was always in dread of the consequences of
> the crime and although I had all the assistance of my solicitor, who
> exercised every possible means, both before and after my trial, to
> rescue me from my untimely end, yet I had my doubts that I should
> escape the penalty which I must now pay by law. I was inwardly
> unhappy throughout but bore up under such a terrible trial with
> the greatest fortitude and courage I possibly could; but when I was
> approaching the day of my execution and fearing that nothing could
> be done to save me, I immediately requested the Governor to send for
> Mr O'Brien, my solicitor, that I might open my mind and reveal all
> things to him immediately, without the slightest hesitation or reserve,
> which I now proceed to do, knowing well that I have no hope of
> mercy in this world.
>
> With respect to the death of Mrs Thomas, the circumstances
> surrounding the murder of that lady are as follows:
>
> I entered the lady's service in the month of January. At first I
> thought her a nice old lady and imagined I could be comfortable and
> happy with her; but I found her very trying. She used to do many
> things to annoy me. When I had finished my work in the rooms
> she used to go over it and point out places where she said I did not
> clean, thus showing evidence of a nasty spirit towards me. This sort
> of conduct made me have an ill-feeling towards her but I had no
> intention of killing her, at least, not then. One day I had an altercation
> with her and we mutually arranged I should leave her service and she
> made an entrance to that effect in her memorandum book.
>
> On the Sunday evening, 2nd March last, Mrs Thomas and I were
> alone in the house. We had some argument at which she and myself
> were enraged and she became very agitated and left the house to go
> to church in that state, leaving me at home. Upon her return from
> church, before her usual hour, she came in and went upstairs. I went

up after her and we had an argument which ripened into a quarrel and in the height of my anger and rage I threw her from the top of the stairs to the ground floor. She had a heavy fall. I felt that she was seriously injured and I became agitated at what had occurred, lost all control of myself and, to prevent her screaming or getting me into trouble, I caught her by the throat and in the struggle she was choked. I threw her on the floor.

I then became entirely lost and without any control over myself and looking on what had happened and the fear of being discovered, I determined to do away with the body as best I could. I chopped the head from the body with the assistance of a razor which I used to cut through the flesh afterwards. I also used the meat saw and the carving knife to cut the body up with. I prepared the copper with water to boil the body to prevent identity; as soon as I had succeeded in cutting it up I placed it in the copper and boiled it.

I opened the stomach with the carving knife and burned up as much of the parts as I could. During the whole of this time there was nobody in the house but myself. When I looked upon the scene before me and saw the blood around my feet, the horror and dread I felt was inconceivable. I was bewildered, acted as if I was mad and did everything I possibly could to conceal the occurrence, keep it quiet, and everything regular, fearing the neighbours might suspect something had happened. I was greatly overcome, both from the horrible sight before me and the smell and I failed several times in my strength and determination, but was helped by the devil in this vile purpose. I remained in the house all night endeavouring to clear up the place and clean away traces of the murder.

I burned one part of the body after chopping it up and boiled the other. I think I boiled one of the feet. I emptied the copper, throwing the water away after having washed and cleaned the outside. I then put parts of the body into the little wooden box which was produced in court and tied it up with cord and determined to deposit it in the Thames, which was afterwards done with the help of young Porter.

I remember the coalman, Mr Deane, coming to the house and knocking at the door. I was greatly frightened but in dread of creating suspicion I opened the door to answer him and spoke to him as he stated in his evidence...

I put the head of Mrs Thomas into the black bag, and being weary and afraid to stay in the house, I carried it to the Porters and had some tea there. I placed the bag with the head in it under the tea table and afterwards took it away from the house and disposed of it in the way and in the place I have described to my solicitor, Mr O'Brien.

The deposition of this black bag gave me great uneasiness as I feared it might be discovered ... and when I heard a black bag had been found I was greatly troubled.[78] I pretended to Mr O'Brien that the bag contained nothing of the kind. The foot found in the dunghill at Kingston was placed there by me, for when I came to realise the true state of things and the great danger I stood in, I resolved to do everything in my power to keep everything secret and prevent [it] being discovered.

When I placed the box in the river and disposed of the head and other parts of the body as best I could ... it was suggested to my mind to sell all that there was in the house and go away; and with that view I went and saw Porter and introduced the sale of the things to him. I gave the chairs to Porter as a gift and also kept ordering things for the house from tradespeople in order to evade suspicion...

At the time of the murder I took possession of Mrs Thomas's gold watch and chain and also of all the money in the house, which was only seven or eight pounds ... I threw the dresses and bonnet of Mrs Thomas into the van which was brought to fetch the furniture and they were taken to Church's ... I determined to proceed to Ireland at once to avoid being discovered but was not surprised at being arrested.

I did not murder Mrs Thomas from any premeditation. I was enraged and in a passion and I cannot now recollect why I did it; something seemed to seize me at the time. I threw her downstairs in the heat of passion and strong impulse ... I never had a hatred towards anybody in my lifetime, certainly not as such as would have induced me to do them bodily injury and I cannot account for the awful feelings that came over me from the time Mrs Thomas came home from church until the murder was completed...

I have now relieved my mind by making a full and sincere confession that myself, without help or assistance of any person whatever, committed the murder. I have accounted for it and described it in this statement to the best of my power and recollection. I heartily exonerate every one from having any hand or part in it.

When I got into trouble in Liverpool it was owing in a great measure to poverty and evil associations which led me step by step

---

78 Three black canvas bags similar to Kate Webster's were found in the Thames during the investigation.

into badness. When I got over that trouble I formed an intimate acquaintance with one who should have protected me and, being led away by evil associates and bad companions, I became, as it were, forlorn and forsook everything that might have kept me in the path of rectitude and prevented my unhappy end.

I was afraid to make known the real state of things to my solicitor lest he might have abandoned my case and taken no interest in it. I therefore concealed the truth from him until I sent for him and he told me of the reply to the memorial sent up for me. I then fully and candidly confessed to him the facts, in order that everything might be cleared up and that I alone should be blamed. I am perfectly resigned to my fate and am full of confidence in a happy eternity. If I had a choice I would almost sooner die than return to a life of misery, deception and wickedness. I die with great fortitude and confidence in my faith and in our blessed God, whom I beseech to have mercy on my soul.

Having made her confession, Kate told Father McEnery that she 'felt relieved having unburdened her conscience', and that she 'would sleep more calmly' on her last night on earth. According to the *Penny Illustrated Paper*, she went to bed soon after ten o'clock and slept 'fairly well'.

On the day of her execution, she rose at about five o'clock in the morning and spoke to the Governor, Captain Colville, thanking him for his kindness to her. At half past seven Father McEnery arrived, followed by the prison surgeon. As required by law, the public hangman, William Marwood (who was paid £11 for his work), had slept on the premises the night before the execution, and had made the final adjustments to the scaffold and rope, arriving at the correct ratio between weight and drop to ensure that death was caused by the instantaneous fracture of the neck, not strangulation.

At a quarter to nine the prison bell began to toll. A few minutes later, her arms pinioned, Kate Webster was led down a flight of steps to the scaffold, accompanied by several officials, the prison Governor and Father McEnery, who was reading the Catholic burial service. Once positioned on the scaffold, a white hood was placed over her head and a strap around her legs – not, as some might imagine, to ensure that her modesty was not compromised as she crashed through the trap-door, but to prevent her kicking out.

As the chaplain read the words, 'Jesus, Good Shepherd, come', Kate said, in a loud voice, 'Lord, have mercy upon me.'

The bolt was drawn. It was all over.

At three minutes past nine, a black flag was hoisted on the flagstaff to signal that Kate Webster was dead. The sight of it was greeted by a few cheers from the large but fairly quiet crowd that had gathered outside the prison.

This comment in the *Penny Illustrated Paper* was typical of many at the time: 'The public must feel greatly relieved at the world being rid of so atrocious a criminal – a criminal who scrupled not to endeavour to incriminate innocent men to shield herself from the consequences of a monstrous crime.'

Later that day, Kate Webster's body was buried in an unmarked grave within the prison.

That Kate Webster's crime was one of the most cruel and callous ever recorded cannot be denied. But what of Church and Porter – what a reprehensible pair they turned out to be. Especially Jack Church, who was anything but an 'honest' broker; he was a character with a dubious past and clearly had something to hide. How, one wonders, had he amassed the sum of £500 without any evident source of income besides the hand-to-mouth running of the Rising Sun beer-house? At the sale of Mrs Thomas's remaining furniture and effects, held at Vine Cottage the day after Kate's execution, Church, said to be in a jocular mood, was the main purchaser, buying a number of items – including the gold watch and the carving knife Kate had used to dismember her victim's body. These trophies were, no doubt, subsequently displayed to great effect in the bar of the Rising Sun, by its exceedingly obnoxious landlord.

Unlike Jack Church, Harry Porter and his family were all hard workers – except, of course, for poor Annie Porter, described by the judge in his summing-up as a 'miserable drunkard' – but the way they, and all their friends, had swarmed over the contents of Vine Cottage, like the proverbial maggots over a rotting corpse, was despicable. They were quite prepared to take anything they could lay their hands on – for nothing or going cheap – and not one of them questioned Kate's legitimate entitlement to the bounty. They knew her background perfectly well; they knew she was a liar and a thief and had, in all probability, come by the house and its contents, the jewels, the dresses and the fancy bonnets, by some foul means or other. Big-hearted, boozy Kate, good for a laugh and free with her affections, playing the lady bountiful with poor Mrs Thomas's worldly goods.

Mrs Loder certainly did her friend Julia no favours when she recommended Kate Webster as a live-in maid. If it was another of Mrs Thomas's attempts to 'tame the savage', it went tragically wrong. Poor Julia, with her veneer of gentility: a fussy ex-school mistress, highly-strung, pernickety in her ways, forever finding fault – and Kate, quick-tempered, devious and deeply resentful. Who can tell what made her snap? Quite suddenly, that Sunday evening, all the envy, hatred, resentment and insecurity of her life culminated in a terrible surge of violence. To commit such a savage act, Kate must, herself, have been a woman deeply brutalised by the circumstances of her life. As a result of her long periods of imprisonment, she was naturally resentful of authority and, forever fighting to survive, she harboured a deep-seated envy of the good fortune of others. The closeting together of these two women was destined to end in disaster. The situation had become so tense that Mrs Thomas had given Kate notice to leave on 28 February but was persuaded to let her stay until Sunday 2 March. As this was her half-day, Kate went out drinking and was late returning to the house to help prepare her mistress for church that evening. A heated argument ensued and Mrs Thomas arrived at church late and extremely agitated.

Kate Webster was, without doubt, a rough and ready young woman, a born hustler, yet she doggedly supported her son against all the odds. She could have so easily abandoned him to the workhouse, sold him to one of the baby-farms prolific at the time, or simply given him away, as an unnecessary encumbrance, a drain on her erratic and ill-gotten resources. With her need to keep one step ahead of the police, he was a severe hindrance. But she chose to keep him, and even when she knew her crime would soon be discovered, and that her arrest was imminent, she did not abandon him and escape – instead, she took him back to the safety of her family in Ireland.

As for her associates, there was little honour amongst this particular band of thieves. Not one of these fair-weather friends, not even one of her family, or the women who had spoken of her kindness, bothered to bring her little boy to Wandsworth so that Kate could see him for the last time.

And what of the child's father – the man Kate called Strong? Was he, perhaps, despite her last-minute denial, involved in the murder (or at least, in disposing of parts of the body)? He was seen in her company on 27 February, three days before the murder. Was he, perhaps, the dark-haired man in the Ulster coat seen walking arm-in-arm with Kate Webster soon after the murder? And did she protect his identity not only because he was her young son?

The *denouément* of this case is quite extraordinary. In October 2010, whilst workmen were excavating part of the garden belonging to the naturalist and broadcaster Sir David Attenborough in Park Road, Richmond, a skull was unearthed. It was suggested that this may have been the missing head of Mrs Julia Thomas, as the location was close to Mrs Thomas's house and extended to the derelict site of The Hole in the Wall public house frequented by Kate Webster and her drinking cronies.

The skull was removed by Richmond Police and subjected to carbon dating tests at the University of Edinburgh. These results, along with historical researches, were presented as evidence at the inquest. On Tuesday, 5 July 2011, the West London coroner, Alison Thompson, formally identified the skull as that of Julia Thomas and recorded a verdict of unlawful killing – the cause of death being asphyxiation and head injury.

In her confession, written on the night before her execution, Kate said that she 'placed the box in the river (containing body parts) and disposed of the head and other parts of the body as best I could'. She does not actually say that she threw the black bag containing Julia Thomas's head into the Thames at Hammersmith Bridge. Yet there was no way she would have had time to walk from Hammersmith to Richmond – a distance of 5 miles – bury the head and then rejoin her friends in the pub twenty minutes later, as indicated in their witness statements.

Kate told her friends that she had arranged to meet someone in Barnes that night and hand over the black bag. Did she meet that person near Hammersmith Bridge and hand over the black bag? Who was this unknown accomplice – the mysterious Mr Strong, perhaps?

Did he then carry the bag all the way to Park Road and bury it behind The Hole in the Wall pub, where it remained for some 130 years?

ACKNOWLEDGEMENTS

My special thanks to the crime-writer Mark Ripper (M.W. Oldridge) for his support, expertise and invaluable assistance whilst researching this book. Also to Cate Ludlow at The History Press for her unfailing enthusiasm and understanding of the theme of the book.

The following crime-writers have been generous with their help and encouragement: Martin Edwards, Douglas d'Enno, and Richard and Molly Whittington-Egan.

I am also grateful to the following for their support: Anne Dewell; Sasha and Anil Mahendra; Andy Dixon; Jim Rogers; Alan Rosethorne; Chris Horlock; Dorothy Allam; Milly Eagle; Noelle Beales; Derek Addyman; and Anne Brichto.

BIBLIOGRAPHY

Books

Boswell, James, *London Journal: 1762 – 1763*

Flanders, Judith, *The Invention of Murder*, Harper Press, 2011

Flanders, Judith, *The Victorian City*, Atlantic Books, 2012

Gaute, J.H.H. / Odell, Robin, *Murder Whatdunit*, Harrap, 1982

Jackson, Graham & Ludlow, Cate, *A Grim Almanac of Georgian London*, The History Press, 2011

Huggett, Frank, *Life Below Stairs*, Book Club Associates, 1977

Ludlow, Cate, ed. *Tales From the Terrific Register*, 1825. The History Press 2009

Lustgarten, Edgar, *A Century of Murderers*, Methuen, 1975

Nash, Jay Robert, *Look for the Woman*, New York, 1981

Rumblelow, Donald, *The Triple Tree – Newgate, Tyburn and Old Bailey*, Harrap, 1982

Sly, Nicola, *Murder By Poison*, The History Press, 2009

Unknown, *Circumstantial Evidence; The Extraordinary Case of Eliza Fenning*, Cowie and Strange London 1829

Watkins, John, *The Important Results of an Elaborate Investigation into the Mysterious Case of Elizabeth Fenning*, London, William Hone, 1815

Whitmore, Richard, *Crime and Punishment*, Batsford, 1978

Newspapers and Periodicals

Bath Chronicle & Weekly Gazette
Belfast News-Letter
Berwickshire News
Birmingham Daily Post
Bradford Observer
British Critic
British Gazetteer
British Medical Journal
Bristol Mercury
Bury and Norwich Post
Caledonian Mercury
Carlisle Journal
Chelmsford Chronicle
Cheshire Observer
Chester Chronicle
Daily Telegraph
Day Newspaper
Derby Chronicle
Dunfermline Press
Examiner, The
Era, The
Freeman's Journal
Gentleman's Magazine
Glasgow Herald
Harpers' Weekly
Hereford Times / Journal
Illustrated Police News
Ipswich Journal
Kentish Chronicle
Leeds Intelligencer
Leeds Times
Leominster Chronicle
Lincolnshire Chronicle

Liverpool Mercury
Lloyd's Weekly Newspaper
London Daily News
London Globe, The
London Journal
London Standard
Manchester Evening News
Manchester Guardian
Middlesborough Daily Gazette
Morning Chronicle
Morning Post
Morning Star
Newgate Calendar, The
Newcastle Courant
Newcastle Journal
Northern Star
Nottinghamshire Guardian
Reading Mercury
Reynold's Newspaper
Rotterdam Independent
Sheffield Independent
Sherbourne Mercury
St James's Gazette
Tamworth Herald
Times, The
Weekly Journal
Wells Journal
Western Daily Press
West Kent Guardian
Westmoreland Gazette
Worcestershire Chronicle
York Herald
Yorkshire Gazette

INDEX

If you enjoyed this book, you may also be interested in...

The Moat Farm Mystery
The Life and Criminal Career of Samuel Herbert Dougal
M.W. OLDRIDGE

In 1903 the unexplained disappearance of Samuel Herbert Dougal's latest *inamorata*, a wealthy spinster named Miss Holland, began to excite speculation. A tireless hunt for the missing lady commenced, now revisited in this fascinating study of a mystery that held England spellbound to its dramatic conclusion.

978 0 7524 6629 3

A Grim Almanac of Georgian London
GRAHAM JACKSON & CATE LUDLOW

The Georgian era was perhaps one of the most shocking, gory and surprising in the capital's history. Londoners met some truly spectacular ends during it, including one unfortunate Fleet Street resident who fell into a sausage-grinder. With more than 100 contemporary illustrations, this book will terrify, disgust and delight readers everywhere.

978 0 7524 6170 0

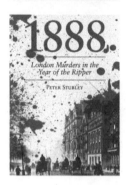

1888
London Murders in the Year of the Ripper
PETER STUBLEY

This book examines all of London's murders in the famous year of the Ripper to build a picture of society. Who were the victims? How did they live, and how did they die? How many died under the wheels of a horse-driven cab? Just how dangerous was London in 1888?

978 0 7524 6543 2

Visit our website and discover thousands of other History Press books.

www.thehistorypress.co.uk